D1630650

Cinema and Society Series
General Editor: Jeffrey Richards

Published and forthcoming:

Annette Kuhn explores the significance of memories of 1930s filmgoing to study patterns of remembrance and their potential causes – rural walking to films, depression's value of a penny, moments of fright, gendered recollections of hopes and pleasures for growing up, and the value of the back row in a theatre. This is an exceptional example of the value of ethnohistory and psychological theory combined with speculation about the meanings of cinema in lives. It sets important standards in researching memories of movies.

Janet Staiger

AN EVERYDAY MAGIC
Cinema and Cultural Memory

Annette Kuhn

U.W.E.
LEARNING RESOURCES
WITHDRAWN

ACC. No.
CLASS 313

CONTROL
186064791x

306.
485
KUH

DATE
17. MAR 2004

SITE

I.B.Tauris *Publishers*
LONDON • NEW YORK

Published in 2002 by I.B.Tauris & Co Ltd
6 Salem Road, London W2 4BU
175 Fifth Avenue, New York NY 10010
www.ibtauris.com

Copyright © Annette Kuhn, 2002

The right of Annette Kuhn to be identified as the author of this work has been asserted by him in accordance with the Copyrights, Designs and Patents Act 1988.

All rights reserved. Except for brief quotations in a review, this book, or any part thereof, may not be reproduced, stored in or introduced into a retrieval system, or transmitted, in any form or by any means, electronic, mechanical, photocopying, recording or otherwise, without the prior written permission of the publisher.

ISBN 1 86064 791 X

A full CIP record for this book is available from the British Library

Project management by Steve Tribe, London
Printed and bound in Great Britain by MPG Books Ltd, Bodmin

Contents

General Editor's Introduction

Writing of inter-war Britain, historian A.J.P. Taylor famously called cinemagoing 'the essential social habit of the age'. But what was the experience of cinemagoing in those years? How did the films affect those who saw them? What was the role of the cinema in the wider popular culture of the time? These are just some of the questions that Annette Kuhn seeks to answer in this vivid and groundbreaking ethnohistorical study. Drawing on an extensive collection of interviews as well as a wealth of contemporary publications, she examines both the phenomenon of cinemagoing and its place in popular memory.

She analyses memories of place, the topography and layout of the cinemas, many of them now demolished, where the films were viewed. She explores the role of cinema in childhood, with memories of negotiating admission, membership of the audience and reaction to individual films. She assesses the importance of cinema to adolescence, its provision of role models, its facilitation of courting and its function in romance and make-believe. She recovers and explains the pleasures associated with film favourites such as Fred Astaire and Ginger Rogers, Jeanette MacDonald and Nelson Eddy, Deanna Durbin and Tom Mix.

Richly detailed, sensitively argued and consistently absorbing, *An Everyday Magic* throws new light on such key topics as spectatorship, canonicity, childhood, adolescence, ageing and film reception. Altogether it constitutes a major contribution to our understanding both of the role of cinema in its heyday and of the nature and function of popular memory in its aftermath.

Jeffrey Richards

Acknowledgements

The research that contributed to the production of this book began more than ten years ago, and indeed it still continues. Over that time, I have received help, support, advice and assistance of myriad kinds from numerous colleagues and friends. They include – with apologies to anyone I have left out – Christine Gledhill and Gillian Swanson, whose commission for a book chapter planted the idea, Amal Treacher, Anu Koivunen, Bruce Bennett, Callie Perks, Ed Gallafent, Ian Conrich, Jean Barr, David Moore, Jeanne Moore, Jeffrey Richards, Jo Stanley, John Caughie, Simon Frith, Philip Schlesinger, John Urry, Marie Rayner, Philippa Brewster, Sarah Smith, Simon Davies, Stephen Peart and Susannah Radstone. Thanks are due also to student intern Veronica Low; and to Eva Parrondo and Ylva Habel, who have translated writings from the project into Spanish and Swedish respectively.

Many people have heard reports of work in progress on the research at academic conferences, colloquia, guest lectures and seminars at home and abroad, and I am grateful for encouraging response and helpful feedback from colleagues at, among other places, Lancaster University, Stockholm University, University of Birmingham, University of Stirling, University of Warwick, University of York; as well as from fellow members of the Film History Seminar, Institute of Historical Research, London and of the Society for the Study of Popular British Cinema. Thanks too to participants at Crossroads in Cultural Studies, Tampere, 1996; Hollywood and its Spectators, London, 1998; Oral History Association Conference, 1996; *Screen* Studies Conference, Glasgow, 1996, 2000 and 2001; Society for Cinema Studies Conference, 1996 and

2000; Archaeology of the Moving Image, UIMP Valencia, 1996; Moving Images, Culture and the Mind, University of Copenhagen, 1997; Historical Reception Studies, University of Bergen, 1992. Enthusiastic comments and additional 'evidence' from audiences outside academe have also been offered at talks given at the Forum, Heversham, Cumbria; the Storey Institute, Lancaster; and Glasgow Film Theatre.

In the course of the research, numerous libraries and archives have been consulted: these are listed in full in the Appendix. I am enormously grateful for the efficiency and helpfulness of their response to what must sometimes have seemed obscure requests.

The research could not have been undertaken without funding support from: the Carnegie Trust for the Universities of Scotland, the Economic and Social Research Council (project number R000 23 5385), the Faculty of Arts and Humanities at the University of Glasgow, and Lancaster University's Faculty of Social Sciences.

Picture acknowledgements: Cover – still from The Long Day Closes, directed by Terence Davies, reproduction courtesy of BFI/FilmFour and the Ronald Grant Archive. Frontispiece – photograph by Humphrey Spender, Bolton Museums, Art Gallery and Aquarium, Bolton Metropolitan Borough Council; p.86 Boris Karloff in The Mask of Fu Manchu, BFI Film Stills, Posters and Designs; p.114 Peggy Kent with friends, collection of Peggy Kent; p.119 Deanna Durbin in Three Smart Girls, BFI Film Stills, Posters and Designs; p.122 Sheila McWhinnie and colleagues, collection of Sheila McWhinnie; p.142 The Astoria, Finsbury Park, courtesy Cinema Theatre Association; p.159 Lili Damita, collection of Denis Houlston; p.160 Madeleine Carroll, collection of Denis Houlston; p.163 Marlene Dietrich in Blue Angel, courtesy the Ronald Grant Archive; p.199 Maytime publicity, courtesy Half Brick Images. Extracts from Crown-copyright records in the Public Record Office appear by permission of Her Majesty's Stationery Office.

Last, but absolutely not least, I owe an enormous debt of thanks to all the 1930 cinemagoers who so generously shared their memories of 'the pictures' in interviews, questionnaires and letters; and to the staff who worked on and sustained the project between 1994 and 1996, without whose skill and dedication successful completion of the ethnographic research would have been impossible. Joan Simpson, the project's secretary, transcribed hundreds of hours of interviews; and Research Fellow Valentina Bold travelled many hundreds of miles to conduct interviews with the most consummate skill and sensitivity.

1

Cinema Memory as
Cultural Memory

T HIS book traces a path through social history and the history of
    cinema, through ideas about popular culture and its place in people's
everyday lives, through memories, life stages and life narratives. The
journey begins where personal and collective memory meet in stories
about cinema and cinemagoing and about what these meant, and still
mean, in the lives of the first movie-made generation[1] – those men and
women who grew up in the 1930s, when 'going to the pictures' was
Britain's favourite spare-time activity. The stories, memories and histories in the chapters which follow emerge from a wide-ranging ethnohistorical inquiry into 1930s cinema culture, conducted over a period of some
ten years.

   In the 1930s, Britain boasted the highest annual per capita cinema
attendance in the world; and cinema's popularity and ubiquity increased
steadily throughout the decade, with admissions rising from 903 million
in 1934 (the first year for which reliable figures are available) to 1027
million in 1940 and a concurrent increase in the number of cinema seats
per head of population. It has been estimated that some 40 per cent of
the British population went to the pictures once a week with a further
25 per cent going twice weekly or more. If this is accurate, something
like two-thirds of the population were regular and frequent cinemagoers:
ballroom dancing was the only pastime that came anywhere close to
rivalling the popular appeal of 'the pictures'.[2]

In his authoritative study of cinema and British society in the 1930s, *The Age of the Dream Palace*, Jeffrey Richards sets out an extensive overview of contemporary data on patterns of cinema attendance, concluding that 'while a large proportion of the population at large went to the cinema occasionally, the enthusiasts were young, working-class, urban and more often female than male'.[3] Richards also notes that as the decade progressed, cinema widened its appeal to the middle classes. This process of embourgeoisement went hand-in-hand with the economy's recovery from the recession of the early 1930s, the development of middle-class suburbs on the fringes of British cities and a boom in the building of 'supercinemas' in these new suburbs and in existing town and city centres.

Often at the leading edge of architecture and design, supercinemas offered – aside from respectability – a luxurious entertainment experience, bringing a taste of the modern and 'essentially democratic' England of J.B. Priestley's by-passes, suburban villas and cocktail bars to the less affluent parts of Britain.[4] And yet cinema was not really a democratising force in these years. Social distinctions within the audience persisted everywhere, manifesting themselves in different types of cinema, from the 'fleapits' at the bottom of the scale to the supercinemas at the top. They are evident, too, in the rigorously stratified organisation of auditorium space reflected in ticket prices, which even within one cinema might range from as little as 3d (just over 1p) right up to 2/6d (12$^{1}/_{2}$p). Nonetheless, it is certainly true that for the British population at large, 'the pictures' was as familiar and taken-for-granted a part of daily life as television is today.

By 1930, Hollywood had long established its dominance over Britain's cinema screens. Even though screenings of British pictures exceeded the legally imposed quota and locally-made films were booked for longer periods than foreign ones, throughout the 1930s something like seven in every ten films shown in Britain were American.[5] Given this state of affairs, British cinema culture was far from synonymous with British cinema. If the influence of Hollywood on British filmgoers' tastes in films and stars was apparent, however, British tastes were highly distinctive.[6] Films aside, a cinema culture is in any case shaped by the contexts and the manner in which films are consumed, and by the people who consume them. The British cinemagoing experience was part of a range of activities, circumstances and experiences peculiar to people's daily lives, and the cinema culture – or cultures – of 1930s Britain was shaped by these peculiarities.

We know about the demographics of British cinemagoing in the 1930s, and we know broadly who the keenest consumers of films were. We also have some idea about British cinemagoers' distinctive preferences in films and stars, and which kinds of films were most popular in Britain during the 1930s. And yet in an important sense we hardly know these people at all. The picturegoing heyday of the 1930s generation lies within living memory, but the cinemagoers' own stories remain largely unrecorded. This state of affairs is in some measure attributable to a condescending attitude towards the 'ordinary' cinemagoer; for in the 1930s, certainly, the stereotypical portrait of the film fan was far from complimentary. She (for the fan is always assumed to be female) is a silly, emptyheaded teenager, thoroughly duped by the cheap dreams purveyed by the picture palaces.[7] It is hardly likely that filmgoers would have pictured themselves in such an unflattering light: this is clearly the tone of voice of the 'concerned' social commentator. What, then, did British film lovers of the 1930s, male and female, bring to their cinemagoing? What did they take away from it? How did going to the pictures fit in with other aspects of their daily lives: school, work, leisure, friendship, courtship? In what ways was this generation formed by cinema? How was cinema experienced by, and what did the pictures mean in the lives of, the 1930s generation?

This book is not just about British cinema culture, nor is it only about people who went to the pictures in a past that may now seem distant. The questions that arise as soon as 'ordinary' media users are taken into account as makers of cultural history are more fundamental, touching on ways of thinking about films, cinemas, and cinema cultures of all kinds, past and present. Pivotal here is the point at which people come into contact with cinema – the moment, that is, of the reception and consumption of films. How do films and their consumers interact? And what, if anything, can we know about this interaction if it has taken place in the past?

These questions may be approached from several disciplinary and methodological angles. A humanities-based study of cinema, for example, will take films as the starting point for exploring the cinema-consumer relationship. As a discipline, film studies models itself largely on literary studies, and to this extent is predominantly text-centred: films as texts are its primary objects of inquiry, and textual analysis its method of preference.[8] Even debates within film studies concerning the nature of spectatorship in the cinema are predominantly about a spectator addressed or constructed by the film text – the 'spectator-in-the text'.[9] The film text remains central, then, and the question at issue is how a film 'speaks to' its spectators, how the meanings implicit in its textual operations may be brought to light. This has nothing at all to do with how the people watching a film might respond to it.

Some confusion arises here because in everyday usage the terms spectator, viewer and audience are more-or-less interchangeable. It is therefore worth restating the distinction between the implied spectator of text-based criticism, the spectator-in-the-text, and the 'social' audience, the flesh and blood human beings who go to cinemas to see films. The social audience is the province of social scientific inquiry, of media audience research and similar types of investigation. However, while one or two sociologists made forays into the study of cinema and its audiences during its heyday as a popular entertainment medium in the 1940s, there is little interest in this area of inquiry among today's media sociologists, for whom contemporary mass media like television are the main focus of attention.[10]

These diverse objects of inquiry – texts and audiences – produce distinctive conceptualisations, methodologies and research procedures. To the extent that film studies privileges the film text, for example, it will downplay not only the reception of films by social audiences but also the social-historical milieux and industrial and institutional settings in which films are produced and consumed.[11] The practice of film analysis has been called into question by critics who find its preoccupation with subtexts and hidden meanings antithetical to the spirit of a popular entertainment medium, irrelevant to the experience of the 'average' cinemagoer, or overweening in its assumption that a spectatorial engagement is somehow built into a film's textual organisation.[12] However, if film analysis is sometimes conducted as if films were not produced and consumed by people at particular times and places, social science-based studies of media and their audiences routinely sideline media texts, treating them as mere epiphenomena of their social, cultural, or industrial conditions of existence.

This division of labour produces a conceptual and methodological dualism of text and context – a divorcing of film texts from their industrial, cultural and historical contexts, and vice versa, and this weakens studies of cinema and other media by ensuring that accounts of media texts and their consumption and reception remain incomplete.

One way of tackling the text-context dualism is to treat texts and contexts alike as discursive practices: thus film texts may be conceptualised as discourses caught up in and informing contexts, and vice versa. This approach is applicable equally to contemporary and to historical studies of media reception.[13]

As a counterweight to text-centred approaches to film spectatorship, Janet Staiger, for example, has proposed that the historical study of film reception could productively adopt a dialectical and 'context-activated' approach:

> the reception studies I seek would be historical, would recognise the dialectics of evidence and theory, and would take up a critical distance on the *relations* between spectators and texts. It would not interpret texts but would attempt a historical *explanation* of the event of interpreting a text.[14]

For evidence, Staiger favours a range of historical sources of information on responses to films, most notably contemporary reviews; and these are then treated as discourses shaping the reception of films. This method offers insight into the discursive features of a film's historical moment, which indeed is what Staiger understands by the context of a film's reception. Rather than the film text proposing the manner of its reception, the film's discursive context performs this work. However, while rightly emphasising the contextual aspects of film consumption, this approach offers no access to the historical social audience.

If neither text-centred nor context-activated approaches to the study of film reception admit the present-day or the historical social audience, and if media audience research admits little else, how might the cinema-goer's experience be investigated in its interaction with films and reception contexts? Media audience research takes a variety of forms, ranging from large-scale investigations based around structured inter-views or pre-coded questionnaires through focus groups to small-scale studies involving depth interviews or participant observation. Inquiries into media use conducted within a cultural studies remit invariably adopt research methods at the qualitative end of the methodological spectrum. Borrowing from cultural anthropology, research of this type calls itself 'ethnographic'.

A dictionary definition of ethnography is 'the scientific description of nations or races of men, their customs, habits and differences'. The key word here is 'description', the presumption being that ethnographic description can be conducted 'scientifically' only if the researcher has been fully immersed in the culture under observation. In its 'description of races and nations' sense, ethnographic inquiry today retains little of its former *raison-d'être* in a post-imperial context, and postmodernity forces issues around cultural otherness, intersubjectivity and the fragmentation of identities to the top of the ethnographer's agenda. A postmodern, post-imperial ethnography must necessarily engage with the dialogic and discursive aspects of ethnographic inquiry, and also accept that it produces new meanings alongside its 'thick description' and interpretation of the 'flow of social discourse'.[15] Furthermore, while holding to these tenets, it must reframe its objects. As James Clifford contends, a renewed ethnography will embrace 'diverse ways of thinking and writing about culture from a standpoint of participant observation'.[16] The object of ethnographic inquiry is no longer 'races and nations', then, but culture; and increasingly it is aspects of the researcher's own culture.

Cultural studies of contemporary media use have taken on board some of these protocols, notably a commitment to qualitative research and to giving serious attention to informants' accounts of their own worlds. To the extent that it is more catholic in its research methods than cultural anthropology and less self-conscious about the dialogic and discursive nature of ethnographic inquiry, though, cultural studies practices an attenuated version of ethnography.[17] As to its objects, with very rare exceptions, cultural studies ethnography concerns itself with contemporary life and contemporary, usually domestic, media. Among the exceptions, Jackie Stacey's study of the written memories of female cinemagoers of the 1940s and 1950s and Helen Taylor's work with female fans of the novel and the film *Gone With The Wind* have brought cultural studies-style ethnographic approaches to the study of historical media consumption.[18] This work may be described as historical ethnography; or, to appropriate another term from cultural anthropology, 'ethnohistory'.

Ethnohistory emerged as a distinct field of inquiry in the 1940s, its object being the historical study of non-literate cultures. This area had been neglected not only by cultural anthropology, which tends not to concern itself with history, but, because of the absence of written records in these cultures, by historians as well. Ethnohistory deployed ethnographic description and interpretation alongside oral historical inquiry and the historian's traditional source materials, in this instance documents produced by conquerors and missionaries. The features of ethnohistory which are of greatest relevance to an historical study of film reception and consumption are, firstly, the use of oral accounts as a research resource and, secondly, the deployment of sources and research protocols of several different kinds. An ethnohistorical study of film reception will aim to keep several balls in play. Following Staiger, it will ideally adopt a dialectical, discursive, and context-aware approach to its source materials and data. Following Clifford and Geertz, it will respect informants as collaborators, and yet make no presumptions as to the transparency of their accounts. In the quest to transcend the text-context dualism, it will aim for inclusivity, bringing together issues around film texts and spectatorial engagements with questions relating to the social audience and the contexts of reception.

The stories, histories and memories in this book are the product of a wide-ranging ethnohistorical study of 1930s cinema culture, conducted over some ten years and involving three parallel sets of inquiries. These inquiries draw on the historian's traditional source materials, contemporary records of various kinds; on ethnographic-style inquiries among surviving cinemagoers of the 1930s; and on readings of selected 1930s films. Although historical, ethnographic and film-based investigations are normally conducted in separate disciplinary and methodological universes, the objective here is to follow the precepts of methodological triangulation, whereby more than one method is brought to bear on a single research problem. The three sets of inquiries have been conducted in parallel with the aim of producing an ethnohistorical account which encompasses all the various objects: the research design is set out in the Appendix. Taken on its own, each inquiry produces a different story; and while each story may be informative in its own right, and even offer new knowledge, it will fill in only a fraction of the picture. For a nuanced and integrated understanding of how cinema works historically, culturally and experientially, it is essential to work at the point where historical, ethnographic and textual stories meet.

The ethnographic element of this investigation consists of a ground-breaking piece of research whose aim is to enter imaginatively into the world of 1930s cinema culture by attending to the stories of those most closely involved, the cinemagoers themselves; and as such it raises conceptual and methodological issues germane to the entire ethnohistorical project. While the cinemagoer's standpoint can certainly be inferred from contemporary records (box-office figures as a measure of the popularity of particular films and stars, say), for an ethnographic inquiry the experience of cinemagoing must be the core and the *raison-d'être*. In consequence, cinemagoers are involved in the research process as inform- ants, and their accounts constitute both the engine and the product of investigation.

Ethnographic inquiry depends upon direct contact between re- searchers and informants, on building a relationship between them, and on researchers treating informants and their stories with respect. If the ideal type of this relationship is participant observation, less sustained qualitative research encounters – in-depth interviews, for example – also involve varying degrees of collaboration and shared productions of knowledge. As far as the principle of collaboration in a non-participant observation context is concerned, oral history interviews offer a good case in point.[19] But even at the other end of the qualitative spectrum, where researchers and informants do not necessarily meet but make contact in other ways, a dialogic process is still at work, and the research encounter will still combine elements of collaboration and maieusis: for in all degrees of ethnographic inquiry, besides actively listening the researcher acts as midwife to the informant's stories.

In ethnographic investigations in which informants are asked to recollect events from the past, their stories may acquire additional value as contributions to historical record. As cultural historian Alison Light observes, 'an understanding of any period might have new things to yield if it acknowledged other perspectives and positions in the culture'.[20] Adding the accounts of marginalised people to the historical record is an entirely worthwhile objective, and indeed is one of the aims of the present inquiry. But it is not its sole nor even its primary purpose; and in any case historical records grounded in remembering have their own distinctive status as evidence. Ethnographic material has been gathered here with the aim of understanding the meanings of cinema for its users and the place of filmgoing in people's everyday lives; to shed light on the ways in which cinema culture figures in history, society and experience; to revitalise and complicate current thinking about the relationship between cinema and its users, past and present; and, above all, to understand how cinema memory works, both in its own right and as a distinctive expression of cultural memory.

As part of the broader ethnohistorical investigation, ethnographic inquiry was undertaken in full recognition of the fact that, in dealing with events of 60 and more years earlier, informants' accounts are memory texts, or recorded acts of remembering, and that particular questions arise concerning the evidential status of accounts which rely on remembering – and thus also on forgetting, selective memory and hindsight. However, memory is regarded here as neither providing access to, nor as representing, the past 'as it was'; the past, rather, is taken to be mediated, indeed produced, in the activity of remembering. When informants tell stories about their youthful filmgoing, they are producing memories in specific ways in a particular context, the research encounter. In other words, they are doing memory work: staging their memories, performing them.

Informants' accounts are consequently treated not only as data but also as discourse, as material for interpretation. Concern is as much with *how* people talk about their youthful picturegoing – with memory discourse – as with *what* they say about it – memory content. For an understanding of cultural memory, it is important to attend to the ways in which memory is produced in the activity of telling stories about the past, personal or shared; to the construction and narration of these memory stories; and in the present instance to the ways in which cinema figures in and shapes these memories. Analysis of ethnographic material is thus conducted on two levels: firstly, it is treated as data which generate insights into the place of cinemagoing and cinema culture in people's everyday lives in the 1930s; and secondly, it is read discursively, for the light it sheds on the nature and workings of cinema memory. This inquiry, in other words, is as much about memory as it is about cinema. It is about the interweaving of the two as cinema memory.

This is not a predictive or a deductive process. As Clifford Geertz observes, ethnography's thick description and interpretation are continuous with one another, the ethnographer's 'double task' being

> to uncover the conceptual structures that inform our subjects' acts, the 'said' of social discourse, and to construct a system of analysis in whose terms what is generic to those structures, what belongs to them because they are what they are, will stand out against the other determinants of human behaviour.[21]

One of the central aims of the present inquiry is to observe the characteristic tropes of memory, of cinema memory, as they present themselves in informants' testimonies. Approached inductively these rich and diverse testimonies yield a limited, but recurrent and pervasive, set of discursive registers. These I shall call repetitive, anecdotal, impersonal and past/present. They differ from each other most markedly in the degree or the manner in which the informant implicates herself or himself in the story and/or its narration.

Impersonal discourse, for example, is characteristically delivered in the third person, distancing the informant from both the content of the account and its narration. This is the register of a witness momentarily standing aside from 'what happened' ('what stupid teenagers we were!'); or, where deployed throughout a testimony, it marks an informant's self-presentation as an expert witness or social commentator rather than as an involved participant ('Hollywood was a dream factory'). At the opposite extreme, anecdotal discourse deploys first-person narration of a specific event or occasion, with the informant constructing herself or himself as a protagonist – more often than not as chief protagonist – in the story ('I remember one time…'). In repetitive memory discourse, the most frequently occurring type, the telling also implicates the informant in events, but both the events themselves and the narrator's involvement in them are represented as habitual ('I always went with my mother'); and often as collective ('we used to hang around outside'; 'you wanted to impress the girls').

The past/present register is about the way in which time is organised in memory discourse, and may embrace a range of relationships between narrator, story and narratee. An extremely common variant of this trope is a simple comparison between past and present, between things as they were long ago and as they are today: this often takes the form of apparently detached observation, and is always firmly rooted in the present, the moment of narration ('the film stars used to be so elegant then, they are all so scruffy now'). This register also incorporates accounts showing greater profundity of engagement on the informant's part with the activity of remembering and with the detail of what is remembered. Often observed in orally transmitted life stories, this discursive register marks accounts in which informants, usually unaware of doing so, shift or 'shuttle' back and forth between past and present standpoints.[22]

Informants' testimonies acquire their idiosyncratic qualities from the degree to which each type of memory discourse is deployed and the manner in which shifts between discursive registers are negotiated. Although observations on these points should be regarded as suggestive rather than conclusive, gender, social class and regional differences in discursive registers do seem to be apparent: the impersonal register, for example, marks a number of the middle-class male informants' accounts. Testimonies characterised by anecdote, often assumed to be the mark of a 'good' storyteller, come across as particularly vivid. Anecdote is relatively rare and does not appear to be the preserve of any one social group, but one commentator has noted that this variant of memory discourse may have a specific function in working-class autobiography, acting as 'a way of mediating between rawer, unformulated experience and more general or formulated truths; it does so by turning such truths into narrative and character'.[23]

If memory stories are not, in the usual sense of the word, fictions, they can certainly be treated as narratives. Considered thus, memory stories share a number of formal attributes, prominent among which is a distinctive organisation of time. Time is rarely continuous or sequential in memory-stories, which are often narrated as a montage of vignettes, anecdotes, fragments, 'snapshots', flashes. Memory texts often display a metaphorical – as opposed to an analogical – quality, and as such have more in common with poetry than with the classical narrative with its linearity, causality and closure. To borrow the terminology of Formalist literary theory, the memory text stresses plot over story, and its formal structure and organisation are typically as salient as its content, if not more so. Often, too, memory texts will deliver abrupt and vertiginous shifts of setting and/or narrative viewpoint.[24]

The formal attributes of memory texts, too, often betray a collective imagination as well as embodying truths of a more personal salience: 'The degree of presence of "formalised materials" like proverbs, songs, formulaic language, stereotypes,' suggests the oral historian Alessandro Portelli, 'can be a measure of the degree of presence of "collective viewpoint"'.[25] Thus memory texts may create, rework, repeat and recontextualise the stories people tell each other about the kinds of lives they have led; and these memory-stories can assume a timeless, even a mythic, quality which may be enhanced with every retelling. Such everyday myth-making works at the levels of both personal and collective memory and is key in the production, through memory, of shared identities. The philosoper Edward Casey uses the word 'commemoration' to describe communal acts of memory: with its sense of a public space of memory, this form of remembering clearly has a ritual quality.[26]

In this project's ethnographic inquiry, interpretation of informants' accounts is approached inductively: the testimonies themselves are the starting-point, and interpretations arise from the material itself rather than from any hypotheses or a priori assumptions. This approach has the benefit of giving priority to what people say about their cinemagoing experiences and memories; and, since historical and film textual materials are likewise treated discursively and inductively, it also offers a point of triangulation between the three sets of inquiries, as well as a common methodological grounding for the ethnohistorical investigation as a whole.

The chapters which follow trace a trajectory from the earliest memories and cinema's place in them, through to what for the majority of the 1930s generation is a significant endpoint, the close of a chapter: 1939, and the rapid coming of age brought on by the outbreak of war. The landscapes of memory are populated by friends and family, long gone; and from this lost everyday world many brief excursions into the out-of-the-ordinary world of the pictures are ventured in memory. Cutting across narratives of formation we witness moments of intensity – images, fragments, vignettes – recollected as if out of time: daydreams of romance, keen longings for life to be somehow better; bodily memories of movement and activity – running, dancing; even out-of-body sensations.

The story starts out from the places of memory, the places of childhood: the paths that lead back into a past that is remembered as a landscape across which cinemas are dotted like beacons in the night, and where all journeys begin and end at home.

Notes

1. This phrase is from the title of Henry James Forman's digest of the findings of the 1930s Payne Fund Studies of the cinema audience in the USA, *Our Movie-Made Children* (New York: Macmillan, 1933).

2. H.E. Browning and A.A. Sorrell, 'Cinemas and cinema-going in Great Britain', *Journal of the Royal Statistical Society*, vol. 117, no. 2 (1954), pp. 133–168; this revises the figures in Simon Rowson, 'A statistical survey of the cinema industry in Great Britain in 1934', *Journal of the Royal Statistical Society*, vol. 99, no. 1 (1936), pp. 67–129. See also Rowson, *The Social and Political Influences of Films*, (London: British Kinematograph Society, 1939).

3. Richards, *The Age of the Dream Palace: Cinema and Society in Britain, 1930–39* (London: Routledge and Kegan Paul, 1984), p. 15. See also Andrew Davies, *Leisure, Gender and Poverty: Working-class Culture in Salford and Manchester, 1900–1939* (Milton Keynes: Open University Press, 1992); Stephen G. Jones, *Workers at Play: A Social and Economic History of Leisure, 1918–1939* (London: Routledge and Kegan Paul, 1986); Nicholas Hiley, '"Let's go to the pictures": the British cinema audience in the 1920s and

1930s', *Journal of Popular British Cinema*, no. 2 (1999), pp. 39–53. For contemporary data, see, for example, E. Wight Bakke, *The Unemployed Man: A Social Study* (London: Nisbet and Co Ltd, 1933); A.P. Jephcott, *Girls Growing Up* (London: Faber and Faber, 1942); London School of Economics and Political Science, *The New Survey of London Life and Labour, Vol ix: Life and Leisure* (London: P.S. King and Son Ltd, 1935); John MacKie, *The Edinburgh Cinema Enquiry: Being an Investigation Conducted into the Influence of the Film on Schoolchildren and Adolescents in the City* (Edinburgh: Edinburgh Cinema Enquiry Committee, 1933); T.M. Middleton, 'An Enquiry into the Use of Leisure Amongst the Working Classes of Liverpool' (MA, University of Liverpool, 1931).

4. J.B. Priestley, *English Journey* (London: William Heinemann Ltd, 1934), p. 401. For a social history of the period, see C.L. Mowat, *Britain Between the Wars, 1918–1940* (London: Methuen, 1955).

5. Kristin Thompson has calculated that in 1930 US films took a 75 per cent share of the UK market and that the proportion remained similar throughout the decade: Thompson, *Exporting Entertainment: America in the World Film Market, 1907–34* (London: BFI Publishing, 1985) p. 219. At 69.5 per cent in 1930, 72.6 per cent in 1931 and 70 per cent in 1932, Margaret Dickinson and Sarah Street's figures are close to Thompson's: see Dickinson and Street, *Cinema and State: The Film Industry and Government, 1927–34* (London: BFI, 1985), p. 42. On British films' share of the market, see Tony Aldgate, 'Comedy, class and containment: the British domestic cinema of the 1930s', in *British Cinema History*, (eds) James Curran and Vincent Porter (London: Weidenfeld and Nicolson, 1983), pp. 257–271; Stephen Craig Shafer, 'Enter the Dream House: the British Film Industry and the Working Classes in Depression England, 1929–1939' (PhD, University of Illinois, 1982).

6. For details, see Appendix; and Annette Kuhn, 'Cinema culture and femininity in the 1930s', in *Nationalising Femininity*, (eds) Christine Gledhill and Gillian Swanson (Manchester: Manchester University Press, 1996), pp. 180–2. See also John Sedgwick, *Popular Filmgoing in 1930s Britain* (Exeter: University of Exeter Press, 2000). Although a distinctively national set of tastes is observable, there are regional variations within this overall profile: see 'Census tells what film stars Britain prefers', *Daily Express*, 14 November 1933, p. 8; 'Conflicting tastes of British film-goers', *World Film News*, February 1937, pp. 6–7.

7. See Kuhn, 'Cinema culture and femininity in the 1930s', p. 177–8, in which it is argued that the stereotype undergoes a change towards the end of the 1930s.

8. Jackie Stacey, 'Textual obsessions: method, memory and researching female spectatorship', *Screen*, vol. 34, no. 3 (1993), pp. 260–274.

9. These debates originated within feminist film studies, and are rehearsed in the special issue on 'The Spectatrix' of *Camera Obscura*, nos. 20–21 (1989).

10. For an informative discussion of cinema audience studies, see Jostein Gripsrud, 'Film audiences', in *The Oxford Guide to Film Studies*, (ed.) John Hill and Pamela Church Gibson (Oxford: Oxford University Press, 1998).

11. Kuhn, 'Women's genres', *Screen*, vol. 25, no. 1 (1984), pp. 18–28.

12. For an interesting debate on this question, see Janet Staiger and Martin Barker, 'Traces of interpretations: Janet Staiger and Martin Barker in conversation', in *Framework*, no. 42 (2000), http://www.frameworkonline.com/42jsmb.htm (17 August 2001).

13. Annette Kuhn, *Cinema, Censorship and Sexuality, 1909–1925* (London: Routledge, 1988), pp. 9–10; Jostein Gripsrud, 'Moving images, moving identities: texts and contexts in the reception history of film and television' (Los Angeles: Society for Cinema Studies Annual Conference, 1991).

14. Janet Staiger, *Interpreting Films: Studies in the Historical Reception of American Cinema* (Princeton, NJ: Princeton University Press, 1992), p. 81 (emphasis in original). See also Staiger, 'The handmaiden of villainy: methods and problems in studying the historical reception of film', *Wide Angle,* vol. 8, no. 1 (1986), pp. 19–28; Robert C. Allen, 'From exhibition to reception: reflections on the audience in film history', in *Screen Histories: A* Screen *Reader,* (eds) Annette Kuhn and Jackie Stacey (Oxford: Oxford University Press, 1998), pp. 13–21; Staiger, 'The perversity of spectators: expanding the history of classical Hollywood cinema', in *Moving Images, Culture and the Mind,* (ed.) Ib Bondebjerg (Luton: University of Luton Press, 2000), pp. 19–30; Staiger, 'Writing the history of American film reception', in *Hollywood Spectatorship: Changing Perceptions of Cinema Audiences,* (eds) Melvyn Stokes and Richard Maltby (London: British Film Institute, 2001).

15. Clifford Geertz, *The Interpretation of Cultures* (New York: Basic Books, 1973), pp. 6, 20.

16. James Clifford, *The Predicamant of Culture: Twentieth-Century Ethnography, Literature, and Art* (Cambridge, MA: Harvard University Press, 1988), p. 9. See also *Writing Culture: The Poetics and Politics of Ethnography* (eds) James Clifford and George E. Marcus (Berkeley: University of California Press, 1986).

17. See, for example, David Morley, *Family Television: Cultural Power and Domestic Leisure* (London: Comedia, 1986); James Lull, *Inside Family Viewing: Ethnographic Research on Television's Audiences* (London: Comedia, 1990); John Tulloch, *Watching Television Audiences: Cultural Theories and Methods* (London: Edward Arnold, 2000); Jostein Gripsrud, 'Film audiences'.

18. Jackie Stacey, *Star Gazing: Hollywood Cinema and Female Spectatorship* (London: Routledge, 1994); Helen Taylor, *Scarlett's Women: Gone With The Wind and its Female Fans* (London: Virago Press, 1989). See also Richard de Cordova, 'Ethnography and exhibition: the child audience, the Hays Office and Saturday matinees', *Camera Obscura,* no. 23 (1990), pp. 91–106.

19. On the oral history interview, see Karl Figlio, 'Oral history and the Unconscious', *History Workshop,* no. 26 (1988), pp. 120–132; Luisa Passerini, 'Memory', *History Workshop,* no. 15 (1983), pp. 195–196; Alessandro Portelli, 'The peculiarites of oral history', *History Workshop,* no. 12 (1981), pp. 96–107; Paul Thompson, 'Believe it or not: rethinking the historical interpretation of memory', in *Memory and History: Essays on Recalling and Interpreting Experience,* (eds) Jaclyn Jeffrey and Glenace Edwall (Lanham, MD: University Press of America, 1994), pp. 1–13. See also Michael Agar, 'Stories, background knowledge and themes: problems in the analysis of life history narrative', *American Ethnologist,* vol. 7, no. 2 (1980), pp. 223–239; Mark Freeman, *Rewriting the Self: History, Memory, Narrative* (London: Routledge, 1993).

20. Alison Light, *Forever England: Femininity, Literature and Conservatism Between the Wars* (London: Routledge, 1991), p. 6.

21. Geertz, *The Interpretation of Cultures,* p. 27.

22. Alessandro Portelli, '"The time of my life": functions of time in oral history', in *The Death of Luigi Trastulli and Other Stories: Form and Meaning in Oral History* (Albany, NY: State University of New York Press, 1991), pp. 59–76.

23. Simon Dentith, 'Contemporary working-class autobiography: politics of form, politics of content', in *Modern Selves: Essays on Modern British and American Autobiography,* (ed.) Philip Dodd (London: Frank Cass, 1986), pp. 60–80. The quotation is from p. 71.

24. For a full discussion of these points, see Annette Kuhn, 'A journey through

memory', in *Memory and Methodology*, (ed.) Susannah Radstone (Oxford: Berg, 2000), pp. 179–9.

25. Portelli, 'The peculiarites of oral history', p. 99.

26. Edward S. Casey, *Remembering: A Phenomenological Study* (Bloomington, IN: Indiana University, 1987), p. 216.

2

The Scenes of Cinema Memory

PLACES that we love, places we feel attached to, have the power to move us. The very idea of attachment to a place implies a bodily relationship to it, even perhaps a merging of boundaries between body and place. This notion is antithetical to systems of thought which propose that humans are set apart from the surrounding world, bounded by their skins; which is perhaps why the potency of *place*, concrete and lived, as against *space*, an abstraction, has been underestimated in Western thought. The idea of place implies a potential for rootedness, an engagement with one's milieu, which is fundamentally at odds with the Enlightenment project.

In phenomenological terms, contends Edward Casey, there is an elective affinity between place and memory:

> To be placeless in one's remembering is not only to be disoriented; it is to be decidedly disadvantaged with regard to what a more complete mnemonic experience might deliver. Places serve to *situate* one's memorial life.[1]

The relationship, Casey argues, may operate at a number of levels. Places are containers of memory: simply being in a place can trigger or produce memories. Places also situate memories, serving as a 'mise en scene for remembered events'.[2] Every place has its own inherent features, its own character; and these are independently instrumental in informing acts of memory. Memory, too, is a *topos* in its own right: it is a place we revisit, or to which we are transported; it is the road we travel along and also the destination of our memory-journey. To this extent, memory not only has a topography, it *is* a topography; and the site of production of place-memories is the lived body, the body which traces out the scenes of memory. Memory, in this view, is at once emplaced and embodied.

Producing an account of cinemagoing in the 1930s from the standpoint, now, of the cinemagoers themselves obviously calls for an engagement with memory. And place is extraordinarily insistent in the memories of 1930s cinemagoers, above all when memories are performed orally, in interviews. To a remarkable degree, interviewees set out their memory stories in terms of place: virtually all of them at some point organise their accounts topographically, locating memory stories in the remembered places of their childhood and youth. These physical, spatial and contextual memories are nearly always offered in the early stages of an interview, for it is clearly considered important to lay out the setting before moving on to the detail.

While every informant 'does' place-memory in his or her own way, an overall sense emerges from interviews of a navigation of psycho-geographies, or mental topographies of familiar remembered territory. A rather limited set of contents or themes emerges from informants' physical, spatial and contextual memories, and these in turn are produced through a circumscribed and distinctive corpus of discursive strategies. Informants' topographical memory talk, too, offers clues to some of the ways in which cinema memory operates as a specific form of cultural memory. To summarise, place-related themes observable across the body of interview material are: recollections of cinemas that lay within walking-distance of the informant's home; an association between proximity and familiarity, particularly apparent in the idea of 'going to the pictures' as an extension of home life, a comfortable and unthreatening early venture into the public domain; distinctions drawn, in terms of accessibility, between cinemas in the informant's neighbourhood and those further away, as for example in city centres (that is, beyond walking distance); and contrasts between topographies past and present.

While place is a concern shared by all informants, there are individual variations in the ways in which it figures in their accounts, in the instrumentality of place in memory stories and in the enunciative standpoint from which place stories are narrated. Basically, though, five types of topographical memory talk emerge with regularity in interviews.

These are: memory maps; the guided tour; discursive distance/immersion in the past; shared remembering; and associations and detours.

A number of informants provide discursive 'memory maps' of the parts of town, the neighbourhoods or the suburbs where they first went to the pictures. These maps vary in style and detail, but their function is always to lay out a mise en scene for the recollections which follow. They are 'establishing shots', in a sense; and like establishing shots in films, they work at the service of a story or stories. In mapping out the locations of their memory stories, informants will either insert themselves fully into the past, or speak from the standpoint of the present, or they may 'shuttle' discursively between past and present.

Interviewees Irene Dennerley and Freda McFarland are among those who offer highly detailed memory maps. Mrs Dennerley was born in Warrington in 1918, moved to Manchester as an infant, and was still living in the city at the time of her interview:

Int What were the cinemas round here that you went to?

ID Well, I suppose, when I was young, when I was really young, I lived in Devonshire Street.

Int Right.

ID So one of them would have been the Devonshire. I don't think it's there now but that's what it was called then. Cause they had a stage there, there were a Charleston competition. Didn't get much, about half a crown I think but still [*laughs*] it was daft. Yeh, what other places, yeh, and there was one in Great Cheetham Street, near the bottom, I think that was called the Empire and then there was the Rialto Picturehouse which was, in a way, I think it's still got the Rialto, that's on Bury New Road, near Cheetham Street. I don't know if you know any of these streets? But that's where it is. Quite busy there. And it's em, I think it's a bingo hall now that, you know, so them were all near to Devonshire Street, you know, so that was the pictures that we used to sort of go to. Again, I think from there we moved, oh we moved quite a few times, we moved to Waterloo Road and [*laughs*] it was one on what they called Broughton Lane, I think they it's still called Broughton Lane but they used to call it the bugshouse, you know, I don't think you'd get anything but it was one of those. In the front was like forms, you know, of course we were only little kids, we didn't care, you know. And what else was there? Higher up, when you up to Great Clowes Street, that was a bit up though, that was the Tower. We were full of picture houses. And then coming up the road, say coming up to Cheetham Hill Road, there was on one side, near Waterloo Road, the Shakespeare, down this other street called the Premier. Now the building of the Premier's still there but of course it's not a picture house. I don't know what it is. Then a bit lower down there was an Odeon near Queen's Road. And I think that's, is it the B&Q? I think it is, that, the building is, so they tell me. Then there was the Temple and that one's taken down. I think that's down now. I think that's near the very old graveyard. St Luke's, it was called, you know?[3]

Born in Wigan in 1916, Freda McFarland moved to Bolton in 1921:

FM   This is St Helen's Road. Beyond. Perhaps about ten minutes from here. Down there. You get the main road. St Helen's Road. Eh there was the [Rumworth?] it was called. And then there was this eh [D?] pictures which went to the Tivoli. And that was all along that road. But going over to Dean Road, there was the Fern Cinema. That's three isn't it? Up to now. And then there was the Regent where we used to go. That's four. And then there was a big one. Eh [pause: 1 second] it turned into a skating rink after. And it began with R. It wasn't the Rialto and it wasn't the Regent. [Pause: 2 seconds]. But it began with an R.

Int   Not the Rex? I've heard of the Rex.

FM   Don't remember that one. No, this was [pause: 2 seconds] it was ordinary name.

Int   Mm.

FM   And it was a big cinema that. And they used to say a lot of courting couples used to go there and sit on the back seat. You know. And that was to, I don't know. I never went in, so I don't know. Em so that was like em what, one, two, three, four, five. And then there was one on St George's Road called the Rialto. [Pause: 2 seconds]. This was called the Imperial. That's six isn't it? There was the Queens on [Rajgate?]. That's seven. And then, there was one opened on [Rajgate?] em called the Lido. Now that's still going [amazed voice]. I don't know that it's still called the Lido. But it's still going. And I can remember when it was being built.

Now I was still at school when that was being built. They used to say, the workmen that were working on it said it would fall down within five years. Well it was still up. That's only about seven. There was one [*pause: 2 seconds*]. There was one called the Gem in [*S?*] Street because that is where guide headquarters is built now. You know. That sort of going up em eh, wait a minute. Not Blackburn Road way. Em [*T?*] Road. I believe there was in their teens of cinemas.[4]

Both of these interviewees lay out maps of their old neighbourhoods, primarily perhaps as a mnemonicon or *aide-mémoire*, and each then sets out from what is clearly, if implicitly, a precise address ('home', no doubt), on a journey through these remembered places in quest of the cinemas that used to be there. Mrs Dennerley's account is particularly fluid in its thematisation of, and shifts between, past ('there were a Charleston competition') and present ('is it the B & Q?'). The *aide-mémoire* function of Mrs McFarland's discursive mapping is perhaps more pronounced: her objective is to convey, from the standpoint of the present, a picture of what was once an abundance of cinemas in the neighbourhood: 'I believe there was in their teens of cinemas'; or, as many informants put it, 'one on every street corner'.

As 'stopping-off places' within topographies mapped in memory talk, cinemas may function discursively in a number of – potentially double-edged – ways. Mrs Dennerley and Mrs McFarland are typical in speaking of the current uses of former cinema buildings – an expression of the past/present trope which crops up throughout all the interviews, and which points to the palimpsest-like quality of topographical memory. Beneath a place as it appears today lie, all still palpably present in memory, layers of its past manifestations; and these can be excavated in memory talk by those who belong to the place. Given the decline in the fortunes of cinemagoing and the disappearance of so many cinemas since the 1950s, this excavation becomes an act of witness as much as an exercise in mental archaeology. And yet at the same time it betokens losses of several kinds – of childhood, innocence, youth, community. 'Stopping off' at cinemas on the memory map also allows the speaker to relive pleasures once experienced as familiar and very ordinary aspects of daily life, but which are now lost.

Some interviewees – those an ethnographer might consider good storytellers – embellish their discursive maps with detail and colour. Mary McCusker was born in 1916 in the Gorbals, Glasgow, and was living in nearby Cowcaddens when she gave her interviews. In her first interview, she offers a lively 'guided tour' of the cinemas of her childhood, and has an interesting story to tell for each stopping-off place:

> The Paragon was the local cinema in Cumberland Street. Eh, oh a wee, what would ye say? A wee fleapit sort of style. Oh, nowadays. Eh, penny matinee on a Saturday. And I can remember, eh, this particular film. *Dr Fu Manchu*. And that night I came home and had a nightmare about Dr Fu Manchu. The Chinese, with a big long nail. And my mother vowed, that's the last picture I was ever to see. I was *never* to get back again. Both of them were up all night with me with this nightmare of Dr Fu Manchu. I could see him walking through [*laughing*] the kitchen. Shows you. And then we had another cinema. Eh, the Crown picture house in Crown Street. We went there on a Saturday morning, eh, the matinee. And if you went upstairs you got an American coloured comic. A wee sheet. If you went downstairs [*pause: 2 seconds*] upstairs was tuppence and if ye went downstairs, it was a penny downstairs. And ye *didn't* get a comic. That I can remember. And eh, oh of course, when you came home you exchanged, you know, the comic and whatnot. Eh, then there was a *beautiful* cinema opened out in Caledonia Road. Oh, it was a *beautiful* cinema [*impressed voice*]. It was new to us, you know. But oh! Pricey! You know what I mean. In our standards, you know. So that was up to I was 12. That was the cinemas that I went to. Never went to any of them in the town of course.[5]

Mrs McCusker's interviews are full of vividly-detailed anecdotes, tales of singular incidents or routine events in which she figures as central protagonist. In this respect Mrs McCusker's account distinguishes itself from the repetitive memory discourse so prominent across the interviews as a whole. The discursive memory map is there – the informant locates the cinemas in their streets – but the events recounted (and in the case, for example, of the cinema in Caledonia Road, the reliving of the feelings evoked at the time by the beauty of the place) are accorded greater prominence in the story than their settings. The informant guides the listener through a memory landscape not so much joined up by lines on a mental map (as in Mrs McFarland's 'Going over to Dean Road, there was the Fern Cinema') as constructed around a series of anecdotes prompted by remembered places ('And then we had another place'). In cinematic terms, this might be a sequence composed of a montage of shots as opposed to a single tracking shot or sequence shot. That Mrs McCusker offers concrete ('real') settings for her stories adds authenticity and at the same time allows her fully to relive the memory by enunciatively placing herself within its setting.

While informants like Mrs McCusker in some degree immerse them-selves enunciatively in the past, others favour a more detached and present-oriented narration for their place-memories. Though by no means confined to this group, impersonal discourse characterises the accounts of a number of middle-class male informants.

For example, Harrow resident Anthony Venis was born in the middle-class London suburb of Hampstead in 1924. He left school at 16 and after war service became a consultant engineer:

AV Anyway the Odeon, to me, is synonymous with eh, with this area's called Metroland. Don't know whether you, have you heard that phrase?

Int No, I haven't heard that.

AV Ah. Yes this is Metroland. Because the Metropolitan railway, when they built the railway line out this way they eh, now this is ehm after [*pause: 2 seconds*] the twenties. No, the turn of the century rather. The railway company built a great swathe of land.

Int Mm.

AV All the way through. Sorry, *bought* a swathe of land all the way through and then could eh, ring their options as to where within that swathe they ran the railway line. And eh, having completed the railways then [*clears throat*] they then went into the eh, into building as well.

[...]

AV One of the things in the thirties of course was the eh, eh *amount* of cinemas that there were. [*Coughs*] Eh, we had eh, although I didn't live in, I mentioned Wembley. Well there were three in Wembley. Eh, now moving out this way, there was one at Rayners Lane, there was one at South Harrow. *Every* small area, shopping area or eh, estate area seemed to have a cinema.

There was in eh Pinner, one in Eastcote, one in Ruislip, this sort of thing.

Int   Mm.

AV   And there was a second one proposed for Pinner. So that indicated that there was quite a demand for cinemas.[6]

Mr Venis's list of the cinemas which existed in the Harrow area in the 1930s implies no personal memory of having used the buildings at the time: indeed, he did not move to Harrow until after his marriage in 1957. This informant is interested in local history, and throughout the interview presents himself not as an 'ordinary' cinemagoer but as an expert witness. His point about the Odeon cinema chain signals a peculiarity of the Harrow area which is discussed below: the enormous changes it underwent during the 1930s.

Ellen Casey was born in 1921, and has lived in the Collyhurst area of Manchester nearly all her life. She too has an interest in local history, and is a member of a reminiscence group called 'Past and Present'. As the group's name suggests, Mrs Casey and her fellow members are, unlike Mr Venis, working with memory as much as with history. During the course of her interview, Mrs Casey shows the interviewer a photograph of the part of Collyhurst where she grew up, using this as a starting point for a discursive 'guided tour' of the neighbourhood, pointing out the locations of her house and her favourite cinema, and tracing the walk from the one to the other:

EC   That's the bridge. Well this is the part I lived. I lived just behind here.

Int   Right.

EC   Yeah. This is just part of Collyhurst I lived. And just behind there. This is the railway bridge. A bridge this were the trains used to go under across.

Int   Right.

EC   Like that. Yeah. I lived just at the back. Just down there. Where it's rounded off. There was a sort of em, an entry. And you went down there and I just lived down there. And em [*pause: 1 second*]. See that big building there.

Int   Yeah.

EC   Well as you just went down there, there's like a street there. If you went down there the cinny [*pause: 1 second*] was next to this building. My em picture house, the cinny, was next to this building.[7]

Here the informant's body joins the discursive tour as she directs the interviewer to look at a spot in the photograph which stands in for a 'real' place: 'Just down there'. The location of cinema in relation to home is demonstrated as much as described in this short passage, which is structured by, and produces, the activity of performing the movement into and through the 'entry', as well as the location of the short walk to 'the cinny'. Past and present, narrator and remembered action, are telescoped here as the narratee is shown, rather than told about, the journey.

As the passages quoted so far show, interviewees consider it important to get the settings of their accounts exactly right. They are specific in their designation of streets, for example, often making considerable efforts to remember names and locations. Such insistence on topographical accuracy is particularly pronounced in interviews with couples or groups, when, in sometimes lengthy duets or ensemble performances of memory, informants quiz and correct each other about the places of their youth.

George and Ethel Cullum grew up in different parts of the largely rural county of Norfolk, met in 1931 and married in 1936 when Ethel was 28 and George about 26. Bringing their discussion of the locations of cinemas in Norwich to an end, they fix the details of an only partly-shared cinemagoing history both temporally and topographically by rounding the story off with a wedding – their own:

GC And they had one of those, a place, I don't remember it. That's before my time. But they had one of those eh, in St Stephen's Road. There used to be a station there called Victoria Station. At the bottom of Queen's Road. And they had one there. But eh, I remember it being talked about because my father's uncle kept a pub at the corner of Queen's Road. And that's how I came to know about it.

Int Ah I see.

GC There's also another one which is a very small one, run by a man named, he was only a young man at that time. Was eh, in Northumberland Street. That was run [*in some public house?*]. I think the public house skittle alley. We used to have what they call skittle alleys.

EC That's the Mayfair. That ain't the one, that's the [*inaudible*]. When we used to go, eh, they were two iron gates there.

Int Ah.

EC See they made that eh, the Mayfair. Then I used to go there when I went to work. Now that's the Electric Theatre, isn't it? No, that's on Prince [*Name?*] Road.

GC Yeah.

EC That is. Next to the Regent.

GC Yeah.

[*Pause: 4 seconds*]

GC The Capitol [*rest inaudible*]. No that wasn't the Capitol. Surely.

EC Yeah.

GC Oh wait a minute. I'm lookin' at the wrong one. The Mayfair.

EC I used to go to the pictures straight from work. First house.

GC Yeah, this is the Mayfair. The Capitol. This Capitol, we lived right near there when we were married.[8]

The five members of the Hamiltonhill reminiscence group in Glasgow have in common a lifelong familiarity with certain parts of the city, and during their first interview they work together to name and locate some of the picture houses they remember from long ago:

HD No, that was further down, down at Cowcaddens.

LB I think there was the one, but, no, see if ye said that name.

DP Oh aye.

SI The Wee Raglan, that's right, aye.

SH Sarah's saying the Wee Raglan.

Int The Wee Raglan?

HD Oh I [remember] that one, it was great.

[…]

HD Where the television place was, now it's the Theatre Royal.

LB They had the Star and oh Mary, on Garscube Road, the Star.

SI Aye, aye, that's right. An' the other one facing it.

All Aye.

SH Was there a lot more than what there is today?

All Oh aye.

HD Away up.

LB The Astoria.

HD Three or four in the street.

LB An awful wee.

JS Another wee theatre.

LB An awful wee theatre, the Astoria, and you had to go away down. You had to watch right enough.

JS Ye'd get taken away, and ye were standing.

LB If it was dark. It was in darkness, if ye didn't fall.

JS In the show [*indecipherable*].

HD The one up at Sighthill, they called it the Coffin. Do you [remember] it?

DP We used to do that as well.

HD They called it the Coffin, because it was next to the cemetery.

[All agree]

LB That's right, I [remember] that.⁹

At some point – usually towards the end of the second interview, when the participants are winding down and the sharp focus of the first interview no longer feels appropriate, informants will permit themselves to stray into what might look like detours on their memory maps. However, these moments of 'going off track' sometimes prove surprisingly informative about the workings of cultural memory.

Born in 1921, Rosalind Avadis lived in Neasden in the 1930s and moved to Harrow in 1946. Both her husband and her father were in the clothing trade:

RA That's why when Mick talked about the fleapit that actually in, it still is, in the Portobello Road. The famous Portobello Road. It's still there.

Int I'll have to have a look out for that.

RA Yeah. Yeah. If you walked with someone.

Int Mm.

RA It's the end near to Kensington Park.

Int Right.

RA Not the end where there's a lot of stores.

Int Mm.

RA Actually, it's in the middle of the stores.

Int Mm.

RA It's on the other side of the road. Yes. Well when I lived in North Kensington. That's where we used to go there. And to the State in Kilburn. And the Coronet. Which is in another part, Archer Street I think it was called. Had another name. I can't remember it. But it was halfway to town.

Int Mm.

RA Between Kensington and town. And they were very, somewhere near Bayswater.

Int Mm.

RA Very smart shops there. But regarding fashion, my own mother who as I say would make me little dresses. And then she'd make herself the most *superb* clothes [*said with awe*].

Int Mm.

RA She was *brilliant*. And very modern. Didn't matter her age. Em, when she was about 75 to 80 an' even much more.

Int Mm.

RA Well into her eighties. She'd make her own clothes. And she looked wonderful. You'd think she'd stepped out of a fashion book. Never old fashioned. Then, you'd have people of 60 who dressed old and looked old. But she never did. We never remember her as old. She lived to 96.

Int Really![10]

As she gives the interviewer directions to a cinema she knew as a child and which she had mentioned in her first interview, Mrs Avadis tries to recall the topographies of the parts of London where she lived and went to the pictures in the 1930s. But she left these areas many years ago, and the directions are vague. Following a topographical association, she then segues into a train of thought which permits her to move onto what, for her, is firmer territory – fashion, and her own well-dressed mother, the association being the recollection of the chic clothes shops in 1930s Bayswater ('Very smart shops there'). This in some respects parallels Mary McCusker's discursive strategy, except that here the remembered stopping-off places on the guided tour associate to memories which are 'off the point'.

That most of the passages quoted so far are from interviews conducted in Manchester and Harrow reflects the incidences and variants in place-memory in the four areas in which interviews were conducted. Inter-viewees from East Anglia produce the lowest incidence of place-memory, no doubt because in this largely rural region cinemas were more geographically scattered, and relatively rarely accessible on foot. This suggests a different relationship between place and memory for town and country dwellers. While the more urban areas of Glasgow, Manchester and Harrow produce similar, and appreciably higher, incidences of topographical remembering, by far the most drawn out, detailed and vivid topographical references are to be found in interviews with Manchester and Harrow informants. Glasgow interviewees are no less prone than their counterparts in Manchester and Harrow to offer topographical memories. However, there is less exposition and less detail in their accounts, perhaps because since the researchers were Glasgow-based informants felt less need to lay out explicit topographies.

Harrow presents a special case as regards topographical practices of memory, however. While Manchester and Glasgow were well established cities before the twentieth century, during the 1930s Harrow was undergoing transformation from a village situated well beyond the outer limits of London into a full-blown suburb of the metropolis. In the 1920s, much of Harrow was still semi-rural; but the area's population quadrupled in the period between 1921 and 1939, and at the outbreak of the Second World War Harrow had become the largest of all the outer London suburbs, with a population close to 200,000.[11]

During the interwar period the construction of new cinemas was at its height throughout Britain: many of these were 'supercinemas' boasting a thousand and more seats, exotic and luxurious decor and fittings, and superior sound and picture projection systems. As new houses and shopping centres sprung up in suburbs like Harrow, building plots were routinely set aside for these state-of-the-art cinemas. In the early 1930s, the prominent cinema entrepreneur Oscar Deutsch undertook to circle London with new picture palaces in his

Odeon chain; and the South Harrow Odeon, which opened in
September 1933, was among the first of these. Where at the beginning
of the 1930s Harrow had boasted only a handful of picture houses, all
dating originally from the pre-talkie era, by the end of the decade a
dozen or so new cinemas had opened in the area. These included the
Langham, which sprung up in a few months in 1936 on the site of a
sixteenth-century farmhouse in what had hitherto been known as the
'village' of Pinner.[12]

More than half of the Harrow informants were born outside the area
and neither lived nor went to the cinema in Harrow during the 1930s:
the detached tone and the divagations in the passages quoted from the
interviews of Harrow 'immigrants' Anthony Venis and Rosalind Avadis
illustrate how migration can inform the contents and discourses of place-
memory. Unlike Mr Venis and Mrs Avadis, however, Nancy Carrington
and her friends Nancy Prudhoe and Elsie Horne have all lived in the
Harrow area since infancy and have known each other since childhood:
in consequence, they share many place-memories and many cinemagoing
memories. Together they eagerly recollect the changes Harrow has gone
through during their lifetimes:

NP   And how about Barnets[?] Farm. [*Pause: 3 seconds*] Used to
be a Barnets Farm there.

EH   Opposite the Odeon?

NP   Yes, opposite the Odeon. You remember Barnets Farm?

NC   Oh yes.

NP   You could get a pint of milk at one o'clock in the morning.

NC   Opposite the cinema.

NP   And sometimes you'd have to wait until they'd milked a cow.

NC   That's right.

NP   Honestly. And the milk was warm when you got it.[13]

The juxtaposition of pastoral idyll and emblem of modernity (milk
warm from the cow a few steps away from a supercinema) in this
delightful story has a certain surreal quality. But the image strangely
echoes contemporary reports of the provenance of the Langham cinema:
from sixteenth-century farmhouse to up-to-the-minute picture palace
in a matter of weeks. Significant in the present context is the mythic
quality of both accounts, and the collectively produced character of one

of them. There is a musical quality, too, in the call-and-response format of the women's memory-talk of the Odeon, something dreamlike about the picture evoked of the pastoral happily co-existing side-by-side with the 'modern'. This must surely rate as a prime example of oral memory's capacity to combine historical, poetic and legendary forms of speech, whilst expressing personal truths and a collective imagination.[14]

All the Harrow informants who were living in the area during the 1930s spontaneously mention the immense changes the suburb has seen. Most of them deploy a distinctive discourse of place-memory, in which a contrast is drawn between the landscape as it was then and as it is now. This is very often done by means of stories about passing immediately from 'home' into a grassy place with wildflowers or grazing farm animals. This, perhaps, is another expression of a collective imagination. It also seems to be a peculiarly place-related variant of the past/present trope; for, while remaining distinctive in its evocation of a primal, unspoiled landscape, this discursive register shares something of the palimpsest-like quality of town- and city-based informants' accounts of changes in their familiar places: as one Harrow informant puts it, there were 'flowers where these houses are now'.

Brother and sister Fred and Gwen Curnick, who have lived all their lives in Harrow, talk about the place where Fred was born:

FC   There was a few houses dotted along the, the lane, cos it wasn't much more than a lane. Few houses dotted along there and of course, a farm down there.

Int   Mm.

FC   And that was, that was it. You was out in the country.

GC   Oh, yes. I mean, I can remember, em, going down Shaftesbury Avenue and you only went a little way down there and you were out in fields, you know. And you were right up to your knees in grass.

Int   Mm.

FC   Well, where she talked about, that was a farm, horse farm.

GC   Yes, that's right.

FC   And eh, you only had to walk through the farmyard [*pause: 3 seconds*] and you were out in the fields![15]

Ashley Bird, another Harrow native, also talks about the fields next to his house: 'Open fields. They weren't cultivated. Em, a few cattle sometimes. Few horses and a few sheep'; while according to Elsie Horne: 'when we came out of our back gate, there was a great big field there [...] you'd go out your back garden and you had horses in your front garden'.[16]

One feature of the pre-suburban landscape stands out with peculiar prominence in Harrow informants' accounts: Harrow Hill. The 'posh' Harrow Hill, of course, is still there, though virtually everything on and around it has changed since the 1930s. In Harrow informants' accounts, the Hill operates as synecdoche: this topographical detail is amplified and it miniaturises the whole, so that the Hill, a prominent feature of the remembered landscape, figures as the whole of Harrow. The past/present trope may be no more than implicit here; but the synecdoche is doubly significant in this context because it also associates with expressions specifically of cinema memory.

Most of the 'indigenous' Harrow informants talk about the cinema that was on the Hill during the 1930s, the Cosy. Although a picture house had opened on the Cosy's site as early as 1920, this had been closed between 1923 and 1927, and in fact the place was known as the Cosy only for the years between 1930 and 1934. Given the brevity of its existence under that name and the number of competing cinemas in the area during the 1930s, the Cosy's prominence in Harrow natives' memories is striking. There are several possible reasons for this: the Cosy's heyday largely predates the supercinema era in Harrow, and the Cosy itself represents the type of small and unpretentious picture house which, as noted in chapter 3, 1930s cinemagoers recollect most clearly from their earliest cinemagoing days. It is significant, too, that whenever the Cosy is mentioned, so is the difficulty of getting up the Hill to it, and so too is the 'luxurious Cosy Coach which has proved a boon to many and runs regularly at intervals of a quarter-of-an-hour to convey patrons to the top of the hill'.[17]

Born in South Harrow in 1918, Olga Scowen remembers the Hill as the lively centre of Harrow, and remarks on the effort required to get up to the Cosy on foot:

OS The Cosy was a funny little place on the Hill and it was completely flat. So if you sat at the back you got heads all in front of you. You weren't up above them at all. I *think* it was an abattoir, eh slaughterhouse before that. I'm not absolutely certain but it was something funny. Because Harrow-on-the-Hill in the old days was the centre. Em, we had the fire station up there. We had the, my father was working for the newspaper up there. And there were shops up there. Nowadays it's pretty dead because the, well there *is* a bus service over the hill now but there wasn't for a long time. And em, so anyway, when you wanted to go to the Cosy Cinema, you either had to walk or go on this little bus. And when we walked it was pretty steep up the last bit. And I can remember my sister pushing [*laughs*] my mother.

Int   [*Laughs*].

OS   Get her up the hill [*laughs*]. I mean we were that keen to go to the cinema that we'd do that.[18]

Fred and Gwen Curnick negotiate a shared memory map and a tour of the area's streets, with the destination the Cosy and the means of getting there not the customary walking but the famous 'Cosy Coach':

GC   And that one, that one that was up on a hill. Eh, they used to run a free bus service.

Int   Really?

GC   Yes. Em, I don't know whether you can remember just where it went but it, it,

FC   It came down [*pause: 2 seconds*] along the high road, down [*name of hill?*] then along [*pause: 2 seconds*] Lower Road, isn't it?

GC   Yes.

FC   Along Lower Road. [Besburgh?] Road to Roxburgh Bridge, over Roxburgh Bridge, down, em [*pause: 3 seconds*] that one's College Road, isn't it?

GC   College Road, yes.

FC   To the foot of College Road, then it turned right, and actually went in front of the Coliseum.

GC   Coliseum. Yes, that's right.

FC   Em, and then back up the hill, up Peterborough Road.

GC   Yeah.

FC   Up to the top of the hill and along the High Road again to the cinema.

Int Ah.

FC And eh, it done that [*pause: 3 seconds*] evening, wasn't it? It wasn't, it, it kept going round like that and you could get on it anywhere and go up to the hill or you could come down. I don't think it was all day. It was evening time. And when the last house was well and truly in, then you walked down the hill cos they stopped it. [*Laughs*]

Int So just to get you up then [*laughing*] and make your own way back.

FC Up there.

GC That's right, yes, yes, yes.

FC But that was a, that was completely free. There was no charge or anything.

GC Not on the bus, no, no.[19]

Traversing the dominant themes of physical, spatial and contextual memories present in the testimonies of 1930s cinemagoers across Britain, and structuring the discursive production of these memories, is the trope of walking. For example, the walk along familiar remembered streets of childhood is reenacted again and again, implicitly or explicitly, in informants' memory talk. For some, indeed, this topographical practice of memory functions as another kind of pathway, a means of returning to and reliving the past for the purposes of the interview: the 'trip down memory lane' may be a cliché, but it possesses considerable cultural resonance. Informants repeatedly perform their memory work through discursively 'walking the streets'.

One informant's 'walking tour' is more than merely virtual. In response to a question about local cinemas, Denis Houlston, who has lived in Levenshulme, Manchester, all his life, gives a long and detailed account of many nearby picture houses, with precise details of their locations and histories of changes in use of the buildings over the years:

So, eh, but then lower down in Longsight we've got these other two, well three, the Queen's which is a, quite an ordinary one, and that was by the side of a little brook. The brook has since been culverted and that's been demolished, em, and now on the right hand side going down was the King's Theatre which was a theatre but also a cinema, more cinema than theatre and I saw my first pantomime there. My parents took me to my first pantomime so I've a soft spot for the King's Theatre. That's demolished and it's now a public library with all the cultural facilities! Then on the opposite side of the road was the Shaftesbury cinema, and that was quite a nice one, now that was just a little bit better quality than the others, that was on the left hand side of the road, well that's now demolished and it's now a Health Centre. But all that area was completely [*pause*] flattened and you wouldn't know it.[20]

As well as talking the interviewer through his remembered pathways, Mr Houlston actually takes her for a walk around the streets near his home, pointing out the sites of three or four of the picture houses that were once within easy reach.

The more common entirely virtual passage through familiar remembered places has a special resonance for this group of informants, in that it references what many of them explicitly construct as a key point of disjuncture between past and present, between the world being produced in memory and the 'now' of the telling. Here, the recurrence of the expression 'within walking distance' is significant. For this generation, walking was the default mode of getting around: accounts, like the Curnicks', of using other means of getting to the pictures by their very lengthiness and detail mark these methods as out-of-the-ordinary. In informants' memory-stories, walking assumes an embodied, kinetic quality.

As an expression of cultural memory, cinema memory organises the embodied walking trope in specific ways. Again, for the 1930s generation, cinema buildings are recalled as familiar features of the everyday landscape, among the places which were close to, and readily accessible from, home. They are, in other words, a taken-for-granted element of what in Cockney parlance is called one's 'manor'. At the same time, as informants (re)construct and revisit their childhood landscapes from the vantage point of old age, a sense of difference and loss enters into their memory talk. The area has changed, or the informant no longer lives where she or he grew up. The cinemas that were once on every street corner are gone – torn down, or the buildings given over to new uses. Along with this comes a further loss – of the freedom, the physical capacity, the desire to walk the streets now. While this is often expressed in conventional turns of phrase ('it just isn't safe to go out at night these days'), the combination of the tropes of loss and of past/present in such statements is clearly of some cultural significance. Paraphrasing Michel de Certeau, a key commentator on practices of everyday life, it might be suggested that in memory discourse what can be spoken designates what is no longer there.[21] Informants' memory talk may be interpreted as a bid to retrieve something that has been lost.

Cultural critics who have looked at spatial practices tend to concern themselves with the practice of urban, and especially metropolitan, space rather than with neighbourhood places.[22] Some of what these commentators have to say does, though, have a bearing on the topographical practices of memory of those 1930s cinemagoers who, in de Certeau's coinage, are 'ordinary practitioners of the city', practising 'lived space' discursively in their accounts. De Certeau's distinction between belonging and not belonging also has purchase in the present context: he associates belonging with walking, and thus by implication with bodily immersion in (urban) space. Not-belonging, on the other hand, goes with looking, and particularly with that peculiar distance between looker and object of the look that is enacted in voyeurism. The walking/looking – or kinetic/optic – opposition is a suggestive one: 'belonging' in a place implies a somatic, sensual, even tactile connection with it.

In their discursive production of places and relations to place defined by the trope of walking, 1930s cinemagoers' practices of memory are pedestrian in two senses: they are ordinary, everyday; and they are negotiated on foot. At the same time, these practices are distinctive as cinema memory in that they construct cinemas as particular sorts of nodes in topographical networks. Furthermore, the settings for topographical practices of cinema memory are by no means homogeneous: not all 1930s cinemagoers are metropolitan, nor even are they all urban. The 'streetwalking' of the 1930s cinemagoer is clearly not that of Walter Benjamin's *flâneur*, for the flâneur, being characteristically detached from the places he wanders through, is more like Georg Simmel's isolated metropolitan type than a member of a local community or neighbourhood. By contrast with this 'botanising' idler, cinemagoers' walking tours are goal-directed: these people belong to the area, and the pathways they tread all lead to the pictures. In their memory maps, local picture houses figure as stopping-off points in familiar, everyday foot-passages from home through remembered streets. These passages, too, are imprinted in the body's memory, for 'places are as much in us as we are in them'.[23]

While the familiar walk to the pictures might end with a virtual excursion to the unfamiliar places, the 'other' worlds, offered up on the cinema screen, it is the places of their 'real' worlds which figure most strongly and consistently in 1930s cinemagoers' memories. For this generation, going to the pictures was the occasion for the very earliest ventures into the world beyond the home. Close to home, almost an extension of home, and yet not home, 'the pictures' is remembered as both daring and safe. Referencing Freud, Michel de Certeau suggests that the back and forth (*fort/da*) movement and the 'being-there' (*Dasein*) which characterise spatial practices re-enact the child's separation from the mother.[24] To translate this conceit to cinema memory, it might be argued that for the 1930s generation, cinema constitutes a transitional object.

Notes

1. Edward S. Casey, *Remembering: A Phenomenological Study* (Bloomington, IN: Indiana University, 1987), pp. 183–4. Emphasis in original.

2. Ibid., p. 189. See also Henri Bergson, *Matter and Memory* (London: George Allen and Unwin, 1911); Gaston Bachelard, *The Poetics of Space* (Boston: Beacon Press, 1969).

3. T95-24, Irene Dennerley, Manchester, 1 June 1995.

4. T95-46, Freda McFarland, Bolton, 7 June 1995.

5. T94-5, Mary McCusker, Glasgow, 22 November 1994.

6. T95-84, Anthony Venis, Harrow, 11 July 1995.

7. 95-182-14, Ellen Casey, Manchester, to Annette Kuhn, 13 October 2000; T95-38, Ellen Casey, Manchester, 31 May 1995.

8. T95-123, Ethel and George Cullum, Norfolk, 25 November 1995.

9. T94-3, Lilian Buik, Helen Donaghy, Sarah Irvine, John Shearer and Davy Paterson, 18 November 1994 (also present Senga Hughes, care-worker).

10. T95-108, Rosalind Avadis, Harrow, 27 July 1995.

11. In 1921, Harrow's population was 49,020; in 1931, 96,656; and by 1939, 190,200. Alan A. Jackson, *Semi-detached London: Suburban Development, Life and Transport, 1900–39* (London: George Allen and Unwin, 1973), pp. 326–7; 95-202-15, booklet, 'From Rural Middlesex to London Borough: The Growth and Development of Harrow Illustrated with Maps', 1981.

12. 'The new cinema at South Harrow', *Harrow Observer and Gazette*, 8 September 1933; 'When film fans were spoiled for choice', *Harrow and Wembley Independent*, 31 December 1980. On the opening of the Langham, see *Harrow Observer and Gazette*, 27 December 1935; Jackson, *Semi-detached London*, pp. 177, 178.

13. T95-101, Nancy Carrington, Nancy Prudhoe and Elsie Horne, Harrow, 25 July 1995.

14. Alessandro Portelli, 'The peculiarites of oral history', *History Workshop*, no. 12 (1981), pp. 96–107.

15. T95-74, Fred and Gwen Curnick, Harrow, 5 July 1995.

16. T95-104, Ashley Bird, Harrow, 26 July 1995; T95-101, Nancy Carrington, Nancy Prudhoe and Elsie Horne, Harrow, 25 July 1995.

17. 'The Cosy Cinema: many improvements recently effected', *Harrow Observer and Gazette*, 13 November 1931.

18. T95-80, Olga Scowen, Harrow, 6 July 1995.

19. T95-74, Fred and Gwen Curnick, Harrow, 5 July 1995.

20. T95-18, A.D. Houlston, Manchester, 26 April 1995.

21. Michel de Certeau, *The Practice of Everyday Life*, trans. Steven Rendall (Berkeley: University of California Press, 1984), p. 108.

22. For example, ibid., chapter 7; Georg Simmel, 'The metropolis and mental life', in K. Wolff (ed.), *The Sociology of Georg Simmel* (Glencoe, IL: Free Press, 1950), pp. 409–24; Walter Benjamin, 'Some motifs in Baudelaire', in *Charles Baudelaire: A Lyric Poet in the Era of High Capitalism* (London: Verso, 1983); Henri Lefebvre, *Writings on Cities*, translated and introduced by Eleonore Kofman and Elizabeth Lebas (Oxford: Blackwell, 1996); Giuliana Bruno, 'Site-seeing: architecture and the moving image', *Wide Angle*, vol. 19, no. 4 (1997), pp. 8–24. John Urry, in *Consuming Places* (London: Routledge, 1995), addresses a wider range of places.

23. Casey, *Remembering*, p. 213.

24. De Certeau, *The Practice of Everyday Life*, p. 109.

3

Jam Jars and Cliffhangers

FOR the 1930s generation, cinemagoing began early in life. When they were very young, it was not at all unusual for mothers and older children to take babies and toddlers along on visits to the pictures:

> I was actually taken in arms, and that was very common, for a kid, for children, to – as soon as you were born you were just taken, wrapped in a shawl and taken... Everybody, but *everybody* went with their baby in their shawl! And the rest of the family, when they could afford it.[1]

> I was... told by my mother that I was first taken to the cinema at the age of six months which was usual in those days.[2]

Nicholas Hiley quotes a cinema manager's complaint in 1924 that his foyer was often crowded with prams during a performance. Others in the film trade took a more pragmatic view, acknowledging that if parents were forbidden to bring their babies to the cinema, business would suffer.[3] In 1932, an investigation of London children's cinemagoing revealed that the film habit started early, with as many as 63 per cent of under-fives regularly attending cinemas. A similar state of affairs is noted in the late 1930s by Richard Ford in his report on children and the cinema: 'tiny tots are often brought to children's matinees in the arms of an older brother or sister'.[4] Babes in arms aside, picturegoing normally started before the age of six. Ford notes an average age at first cinema visit of four or five; and among a group of 1930s cinemagoers who took part in the present investigation, the median age at first visit was six.[5]

Those who say they were taken to the cinema 'in arms' are unlikely to remember the experience: they will have heard about it from family members. Norman MacDonald, for example, was taken by his mother to see the Charlie Chaplin film *The Kid*:

> I remember Mother telling me that, eh, the manager or someone in charge'd come along during the course of the performance and he said, 'If you don't keep that child from making so much noise, he'll have to be taken away!' ... I was screaming with laughter at what was going on on the screen![6]

Nonetheless, some 1930s cinemagoers do remember being at the cinema at quite an early age. Margaret Young can just recall an occasion when she was at the pictures with her mother at the age of about five:

> It was a comedy with, I think, Harold Lloyd. He got his foot stuck in a spittoon and while everyone was in fits of laughter I was crying my eyes out as I thought he would have his foot caught forever. My mother had to take me out of the picture house. This would be 1930.

In 1926, Ellen Casey started going to the pictures with her grandmother, who could not see well, or perhaps was illiterate. It fell to the five-year-old Ellen to read out the intertitles of the silent films. Douglas Rendell reckons he must have been five or six when he saw *The Kid*. Mary McCusker was 'five years old when I first went to the Paragon Cinema in Cumberland Street in Gorbals'; and Arthur Orrell, who was born in 1920, thinks he would have been about six or seven when he saw a rerun of the 1916 picture *The Battle of the Somme* at the Theatre Royal in Bolton.[7]

Memories like these stand out for reasons that rarely have anything to do with the cinema or the film: the extremity or inappropriateness of the informant's behaviour, perhaps (Margaret Young's being upset and having to be taken out of the cinema), or the proud memory of being a proficient reader at an early age (Ellen Casey). Where an account is unusually detailed, there is often a sense that the feeling of the occasion is being relived in the act of narration. Oliver Dewar writes:

> My earliest recollection is of a silent film 'Atlantic' [about Titanic]. The pianist played... as the water rose eventually to cover the

sinking passengers as the ship sank. I can still visualise the scene. Everyone cried.[8]

Few informants can recall the details of their very first visit to the cinema; but all are able and willing to talk about their earliest memories of picturegoing. Whether spontaneously or in response to the interviewer's prompting, beginning their stories with recollections of early trips to the cinema appears to provide informants with a helpful means of entry to this particular past:

Int   Em, the first thing I really wanted to ask was about your earliest memories of going to the cinema.

AO   Oh yes.

Int   You were about seven or,

AO   Yes. I'd be, yeah, earliest memories would be about 1925. Yes, yes. If not 24.

Int   Yeah.

AO   Just between those. And that was at Farnworth.

Int   Right.[9]

I was born on 31 December 1926 in Edge Hill, Liverpool. This was, and is, a working-class area... I was probably aged about seven years old [sic] when my cousin Gordon took me to the Children's Matinee for the first time at the Coliseum...[10]

Discursively, memories of early cinemagoing are marked by a mix of anecdotal and repetitive memory. A few informants offer anecdotes which include details of place or occasion and of their own involvement as protagonists. Margaret Young's memory of being at a screening of a Harold Lloyd comedy, for example, includes details of a scene in the film and records the feelings of distress it provoked: the story is rounded off with the narratively satisfying closure of the protagonist's removal from the scene. Mike Mitchell narrates an 'indelicate memory' of his first cinema visit which also involves inappropriate behaviour in a public place: 'I wanted to go for a "wee", and started crying. My cousin, impatiently, told me to do it on the floor – which I did!'[11]

More common in accounts of early cinemagoing, though, is repetitive memory discourse implying various degrees of individuality or collectivity. In recollecting habitual cinema visits with her mother as a little girl, Mary McCusker places herself at the centre of the story:

> When mum got her wages on a Friday she would splash out and take us to the Astoria on Possil Road, it cost sixpence for adults and threepence for kids. Beside the pictures there was a wee shop that sold homemade sweets… I used to press my face against the window and drool, candy bars, humbugs, macaroon, pink and white tablet, yum![12]

Mrs McCusker is unusual, however, for in stories of early cinemagoing repetitive memory discourse nearly always implies collectivity: 'Sometimes when funds were low', writes William Ward, 'we would go to what was known as the flea pit… The entrance fee was one penny plus either an orange or an apple was given to each patron entering'.[13]

Six themes emerge recurrently from oral and written memories of early cinemagoing. First, everyone makes an effort to record the name and location of the first *cinemas* they went to. Second, nearly everyone recollects, even if only vaguely, the *companions* of their earliest visits. Third, informants invariably talk about negotiating *admission* to the cinema. Fourth, some also offer descriptions of the *interiors* of the first cinemas they remember. Fifth, there are some descriptions of what was on the *programme*. Finally, a number of informants record their own and others' *responses* to films, or describe the behaviour of the audience.

Invited to recall their earliest cinema visits, interviewees launch into their stories by specifying first of all where these took place, often making considerable efforts to recall, correctly and to their own satisfaction, the names and locations of the cinemas involved. This generally involves specification of street names or descriptions of nearby buildings or other neighbourhood landmarks. The details vary, but the impulse to name and place one's first cinemas appears to be shared by everyone:

> In one, they called it the Bees, I don't know why they called it the Bees, it was South Wellington Street and it, Lawmuir [?] Street it became.[14]

> *TM* [T]he first time I ever [remember] being to a cinema was the Old Annfield cinema in the Gallowgate. Now, I don't know if you know that area.
> *Int* Not very well.

TM But there's a hotel down there, it's used as a working man's club nowadays, you know. But it used to, it was the Bellgrove Hotel. Now, on that side, where the Bellgrove Hotel stood, was the old Annfield cinema. And that was the first picture house that I was ever in. That I can remember. My dad took me to it.[15]

JC So my first experiences of the cinema would be in Bolton, round about the eh, from about 1924 to about '27. When I moved out of Bolton. And I was a boy then. A boy. There were many picture places in Bolton then. My nearest from where I lived in an industrial community, was about five minutes walk away. It was called the Atlas. That's its name.[16]

And it started like that. The little cinema we used in Harrow, em, was right on top of Harrow Hill where the Harrow school is. Em, that's the posh part.[17]

Many informants, besides making every effort to recall the names and locations of cinemas as they were at the time, also note subsequent changes to these cinemas and their surroundings. Mrs McWhinnie mentions a change of street name, Mr McGoran an alteration in the use of a building close to his first cinema.

Mike Mitchell's mapping of the location of his first cinema (the Coliseum, Paddington Street – one of three situated within three-quarters of a mile of his home in Liverpool[18]) suggests how ubiquitous cinemas once were; and other informants who grew up in towns and cities also emphasise the proximity of cinemas to their homes. For these informants, home and the streets of the immediate neighbourhood are contiguous, and the picture house down the road or on the street corner is sited in memory within that spatial nexus taken for granted as part of one's territory, sometimes even figuring as an extension of home:

[W]herever the cinema was situated the population from the surrounding streets 'adopted' this cinema as their own, if ever you wanted to find someone quickly you just went to the cinema they frequented! … Whole families used to take over and monopolise 'their' cinema at the top of the street, and woe betide any stranger that inadvertently sat in their rows of seats.[19]

The significance of place in cinema memory is considered in Chapter 2; but it is worth revisiting the issue because, in memories of early cinemagoing, details of the settings of first-remembered cinemas assume narrative primacy. These details are always laid out before other aspects of early cinema visits are dealt with – what the interior of the cinema was like, for example, or the sorts of films seen there. It does not follow that these details are of less importance than setting: it is simply that their proper place comes later in the story.

A small number of informants were interviewed with friends or relatives whom they had known since childhood and who had been picturegoing companions when young. Those with shared early cinemagoing memories exhibit a highly distinctive style of memory talk. Their interviews are an occasion for reinforcing, in the present, a longstanding relationship, and indeed for putting it on display for the benefit of the researchers. Encouraging one another to call details to mind, these interviewees collaborate in laying out their memory-stories.

Margaret Young and Molly Stevenson are sisters who have always shared a passion for cinema, and their interviews are in many respects a continuation of conversations they have conducted throughout their lives. Invited to talk about their earliest picturegoing memories, the sisters immediately start prompting each other:

Int Eh, the first thing that I would like to ask you both about, eh, are your earliest memories of going to the cinema because I know you were talking about going to the cinema, sort of the age of five.

MY A lot!

MS [*Laughs*]

MY Is it on just now?

Int Yes it is.

MY Well you start with yours.

MS Well, there's a funny one that I can remember. My earliest one was going to the picture house in Sauchiehall Street with my mother, my aunt and yourself.[20]

Mrs Young cedes the floor to her elder sister, who launches into a typical piece of scene setting ('My earliest one was going to the picture house in Sauchiehall Street') before placing Miss Stevenson, presumably too young at the time to remember the occasion herself, on the scene alongside their two adult companions.

Brother and sister Fred and Gwen Curnick, though less enthusiastic about cinema in their youth, also collaborate in coming up with some early picturegoing memories:

Int   Did you go to the cinema much when you were children?

GC   Em [*pause: 3 seconds*] we didn't go. We weren't really taken by our mother and father but [Chummy?] used to take us, didn't she?

FC   Well.

GC   Or she used to take me.

FC   Yeah, well, I, I [*pause: 2 seconds*] I think I used to go with, you know, Dennis Stratton next door.

GC   Mm.

FC   As much as anything. He was a couple of years older than me and eh, and I seem to think that we used to go together.[21]

Recollections of early cinemagoing companions provide an occasion for memorialising deceased loved ones; and the vagueness of the Curnicks' memories here may have something to do with the fact that they are not associated with family members ('we weren't really taken by our mother and father').

Where companions are named, the occasion is often remembered as in some way special or set apart from ordinary routines. Bernard Letchet's recollection of seeing *Congress Dances* is tied to memories of his mother and her quirks, for the story he tells is not about his own memory of the film so much as his mother's response to it:

My first film I think I was about nine. And I was taken to see Jackie Coogan in *The Kid*. Which I can't remember seeing. But the other films, the *Congress Dances*, which you've probably never heard of [*amused voice*]. My mother was horrified because it was girls dancing on a stage![22]

Some memories of childhood cinemagoing companions, though, explicitly evoke feelings of lack or loss. The family of Ashley Bird, who was born in 1917, was broken up when his father was killed in the First World War:

Int   So was that with your parents? Did they take you, or…?

AB   Em. You know I don't know whether they did. I think I went

with an uncle the first time. I was a step-child. My father got killed
in the First World War so I was a step-child. And, I very much
spent a lot of my time with my grandmother. So I, no I didn't go to
the cinema much with my family. I remember going as a… My
uncle took me once. And I think that was the time I saw Lon
Chaney in *The Hunchback of Notre Dame*. Em, but em, after that,
mostly as kids, you know, sixpence Saturday afternoon.[23]

Mr Bird's recollection of being taken to the pictures by a relative stands
out as special, on two counts. It figures in his story as an isolated occasion, in that he recalls having no real family with whom to share the
pleasures of picturegoing. At the same time, his memory is of seeing the
kind of 'frightening' picture which, as noted in Chapter 4, left a lasting
impression on many young cinemagoers of the 1930s.

May Godden's first visit to the pictures, on the other hand, took place
when she was grown up. It stands out in her memory largely because
she was accompanied by her husband and brother:

MG I was nearly 23 the first, before I ever went to a film.

CP Mm.

Int Really?

MG I was married then. My brother was in the navy and he was
home on leave and there was one that he thought we would like.
And my husband and I and my brother went to see it.

Int Mm.

MG And there was no talking you know. Silent film as you say.
And I wasn't very smitten. So, we didn't go any more.[24]

Born in 1897, Mrs Godden is the oldest of the interviewees, and unlike
members of the generation born between the wars did not acquire the
cinemagoing habit early in life.[25]

Other stories about early picturegoing companions recall treats,
generosity, abundance and plenty of many kinds. Mary McCusker's
account of Friday night outings to the pictures with her mother relives
a little girl's delight at the profusion of tempting sweets on the other
side of a shop window ('candy bars, humbugs, macaroon, pink and white
tablet, yum!'), and she associates these pleasures with happy memories
of her mother's largesse ('she would splash out'). Beatrice Cooper also
celebrates the generosity of her first picturegoing companions:

Int   But you were saying that your first memory was of going to the cinema at about six or,

BC   Em, yes. Well we had maids in those days and em, and they were very often more eh, not more important. They were, they were *good* girls. And they used to, on their days off, sometimes take me to the cinema.[26]

This story is in some respects unusual. Firstly, the companions Mrs Cooper remembers were servants of the family rather than friends or relatives. Also, while she goes on to mention a particular visit to the pictures, the story, discursively speaking, is repetitive rather than anecdotal ('they used to... sometimes take me to the cinema'). The suggestion is that there were a number of trips to the cinema with a series of different maids. While serving as a reminder that until around the mid-1930s cinema was regarded as somewhat *déclassé*, fit only for children and servants, Mrs Cooper's story is pre-eminently a tribute to the kindliness of the 'good girls' whom she barely manages to refrain from calling 'more important' than family members. There is also a hint that these visits to the pictures were a welcome departure from the day-to-day routines of an upper-middle-class little girl's life, and a suggestion of subversiveness in that she had access to places and amusements of which her parents would in all probability have disapproved.

Early cinemagoing companions are not always named, especially in accounts of visits to children's matinees. Matineegoing memories typically enact a repetitive and collective discourse while operating a category distinction between being taken to normal picture shows by adults and going to matinees with other children. Ashley Bird's story about being taken to the cinema by his uncle, for example, underlines the rarity in his memory of occasions of this sort by comparison with his more customary kind of cinemagoing, 'as kids, you know, sixpence Saturday afternoon'; and Beatrice Cooper's account of outings to the pictures with the various unnamed maids, her peers for the duration, shares some of the features of other informants' memories of visits to matinees with contemporaries.

In the particular collective/repetitive discourse which characterises memories of matineegoing, the space of the cinema is constructed as divorced from that of the adult world, set aside exclusively for 'us kids'. 'The Plaza stands out best because every Saturday afternoon crowds of us kids managed to procure a penny to go in', writes Eric Williams;

while Alice Close recalls that 'a gang of us went to see matinees at the Globe Cinema in Cornbrook Street, Old Trafford'.[27] In the matinee, the boy or girl becomes part of the crowd, and with the merging of individual and collective in a children-only space comes temporary freedom from the strictures of the adult world. Significantly, memories of subversions of adult rules, particularly those surrounding admission to cinemas, are similarly discursively organised along collective/repetitive lines.

It seems that everyone who was a child in the 1930s can remember what it cost to get in to the pictures. In cash terms, the price of admission is normally remembered as between a penny and threepence in predecimal currency (less than $\frac{1}{2}$p to just over 1p), but it is evident from the way the stories are told that more than mere money is at stake. First of all, the careful specification of such tiny amounts is intended to emphasise that going to the pictures was a very inexpensive amusement, and not just by comparison with what a cinema ticket costs today: it was cheap then, too. At the same time, it is clear that a mere penny or tuppence could be a formidable barrier between hanging around hopefully on the street outside the local picture house and being securely ensconced on the benches inside.

If money looms large in childhood memories of cinemagoing, it is by no means the only obstacle in the way of the much-desired pictures. Some informants note that their parents disapproved of the pictures in general, or imposed a veto on certain kinds of films. Marion Cooper wistfully recalls that, unlike her husband, she was 'not encouraged' to go to her local cinema as a child:

> Most of my schoolfriends would go, at least twice a week. But we sort of weren't em [*pause: 2 seconds*] oh, not encouraged. It was just never [*pause: 3 seconds*] *dreamt* that we would go at all. I suppose at home we would be reading or, I don't know what we did. But we certainly didn't go to the cinema in Little Lever. In fact I didn't go to that cinema until I was quite grown up. [*Laughs*][28]

And Mrs B.M. Duncan's father was 'a very religious, very strict man, who considered picturegoing terribly sinful, so he wouldn't allow his daughters to go'.[29]

Films considered likely to frighten children were often the subject of specific parental vetoes; and prohibitions surrounding children's picturegoing extended beyond the family, too. In most parts of Britain, for example, children unaccompanied by adults were not supposed to be admitted to certificate 'A' films – a rule honoured more often in the breach than in the observance, but nonetheless widely remembered as yet another obstacle to be overcome.

And so while the local picture house might figure in memory as a familiar neighbourhood feature, it is not remembered as freely accessible. From the absolute parental veto to the simple necessity of organising the cost of getting in, the passage from outside to inside the cinema always required negotiation. Accounts of early cinemagoing are full of gleeful tales of the wheedling, opportunism, disobedience, even the downright dishonesty, resorted to in the noble cause of getting into the pictures.

Thomas McGoran still recalls the rare delight of having more than enough cash in his pocket for a visit to the cinema:

> And if you had threepence, a wee silver threepenny bit, then you were rich! That was a night at the pictures and a bag of sweeties to go in. Tuppence for the pictures and a penny for sweeties.

But, pausing for a moment, he soon follows up this tale of untold wealth with stories of how you could get by in more normal, leaner, times:

> [*pause: 1 second*] And when we were younger, we used to go round the middens, we used to go down there with the midges and rake out ginger [beer] bottles and jam jars, and maybe you've heard of people saying they got into the pictures with a jam jar. *I* don't think they had but I mind getting the jam jars, washing them, taking them to the shop and getting a penny on the jam jar and then going to the pictures. But you didn't, you maybe needed to get a lemonade bottle, and a jam jar and that got you into the film, penny on the lemonade bottle, a penny on the jam jar, that was the money for the bottles.[30]

Mr McGoran's jam jar story is part of a rich seam of popular memory of childhood cinemagoing, and versions of it surface again and again in informants' accounts. Jimmy Murray recalls that in the currency of jam jars, three were worth one cinema ticket:

> Three jam jars. Eh, or one vinegar bottle. For one vinegar bottle you got a penny. And for three jam jars you got a penny. So, if you had

any relation they'd to empty the vinegar bottle. Or eh, get the jam out and put it on a plate. [*Chuckles*] You know. Aye. That was it.[31]

Pamela Johnson writes: 'If really short of cash you could get in by taking empty jam jars to some cinemas – I never did this but people I know did.' Remembering his Liverpool childhood, Mike Mitchell writes: 'Over in Everton was a cinema named the Lytton. If you were too poor to pay in money, you could pay with jam jars'. Brigadier J.B. Ryall 'can still remember the Ionic [Golders Green] accepting jam jars as an entrance fee – I think that finished about 1930'. Bob Surtees is precise about the monetary value of a jam jar: 'One cinema cost 1 penny or half a penny and a jam jar. The one I went to cost 1 penny'. Mr A.M. Peary writes: 'We could normally raise the price of admission [to fleapits] by scrounging empty lemonade bottles on which we could redeem the one penny deposit'. And Mrs B.M. Duncan says that her husband remembers taking 'empty jam jars to "Old Man Warminger" in Northumberland Street [a local cinema proprietor], who then gave him free admission to "the pictures".'[32]

Variations on this theme of barter surface in the testimonies of several informants who grew up in rural areas. Phyllis Bennett of Norwich recalls a cinema where 'If you didn't have enough money to pay, I think it was a penny or tuppence to get in in them days, you could take a jam jar or a rabbit skin':

Int A rabbit skin!

PB That's right. Yeah. It's true. [*Laughs*]

Int Aw.

PB Oh, we used to have [*laughs*]. Oh, yeah, that's right. Yeah, cos my brother, my brother could remember that.

Int A-ah.

PB My youngest brother.[33]

Two letter writers from East Anglia mention cinemas which accepted eggs in lieu of cash: Eric Williams recalls the Plaza in Great Yarmouth, where 'every Saturday afternoon crowds of us kids managed to procure a penny to go in, sometimes an egg was the entrance fee, the eggs were then given to Great Yarmouth hospital'. Mr S.G. Leggett mentions the Coliseum, a cinema in Gorleston where he grew up, whose manager charged 'an egg entrance fee for the local cottage hospital – there was many a tear if your egg got broken but you were always allowed in'.[34]

The spirit of munificence implicit in these egg stories – a charitable gift, an act of kindness to a tearful child – is echoed in the memories of other East Anglian informants. Jim Godbold, for instance, talks about the unemployed people who waited outside one cinema he went to:

> *EG* When the unemployed were waiting round the door like this, and they all used to pile in. They hadn't paid, you see [*laughs*]. But they hadn't got the money. I think we all realised that, you know. You didn't do nothing to stop them. Because you knew they hadn't got much money.
>
> *Int* Mm.
>
> *EG* And they used to pile in and see the main film, you see [*laughs*].[35]

This recalls the association already noted between early childhood memory, the pictures and abundance or plenty. Going to a children's matinee sometimes involved receiving free gifts, and a number of informants remember being given comics, fruit or sweets. Mrs Fodden writes: 'Every Easter we children got a candy egg'; and Bernard Goodsall remembers 'the Saturday morning children's shows with their free packets of sweets'.[36] But this generosity is sometimes remembered as double-edged:

> And then we had another cinema. Eh, the Crown picture house in Crown Street. We went there on a Saturday morning, eh, the matinee. And if you went upstairs you got an American coloured comic. A wee sheet. If you went downstairs [*pause: 2 seconds*] upstairs was tuppence an' if you went downstairs, it was a penny downstairs. And you *didn't* get a comic. That I can remember.[37]

> *OP* Yes well, I never was a great cinema [goer?]. But, eh, I remember in my school days, I used to go to a thing called a Hole in the Wall, it used to be called. And eh, it used to have these cowboys. Saturday morning.
>
> *Int* Yeah.
>
> *OP* The entrance fee, I think, was *tuppence*.
>
> *Int* Yeah.
>
> *FC* We used to go to that, it was the Elite when we I was a kid,

the Cosy. And we used to go up there. I think it was fourpence and we used to get an out of date comic as well.

OP Mm.

FC They'd give you a comic when you went in.

Int Really?

FC And it was out of date.[38]

Stories of gifts received combine a child's delight at getting something for nothing with the sense of economic deprivation that colours the memories of many members of the 1930s generation. To this extent, they are of a piece with stories of cash-free picturegoing in general, and with jam jar stories in particular. Informants greatly enjoy telling these stories of getting by in the face of hardship, and their enthusiasm is particularly apparent when they are encouraged to elaborate, or can bounce memories off contemporaries in group interviews:

Int But some of them you were saying you could get into with a jam jar [*said in amused voice*].

NC Oh yes. That in, eh, Harrow.

Int Yes.

NC That was in a little tiny one, you know.

SN That was, em, three, three pence. Threepence.

NC Three pennies.

SN So how many jam jars did ye have to take to get threepence?

NC Oh, we'd probably get, eh, penny on each jam jar. We saved them for that. Special.

SN An you took the jam jars to a shop nearby.

NC Yes, well, anywhere.

SN Yeah.

NC We flogged them there, ye see. And we got in for the threepence, you know.[39]

DP At the kids' matinees, it was bedlam!

LB At the ones in the evenings, we used to go to the ones in Raglan Street, they called it the…

SI Oh aye, I went there and all! [*Laughs*]

LB   They called it the, I cannae mind it.

SI   [*Laughs, prolonged*]

LB   They called it the, foot of Raglan Street, where we used to get in with jeely [jam] jars.

All   Aye.

Int   Is that right?

All   Aye.

JS   There used to be one at Bridgeton.

SH   The Wee Raglan?

LB   Away down at the end, the end of Raglan Street.

SI   At the foot of Raglan Street, Oh aye! [*Laughs*] Oh aye.

LB   You used to get in with your jeely jars. Oh, you were quite happy with your jeely jars!

JS   At the cinema, you'd take your jeely jars, you got in with your jeely jars.[40]

In discursive terms, jam jar stories – and indeed other memories of getting around the problem of obtaining money for admission to the pictures – are invariably collective/repetitive ('we used to go round to the middens and rake out… jam jars'; 'you got in with your jeely jars'). The furthest these stories ever stray from collective/repetitive discourse is when, urban myth-like, informants claim to have known someone else who, say, paid their entry to the pictures with jam jars ('my brother could remember that'; 'I never did this but people I know did'). The distinction between using actual jam jars as currency at the cinema box office and collecting empty jars and bottles and getting cash by redeeming them for deposits is often elided, probably because this distinction is beside the main point of these stories, which are about resourcefulness in the face of difficulties.

If jam jar stories testify to a specific relation to childhood culture, other memories of devising ways and means of getting into the pictures are a testament to more overt engagements with and challenges to the adult world. Such tactics have about them something of what Michel de Certeau calls 'making do'. These 'clever tricks of the "weak" within the order established by the "strong"' are recollected with all the satisfaction that comes with successfully 'getting away with it' or, in de Certeau's words, 'getting around the rules of a constraining space'.[41] But the innocent utopianism of the jam jar stories contrasts with the knowing subversiveness of other ruses for getting into the pictures free. Brigadier Ryall, who grew up in Golders Green in north London, recalls boyhood raids on a local cinema: 'Normally when we went to the Ionic, one of us would pay and then… go to the toilet and open the emergency exit doors and let our friends in for free.'[42] Tom Walsh's account of employing the same subterfuge in his native Glasgow is unusual in enacting anecdotal rather than repetitive memory discourse:

TW Oh, yes there was the Strathclyde, eh. One historic occasion I can remember. One Easter Sunday, now I'd be about maybe 15 or 16, I was still at school, eh, we walked all the way to Eaglesham which, do you know where Eaglesham is? … away out.

Int It's quite far isn't it?

TW Good walk, good walk, aye. And eh, as you know the spring of the year's very treacherous and it snowed on the way and we got soaked to the skin but we, I remember trying to light a fire out on the moors to try and get some tea going but however! to make a long story short, we came back on the bus and eh, we devised a plan. Top Hat, Fred Astaire in Top Hat was performing in the Strathclyde cinema. And we devised a plan… we hadn't enough money to get in but we put together an' one guy got in and he went up to the balcony and then he came down and he opened the push bar to open the emergency exit and we all got in, six of us [laughs] got in for the price of one![43]

The adult world appears for the most part to have turned a blind eye to another, and frequently recollected, piece of rule-breaking. During the 1930s, the British Board of Film Censors recommended two certificates for films: U (Universal) and A (Adult). In most districts, cinema licensing conditions forbade admission of children un-accompanied by parents or guardians to programmes which included an 'A' picture. However, it was common practice for unaccompanied children to ask adult strangers to take them into the cinema if an 'A' film was showing. Numerous informants, letter-writers in particular, recall doing this themselves or witnessing others doing it. Among them is Trevor Hillyer, who remembers that if an 'A' film was showing 'I had to approach any adult going into the cinema, asking if I could accompany them. I must have had a sympathetic face as most people generally agreed to co-operate.' Mrs B. Verdant writes: '[I]f you were [unaccompanied] you could wait outside and ask a grownup if you could go in with them'. And Don West recalls asking '"will you take me in please?" Usually this ploy succeeded and once inside our "adopted parents" were deserted'.[44]

This practice appears to have been so widespread that it perhaps hardly rates as subversion. Nevertheless, even if unpoliced, such barriers of formal prohibition dividing the worlds of child and adult retain considerable cultural purchase. This one certainly figures prominently in informants' memories, suggesting that the 'A' films issue was an important site of negotiation of the passage from childhood to adulthood. While every generation must manage this passage, it is significant that for the 1930s generation cinema was centrally involved in it.

The trials and tribulations surrounding getting in to the pictures appear to be more prominent in 1930s cinemagoers' memories that what they discovered once inside; but some do talk about the interiors of their first cinemas. Their descriptions always stress how plain, unadorned and sometimes insalubrious these places were:

> I would like to describe our wonderful little place of entertainment. It was a long narrow type of building with corrugated iron sides and roof, inside bare floors. The seating was mostly long wooden forms...[45]

> My earliest recollection of the cinema was when my big brother took me... The picture house was basic to say the least but magic was what we experienced.[46]

> [My first] cinema was very poorly furnished. The admission charge would be about 2d, and during the show, a uniformed attendant/ fireman would walk up and down the aisles discharging a cloying, sweet smelling disinfectant.[47]

This telling sense-memory of disinfectant, sprayed about the auditorium, presumably to stop the spread of headlice and infections, surfaces in a number of accounts, including that of Mark Sandoz, who recalls 'the uniformed commissionaire [who] came round with a brass spray, which engulfed the audience in a perfumed disinfectant mist'.[48]

Our simple, cheap picture houses might not have been much, these testimonies imply, but they belonged to us and they met our needs.

This tone is very different from that adopted in descriptions of another kind of cinema, the sort that offered comfort, luxury and a milieu altogether different from one's usual surroundings. As discussed in Chapter 6, when cinemagoers of the 1930s mention these cinemas, they are never talking about their earliest cinemagoing.[49]

Embedded in these descriptions is a certain past/present trope: there was poverty then, but there was also a sense of community that no longer exists today. A similar picture of a somewhat ambiguously prelapsarian world emerges in the numerous accounts which equate early cinemagoing with cinema's pre-talkie era. In the years that followed the introduction of sound in the late 1920s, many cinemas continued to show silent films. These tended to be the oldest establishments with the most basic facilities and the lowest admission prices: the very sort of cinema that figures so prominently in early cinemagoing memories. While, since most informants were born before the mid 1920s, memories of seeing silent films are quite likely to be accurate, historical accuracy is not really what is at stake here. For this generation, memories of seeing silent films are a form of witness to an era of picturegoing that was already history by the time most of them entered adolescence. Their moment of initiation into cinemagoing is located in a long-lost time of primal innocence, the cinema's as well as the narrator's own, when cinema was unsophisticated and looked down on, just as they were themselves, as children.

The earliest films remembered, then, are silent films. However, specific, named films rarely appear in early memories of cinema programmes, figuring only in anecdotal memories of cinema visits with older companions, family members in particular. In this context, the film most often mentioned is Charlie Chaplin's *The Kid* whose co-star, the six-year-old Jackie Coogan, made a lasting impression on a number of male informants. Otherwise, informants refer to films by type or genre. Westerns, for example, are firmly associated with memories of children's matinees:

> JC   In the early days I went to the Saturday afternoon matinees, which were mostly all, I'm telling my memory this, cowboy films. Tom Mix and those other, eh, actors of the day. Eh, cowboy films mainly, the things that stand in my mind. Wild West and the like. Those drama things.[50]

So, we used to go to the Saturday matinee. I didn't like the Saturday matinee because [*pause: 1 second*] they was mostly westerns. I didn't like westerns. I didn't like westerns. You know all this shooting one another and the Indians. I was terrified. So, it was very rare I went to the children's matinee. If it was a western. I didn't like them.[51]

Most keenly remembered, though, are film serials, especially the 'cliffhangers' that ended every episode:

DH As I said the children's matinee was on a Saturday afternoon and we used to go and see these silent films with black and white with the piano playing.

Int Mmm.

DH Which were made up of serials and some of the serials – I'm sure they started turning my hair white. I remember one, *Tin Billy*[?] which was *horrendous*, when he came on the scene and all it was, looking back, was a man in a suit, great big massive suit a bit like a coloured diving bell.

Int Right.

DH You know these big diving bells where Jean Cocteau, eh, Cocteau, whoever he is, going down, exposing.

Int Yeh.

DH Well that sort of thing. If you can imagine that walking toward you in a silent this was horrifying. And then *Elmo the Mighty*[?] was another one. He was a bloke who come, oh it was *horrible*! Then, they filmed a lot of Sax Rohmer's books, Dr Fu Manchu, the evil Chinaman. We used to die the death at those so we used to come out of the Saturday morning serials having laughed at the comedies but having seen the big film, terrified but drawn back the next week to see episode 23![52]

I do remember a series of Dr Fu Manchu in which the episode was very short but always threatening and ending in dreaded suspense.[53]

The serials were very gripping, mostly Flash Gordon with lots of robots or somebody hanging from a skyscraper until the following Saturday.[54]

PB 'Cos you had to go, you see. 'Cos they had a serial on. Every week! Like Buck Rogers or, oh, old cowboy films. And it got to an exciting part [*laughs*] and that went off until next week. So of course you had to go.

Int   Yeah.

PB   You had to save up your pennies then, to get in. [*Laughs*] Aw dear.[55]

They always managed to leave some poor female in a perilous position such as on a ledge of a burning building or best of all rolling down a mountain side towards a steaming mass of molten lava and up would come the words on the screen 'TO BE CONTINUED NEXT WEEK'.[56]

That meant we had to go to the cinema thirteen weeks in succession [*with rising emphasis*]. But you know, it couldn't come quick enough! See when you come out of the cinema, on a Saturday afternoon? You'd say to yourself, 'I wonder what'll happen next week? I wonder if he'll get out of that mess that he's in'.[57]

An unusually detailed memory of seeing a serial at a matinee is offered by Marion Cooper. She recollects the situation in such detail precisely because it was so out of the ordinary for her: 'the pictures' were frowned on in her family, and the feeling of frustration at being unable to find out how the cliffhanger was resolved, and so to share in the pleasures enjoyed by her peers, is palpable in Mrs Cooper's account:

MC   Em, some Saturdays, my father would take my sister, and me, to Bolton. He, mainly, to go to the [county?] library in Bolton. We didn't have a library in the village. Then. And he would go up there. He would dump us in the reading room while he went to choose a book. And I can remember the titles of the books that he left us looking. *The Lady*. [*Posh voice*] *The Queen*. What peculiar books they were. Now all this was preliminary to being taken to the cinema. We got to the cinema, and my father knew the lady in the, what d'you call it? Where you paid. In the thing. They always had a few words together. And I should think that we got in very cheaply. Would think so. I think I would be about eight, and my sister would be ten. Always got quite good seats. And it always finished up with

em, what d'you call those things? That, repeat, one that em, was
continued next week. Some desperate thing was happening and we
never saw it again. As we never went the following weeks.

Int [*Laughs*]

MC We never knew what happened. [*Laughs*] And then we walked
home again. And then it was three miles to walk home. [*Laughs*][58]

The prominence of 'chapter plays'[59] in informants' accounts, the
manner in which these memories are narrated, and above all their
repeated and sometimes affect-laden allusions to cliffhangers, are highly
revealing about cultural memory and how it works. Some investigations
of children's cinemagoing conducted during the 1930s suggest that in
the years up to the middle of the decade, the period when many
informants would have been going to matinees, matinee programmes
were usually comprised of the pictures that were on exhibition in the
cinema's normal shows for that week, including 'A' films.[60] In other
words, as children, they were just as likely to be exposed to feature
films as to serials at the matinees they went to. Why, then, do serials and
cliffhangers figure so insistently in their memories?

Anecdotal memories of early cinemagoing are few and far between,
and all of them centre on informants' responses to films and behaviour
in the cinema. These are always represented as excessive or in some
other way inappropriate. In recounting such memories, informants
are clearly constructing themselves – like the legendary audience fleeing
in terror from a screening of the Lumieres' film of an approaching
steam engine – as not yet versed in the proper ways of 'reading' films
and of conducting oneself in the cinema. Many of these initiation
narratives are obviously treasures from family legend rather than direct
memories: Margaret Young's and Norman MacDonald's stories about
having to be removed from the cinema by their mothers are cases in
point. The earliest direct memories of responses and reactions to films
are overwhelmingly repetitive in character, and rarely convey affect
on the narrator's part. Even references to cliffhangers, which sometimes
do convey something of the sense of frustration at having to wait a
week to see what happened next, typically lack detail or are formulaic
in content and expression.

Memories of visits to matinees in particular emphasise collective
audience behaviour as against the informant's own responses and

activities. Stories of children yelling at characters on the screen ('he's behind yer!'), booing and cheering, rushing around the auditorium, and using nuts and fruit as missiles abound:

NM And, eh, that's where I went when I was… The first cinema I went to was at, I can't remember what the name of it was but it was at Patrick Cross anyway.

Int What was that one like?

NM That was the same as the Gem, it was very much [*pause: 3 seconds*] there were no refinements, just a basic cinema with, I think, wooden benches seats. It might have had. It was later, I think that there were long wooden benches. And it was usually crowded with kids, all screaming and shouting.[61]

EC [T]here was forms at the front. There was about a dozen forms at the front which was only tuppence. So we used to sit on the back row. The form on the back row. And em [*pause: 2 seconds*] the other forms were occupied you know, mostly by children. If children were on their own they put them on the first four. Put them on the first four forms.

If it was a film that wasn't very interesting, [children would] be running about. They'd be going backwards and forwards to the toilet. Well with it being silent films it was never quiet you know. Or some kids'd have clogs on. Well it was only bare floor. You know, no carpets. And em, there was nobody in. There was nobody in to, eh, sell things. You know like the cigarette girls or you know, the one with the tray like they did. [*Voices in background*] So you took your own sweets in or whatever. And em, mostly it was, em, monkey nuts with shells on. Used to be shelling em. Take [*amused voice*] the shells off!

Int [*Laughs*]

EC Used to be shelling the nuts on the floor, and then they'd take an orange, peel'd be on the floor. All these were going backwards and forwards. And em, you sit next to some children you could smell camphorated oil. You know, they'd have their chests rubbed with camphorated oil. Or whatever stuff on. You know, to keep it clean. And when I think back there was no, no peace at all [*amused voice*].[62]

We stamped our feet and whistled and clapped until our hands were sore and the building shook.[63]

Soon we get to the door and push in the dimly-lit hall and it would appear all seats are taken. The noise is deafening, with shouts – screams from the girls – stamping, fighting here and there, children climbing over and crawling under seats, banging seats down, running up and down the aisles.[64]

In all these accounts, the picture house figures very much as the children's domain, beyond the writ of adult sanction. And yet while such memories of mayhem are vividly, even gleefully, recounted, their narration often has a detached quality, as if the informant is distancing himself or herself from such bad behaviour.

There is a quality at once universal and particular about the earliest cinemagoing memories of the 1930s generation. A combination of idiosyncratic detail and collective voice marks these stories, sometimes lending the histories they embody a timeless, even mythic, quality.

Britain in the 1930s was for the most part a preconsumer society marked by economic privation, certainly for the working class and for those living outside the relatively prosperous south-east of England.[65] This was a time when, for the majority of children, growing up was about prohibition rather than permission. It was also a time when children enjoyed considerable freedom to roam the streets of their neighbourhoods without adult supervision. These were the children who were growing up just as cinemagoing was becoming a respectable as well as a popular pastime. For these children 'the pictures' was undoubtedly the place to be, 'the main attraction'. The background and details of this generation's early memories of cinema are inevitably informed by these social and historical circumstances.

And yet their stories also exceed the particularities of personal, situated, lives. Alessandro Portelli's observations on collective viewpoint in individuals' narratives relate to oral testimonies of members by non-hegemonic social groups, which he suggests are linked to the tradition of the folk narrative. But the argument works equally well for the childhood memories looked at here, most of which are indeed 'narratives in which the boundary between what takes place outside the narrator and what happens inside, between what concerns the individual and what concerns the group, may become… elusive… so that personal "truth" may coincide with shared "imagination"'.[66] To this extent, the early cinemagoing memories of the 1930s generation may afford access to a collective, perhaps even universal, world of childhood, a view into the child's imagination and preoccupations, and an understanding of the cultures of childhood.

Informants' manner of beginning their stories of early cinemagoing is a case in point. They start by specifying the places where they saw their first films, often mapping in their memory-talk the path trodden between home and picture house. This provides a narrator with a spatial setting in which imaginatively to place herself or himself, and gives access to a past that may in some sense be reinhabited in the act of narration. It also constructs a spatial metaphor for a developmental, psychical process – that of becoming a subject, a separate individual. This process is concretised in the repeated theme of venturing from the enclosed space of home into a more public space, the streets of the neighbourhood and the local picture house. This trope constructs private and public spaces as conjoined, and both as part of an everyday, familiar, and above all shared, world.

Jam jar stories and cliffhanger memories, which appear to be enshrined in the collective memory of this entire generation, are pivotal in this regard. Their very prominence, as well as their distinctive discursive features, suggests that these stories are of considerable cultural and psychical significance. Jam jar stories, which are about resourcefulness in the face of poverty and constraint, reveal a great deal about childhood culture, especially about how children find ways of coping with what they may experience as the overwhelming restrictions and limitations imposed by the adult world on their quest to pursue individual and collective goals. These stories also locate that quest in a particular historical moment; for in the 1930s the goals, and indeed the obstacles standing in the way of attaining them, are focused around what children at the time wanted: cinema. Cinema was desired both for itself and, perhaps more importantly, because it was the place where the child could inhabit a world separate from the adult one. If the object of desire was 'the pictures', the obstacles to fulfilment and, conversely and very importantly, the freedoms permitting fulfilment – poverty and the freedom of the streets respectively – are also peculiar to that historical moment.

Cliffhanger memories are about the cultural resonance of serial narrative forms and the suspense they generate. The repeated return to the cinema demanded by film serials is homologous with the repetitive discourse that structures informants' memory-talk about them. This in turn suggests a continuity with the habitual quality of cinemagoing for children of this generation. Indeed, it has been argued that at the moment when the film industry was establishing itself as the provider of Britain's favourite leisure pursuit, the serial was creating an audience of consumers ready and willing to return to the cinema on a regular basis.[67]

The emphasis on suspense in memories of serials throws into relief the more general fascination exerted by the pictures ('you had to go back', as one informant puts it), and affords insight into the power in the collective imagination of the combination of ordinariness and magic in the activity of cinemagoing. For just as going to the pictures on a Saturday is remembered as part of a weekly routine, so memories of serials and suspense convey something of the structure of feeling of the compulsion to repeat this pleasurable but incomplete experience, with its 'intervals of gratification and interludes of anticipated gratification'.[68] And just as all Saturdays were the same as each other and yet different from every other day of the week, so what you remember seeing at the Saturday pictures was comfortingly the same each time (another western, perhaps) and yet different, too (a fresh cliffhanger every week).

In essence, jam jar stories are about coming to terms with money, and thus with exchange and value, while cliffhanger memories are about the child's struggle with frustration and deferred gratification. Where cinema happens to be the hook on which these processes are pegged, it is functioning as an imaginative locus for narratives of the entry of the psychical into the cultural. The memories acquire whatever historical specificity they have through their construction of cinema as the site where these psychical and cultural processes are enacted, be this the quest for money to get into the pictures or the necessity of going back to the cinema every week so as to find out what happens next in a story.

If early cinemagoing memories describe psychical and developmental processes hinging on desire, and collective and cultural processes hinging on negotiating getting what you want, they are also testament to the imbrication of these processes with children's inner and outer struggles for collective and individual autonomy. For the 1930s generation, cinema provided a safe space for challenges to adult rules and for assertions of independence from parents, teachers and other authority figures. It also offered a safe space for the exploration of fears and horrors.

Notes

1. T94-4, Sheila McWhinnie (b.1919), Glasgow, 21 November 1994.

2. 95-79-1, Iris Alder (b.1924), Hampshire, to Annette Kuhn and Valentina Bold, 8 February 1995.

3. Nicholas Hiley, '"Let's go to the pictures": the British cinema audience in the 1920s and 1930s', *Journal of Popular British Cinema*, vol. 2 (1999), pp. 39–53; see p. 47.

4. London County Council, Education Committee, 'School Children and the Cinema' (London: London County Council, 1932); Richard Ford, *Children in the Cinema* (London: Allen & Unwin, 1939), p. 40.

5. Ibid.; Annette Kuhn, 'Cinemagoing in Britain in the 1930s: report of a questionnaire survey', *Historical Journal of Film, Radio and Television*, vol. 19, no. 4 (1999), pp. 531–43.

6. T94-1, Norman MacDonald (b.1915), Glasgow, 17 November 1994. *The Kid* was first released in 1921.

7. 92-1-4, Questionnaire, Margaret Young (b.1925), Glasgow, n.d. 1992; T95-37, Ellen Casey (b.1921), Manchester, 31 May 1995; T95-66, Douglas Rendell (b. circa 1919), Manchester, 12 May 1995; 92-8-4, Mary McCusker (b.1916), Glasgow, to Annette Kuhn, n.d. 1992; T95-50, Arthur Orrell (b.1920), Manchester, 9 June 1995.

8. 95-287, Questionnaire, Oliver Dewar, Norfolk, December 1995.

9. T95-68, Arthur Orrell, Bolton, 12 May 1995.

10. 95-24-6, 'Some recollections of cinemagoing', Mike Mitchell, Manchester, n.d. 1995.

11. Ibid.

12. 92-8-5, Press clipping, 'Going to the pictures', Mary McCusker, Glasgow, December 1990.

13. 95-83-1, William Ward, Cheshire to Annette Kuhn and Valentina Bold, 9 February 1995.

14. T94-4, Sheila McWhinnie, Glasgow, 21 November 1994. Mrs McWhinnie is referring to Bennell's Bright and Beautiful Cinerama: see Peter, Bruce, *100 Years of Glasgow's Amazing Cinemas* (Edinburgh: Polygon, 1996), p.67.

15. T94-12, Thomas McGoran, Glasgow, 30 November 1994. Mr McGoran is referring to Scott's Annfield Electric Theatre: see Peter, *100 Years of Glasgow's Amazing Cinemas*, p. 165.

16. T95-58, John and Marion Cooper, Bolton, 8 May 1995.

17. T95-88, Ashley Bird, Harrow, 12 July 1995.

18. 95-24-6, 'Some recollections of cinemagoing', Mike Mitchell, Manchester, n.d. 1995.

19. 95-35-1, Ray Rockford, Manchester, to Cinema Culture in 1930s Britain, 11 February 1995.

20. T94-16, Margaret Young and Molly Stevenson, Glasgow, 5 December 1994 (Mrs Young was born in 1925, Miss Stevenson in 1923).

21. T95-74, Fred and Gwen Curnick, Harrow, 5 July 1995.

22. T95-97, Irene and Bernard Letchet, Harrow, 21 July 1995.

23. T95-88, Ashley Bird, Harrow, 12 July 1995.

24. T95-103, May Godden and Celia Piggott, Harrow, 25 July 1995.

25. Hiley, '"Let's go to the pictures"', discusses age and generation differences in interwar cinemagoing in Britain.

26. T95-96, Beatrice Cooper, Harrow, 20 July 1995.

27. 95-276-3, Eric Williams, Norfolk, to Stephen Peart, 14 September 1995; 95-324, Questionnaire, Alice Close, Lincolnshire, December 1995.

28. T95-58, John and Marion Cooper, Bolton, 8 May 1995.

29. 95-316-1, Mrs B.M. Duncan, Norfolk, to Stephen Peart, 8 September 1995.

30. T94-14, Thomas McGoran, Glasgow, 30 November 1994.

31. T95-62, Jimmy Murray, Manchester, 9 May 1995.

32. 95-22, Questionnaire, Pamela Johnson, Surrey, May 1995; 95-24-6, 'Some recollections of cinemagoing', Mike Mitchell, Manchester, n.d. 1995; 95-48, Questionnaire, Brigadier J.B. Ryall, Sussex, May 1995; 95-96-1, Bob Surtees, Gwent, to Annette Kuhn and Valentina Bold, February 1995; 95-119-1, A.M. Peary, Suffolk, to Annette Kuhn and Valentina Bold, 21 February 1995; 95-316-1, Mrs B.M. Duncan, Norwich, to Stephen Peart, 8 September 1995.

33. T95-127, Phyllis Bennett, Norwich, 27 November 1995.

34. 95-276-3, Eric Williams, Norfolk, to Stephen Peart, 14 September 1995; 95-279-3, S.G. Leggett, Norfolk, to Stephen Peart, n.d. 1995. In the 1930s, the manager of the Plaza gave free admission to the unemployed: see Stephen Peart, *The Picture House in East Anglia* (Lavenham, Suffolk: Terence Dalton Ltd, 1980), p. 157.

35. T95-113, E.J. Godbold, Suffolk, 17 October 1995.

36. 95-61-1, Mrs Fodden, Northumbria, to CCINTB, February 1995; 95-81-1, Bernard Goodsall, Avon, to Annette Kuhn and Valentina Bold, February 1995.

37. T94-5, Mary McCusker, Glasgow, 22 November 1994.

38. T95-78, Fred and Gwen Curnick, Harrow, 5 July 1995 (during the interview, the Curnicks were joined by another person [OP]).

39. T95-82, Nancy Carrington, Harrow, 7 July 1995 (also present Sue Nicholls of Harrow Housebound Readers Service).

40. T94-3, Lilian Buik, Helen Donaghy, Sarah Irvine, John Shearer and Davy Paterson, Glasgow, 18 November 1994 (also present Senga Hughes, care-worker).

41. Michel de Certeau, *The Practice of Everyday Life*, trans. Steven Rendall (Berkeley: University of California Press, 1984), p. 40, p. 18.

42. 95-48-1, J.B. Ryall, Sussex, to Annette Kuhn and Valentina Bold, 8 February 1995.

43. T94-8, Tom Walsh, Glasgow, 25 November 1994.

44. 95-149-1, Trevor Hillyer, Wiltshire, to Annette Kuhn and Valentina Bold, 12 February 1995; 95-110-1, Mrs B. Verdant, West Midlands, to Annette Kuhn and Valentina Bold, 19 February 1995; 95-105, Questionnaire, Don West, Bristol, 4 June 1995.

45. 95-182-14, Ellen Casey to Annette Kuhn, 13 October 2000.

46. 92-33-1, Rose Mint, Edinburgh, to Annette Kuhn, 11 May 1992.

47. 95-24-6, 'Some recollections of cinemagoing', Mike Mitchell, Manchester, n.d. 1995.

48. 95-65-1, Mark Sandoz, West Midlands, to Annette Kuhn and Valentina Bold, n.d. February 1995.

49. Nicholas Hiley's distinction between two patterns and styles of cinemagoing in the interwar years echoes the distinctions implicit in 1930s cinemagoers' memories: see 'Let's go to the pictures', p. 45.

50. T95-58, John and Marion Cooper, Bolton, 8 May 1995.

51. T95-37, Ellen Casey, Manchester, 31 May 1995.

52. T95-20, A.D. Houlston, Manchester. 26 April 1995.

53. 95-54-1, Sidney Beadle, Sussex, to Annette Kuhn, 16 February 1995.

54. 95-135-1, Hilda Moss, mid Glamorgan, to Annette Kuhn and Valentina Bold, n.d. 1995.

55. T95-127, Phyllis Bennett, Norwich, 27 November 1995.

56. 95-87-1, Joan Donoghue, Cardiff, to Annette Kuhn and Valentina Bold, 11 February 1995.

57. T94-14, Thomas McGoran, Glasgow, 30 November 1994.

58. T95-58, John and Marion Cooper, Bolton, 8 May 1995.

59. William K. Everson, 'Serials with sound have steadily declined in quality and quantity', *Films in Review,* vol. 4, no. 4 (1953), pp. 269–276.

60. Public Record Office, HO45/14731/91, report of inquiry by Sheffield Social Survey Committee on films shown at children's matinees, July 1931; Birmingham Cinema Inquiry Committee, 'Report of Investigations, April 1930–May 1931' (Birmingham: Cinema Enquiry Committee, 1931). After about 1936, the new children's matinee movement devoted itself to encouraging programming more suitable for children: see Chapter 4.

61. T94-1, Norman MacDonald, Glasgow, 17 November 1994.

62. T95-37, Ellen Casey, Manchester, 31 May 1995.

63. 95-98-1, Mrs V.A. Tucker, Cardiff, to Annette Kuhn and Valentina Bold, 6 February 1995.

64. 95-33-1, 'Mainly about Ardwick', Les Sutton, Manchester, n.d. 1995.

65. For contemporary accounts of regional economic variations, see J.B. Priestley, *English Journey* (London: William Heinemann Ltd, 1934); George Orwell, *The Road to Wigan Pier* (London: Victor Gollancz, 1937).

66. Alessandro Portelli, *The Death of Luigi Trastulli and Other Stories: Form and Meaning in Oral History* (Albany, NY: State University of New York Press, 1991), p. 49.

67. Roger Hagedorn, 'The serial as a form of narrative presentation', *Wide Angle,* vol. 10, no. 4 (1998), pp. 4–12; see p. 9.

68. Tudor Oltean, 'Series and seriality in media culture', *European Journal of Communication,* vol. 8, no. 8 (1993), pp. 5–31; see p. 13.

4

When the Child Looks

Oh, I remember the first film we went to see [Boris Karloff]
in. Em, at the Globe, in [*pause: 3 seconds*] where was it? Old
Trafford, I think it was. And it was *The Mummy*. Well there
were benches then, you know, not seats. I don't know
whether I'd left school. Probably I'd left school. Anyway, I
went to see him. I was sat there, dead quiet. And when they
opened the lid and it shows him like, you know, and he
moves his hand. Well I let out one [*bursts out laughing*]. I
slid along the seat. I was frightened to death! It wouldn't
frighten me now, but. Oh dear.[1]

IN her recollection of seeing Boris Karloff in the 1933 film *The
Mummy*, Annie Wright carefully sets the scene by giving the location
and the name of the cinema where she saw the film, then puts herself
firmly into the picture, sitting on a bench inside the picture house, 'dead
quiet'. In her story, she rehearses a moment of terror caused by a scene
in the film, and her bodily expression of that fear: 'I slid along the seat'.

Mrs Wright is not alone among cinemagoers of the 1930s in remembering being scared at the cinema. Many interviewees and correspondents
offer similar recollections of frightening films. Often just as colourfully
told as Mrs Wright's, these accounts are precise in their recollection of
the images and scenes which terrified their narrators. So uncommonly
vivid and detailed are these stories that it sometimes seems as if, in the

process of narrating them, informants are accessing the 'child's voice' within themselves and reliving the experience of being scared out of their wits. Like Mrs Wright, most then disengage from the past and distance themselves from their impressionable younger selves by passing amused judgement ('It wouldn't frighten me now'). Laughter is a common accompaniment to these stories.

While being frightened – and enjoying being frightened – by horror stories is a normal, perhaps even a universal, childhood experience, the fears of a generation that grew up in the years between two wars and who spent much of their free time at 'the pictures' have a distinctive structure of feeling and cultural resonance. At the beginning of the 1930s, a new type of Hollywood film appeared on British screens, causing a stir verging on moral panic. This genre – dubbed (usually complete with quotation marks) 'horrific' – stands at the centre of a number of shifts in public discourse and official policy surrounding cinema and its audience.

At the height of the 'horrific' films furore, most informants had not yet reached adolescence, and some were still very young indeed. While many of those who went to the pictures as children during the 1930s still retain strong memories of seeing films that frightened them, they can scarcely have been conscious at the time of the extent of the adult world's anxieties about their passion for the pictures; nor indeed does their memory-talk betray any sign that they became aware of this in later years.

The slight sense of subversion of adult rules attaching to picturegoing for many of this generation has particular resonances in relation to the 'horrific' film. To the general fascination exerted by the pictures, to the feeling that getting into the cinema was something that had to be carefully negotiated, is added the ambiguous lure of the frightening. If there is any sense of engagement with the adult world in informants' accounts, this is its extent, and it is invariably articulated in the child's terms. The child's voice which speaks through informants' memories of frightening films could not be more different from the concerned tones of the adult 'experts', the moral guardians, officials and politicians, who were so exercised by children's exposure to these pictures.

At the same time, informants' memory stories of being frightened by films have a tenor all their own. 'Horrific' film memories are relatively numerous, they are told in some detail, and are very often recounted as if the narrator were reliving a memory in the telling. What do cinemagoers of the 1930s remember about frightening films, and how do they organise these memories in their spoken or written accounts?

What they remember most of all are their own responses or reactions to 'horrific' films. When talking about the emotions a film stirred up at the moment of viewing, informants will simply say they were terrified, scared, or, like Annie Wright, 'frightened to death'. But while they rarely elaborate verbally on their feelings, they convey a sense of the films' impact in other ways. Accounts of coping strategies resorted to inside the cinema, for example, always reference physical activity, as if bodily memory is primally imprinted, or as if recollecting a bodily memory involves less secondary revision than verbal articulation of remembered feelings.[2]

Annie Wright, quoted above, recalls sliding along the bench; Joan Donaghue and her friends would 'cling to each other and squeal or shut our eyes'; Hilda Moss 'was always under the seat if things got too scary'.[3] The stereotypical phrase 'under the seat' is not necessarily to be taken literally, as Margaret Stevenson points out:

> *MY* Yes, that's right it was [*I Am A Fugitive From A Chain Gang*]. That was way back.
>
> *MS* That, that *really* scared me. That's when I was under the seat. Mind you, I don't remember much about it because I was under the seat. [*Pause: 3 seconds*] Not that you could get under a cinema seat because it went flat back, but I was down on the floor at any rate. I mean they never stayed put.
>
> *MY* Uhuh.
>
> *MS* They always came back up with such a noise.[4]

Vee Entwistle, one of several informants who admit to having enjoyed being frightened, amusedly recalls a companion's less sanguine reactions to frightening films:

> I used to like being frightened, you know. Used to go and watch *Frankenstein*. And my friend used to be [*makes face*]. [*Laughs*] 'Tell me when he's gone off! Tell me when he's gone off!'[5]

Jim Godbold was not above taking advantage of a girlfriend's fears:

> *Int* Did you like horror films yourself? Were they...
>
> *EG* Yeah. It was, eh, all right at the time. As you say, specially if you was with a girl cause you, em [*laughs*]

Int [*Laughs*]

EG Cuddle close to you. It really used to frighten em.[6]

Many informants recollect how films that scared them could keep their psychological grip outside the cinema, sometimes for a long time afterwards:

BP Em, you mentioned *Night Must Fall*. Now although that isn't in my three...

Int Mm.

BP That was a most impressive film. Yes it did. It was very good.

LB We were in college, right on top of Bingleys Hill. We went to Shipley, on the bus. And when we came out, we caught the bus back to Bingley. And I can remember saying, 'I'm not walking up that hill.' You know 20 minutes up a hill. Lonely. Quiet. So we had a taxi back! [*Bursts out laughing*][7]

EC Now the frightening films. You had to go in with somebody for these. Now I shouldn't have gone to one but I wanted to see [Boris Karloff] in *Frankenstein*. *The Mummy's Hand*, *The Old Dark House*. They were all Boris Karloff. And, eh, I'd only be about, eh [*pause: 1 second*] ten then. Nine, ten. *Dracula*. 1931. *Dr Jekyll and Mr Hyde*. The first one.

Int Mm.

EC I used to be terrified [*said in small voice*]. I used to be run home terrified. I used to run home all the way. And then we didn't have no lighting up the stairs and there used to get saucer [*sniffs*] or whatever, a tin lid. Anything what we had. We used to get a candle lighted. Then we used to put the wax on [*pause: 2 seconds*] stick the candle in and then go up the stairs you see. [*Next few words inaudible*] I remember going up the stairs my hand shaking like that. The flaming candle fell off and rolled down the stairs! [*Laughs*][8]

Jessie Boyd, who lived in Middleton, Lancashire, in the 1930s, recalls the occasion she saw *Dracula*:

[A]dmission was supposedly only for 16+ people... but I begged Mum to take me along and she pleaded with the doorman: 'My little girl has been *so* looking forward to this'. He was moved by her appeal. Consequence – the 'little girl' took her FASCINATED terror home, and was haunted by vampire dreams for years![9]

Dorris Braithwaite was frightened by a werewolf film:

> But I remember going to see a werewolf one. And I were sleeping with my friend. And she had a dog. And that was howling in the night. And I was dreaming about this werewolf. I was terrified! [*Laughs*][10]

Hilda Moss writes about what happened after she saw *Dr Jekyll and Mr Hyde*:

> I can remember seeing Jekyll and Hyde which was a creepy film, when we came out it was thick fog and we had to walk about half a mile home. When we got to the end of our road there were two figures shrouded in the mist clad in black cloaks. We were very relieved to find they were two local policemen... having a vivid imagination I frightened the others with tales of who they might be.[11]

Tom Affleck tells of being affected for many years after seeing *The Werewolf of London*:

> The picture that sticks in my mind, *The Werewolf of London*, the most horrific one I ever remember. Coming out of the picture house I went to my Granny's to meet my mother and after tea we made our way home. It was now dark and arriving there, having got the light on, my mother told me to pull the blind while she got a shovel of coal for the fire. As I went to the window there was a tap on it from outside and with the inside light on I could not see out. I only heard the tap and flew through to the scullery shouting that the werewolf was after me. Later I found out that the train had come in and one of the people passing was my cousin who tapped on the window.
>
> Resulting from this incident, about eleven at the time, I took a nervous condition, continually blinking my eyes but a doctor diagnosed nothing seriously wrong...
>
> I finally laid the werewolf to rest when I saw that old picture on television some years ago, although it brought back painful memories.[12]

Many informants make briefer mention of nightmares and waking fears brought on by seeing 'horrific' films. James Barton recalls seeing an 'A' film called *Seven Keys to Baldpate*, which resulted in 'a couple of weeks' nightmares and protests at having to fill the coal scuttle from the cellar!'. Rose Mint remembers 'a serial about a mechanical man who haunted my worst nightmares for years'. Mary Cecil Pook is still haunted by 'a film about the Ripper called "The Lodger"'. Reg Ireland thinks he must have seen *King Kong*, 'for I have recollections of a huge gorilla. I have never confessed to it before but as a boy I was never again so brave in the dark!'. And Trevor Hillyer recalls that 'Two horror films which gave me nightmares were "The Old Dark House" and "The Cat Creeps"'.[13]

Descriptions of the films themselves are rather fewer than memories of the impact they made, and often informants will simply note the title of a film that scared them. Others, however, elaborate on what it was about a film that they found so terrifying. Plot details are rare in such memories: what emerge are vivid visual descriptions, recalled in isolation from each other and from the film's plot, of individual scenes, shots or images which seem to have branded themselves on each informant's consciousness.

The tendency to describe isolated visual impressions is a recurrent and distinctive feature of memories of frightening fims. Annie Wright's description of what is in fact no more than a single shot from *The Mummy* is characteristic. So, too, is Helen Donaghy's memory of seeing a film whose title she does not give. She could well be referring to the same scene as the one that frightened Mrs Wright: 'He had one where he sorta come out the coffin, ye seen the hand coming up and oh I was in *terror* with that one'.[14]

Lois Basnett's and Bert Partington's memories of *Night Must Fall* end with an account of a chilling moment in the film:

BP And the Welsh villain if you like, the, the Danny.

LB Danny.

BP Was played by Robert Montgomery! [*Amazed voice*]

LB Mm.

BP Who was a suave, sophisticated,

LB American.

BP Very suave actor. Was noted for his appeal you know.

LB Mm. Yes. He was a pin-up.

BP He was a tremendous… and Rosalind Russell was the girl, wasn't she? The sort of slightly impressed by him and almost in love with him. And he has [*amused voice*] this hat box with [the head in it?]. [*Laughs*] And there's this *terrible* ending.[15]

Dorris Braithwaite remembers a decapitated head in another film:

Well I once remember seeing a film with Spencer Tracy. I think it was called *North West Passage*. I don't know who the other stars were but, eh, there was one chap in it and he was carrying this bag. And everybody was sort of keeping away from him. And, you know, it was a while before you realised. And then he brought out what was in the bag and it was a skull! [*Laughs*] I was under the chair! I was absolutely terrified! Yes. And I've never forgotten it.[16]

In the last two stories, relatively detached in tone, the narrators are talking about their adolescence rather than their childhood. When frightening moments in films seen very early in life are recalled, accounts are less articulate, and the frightening moment itself stands out in strong relief against a background usually somewhat vague and lacking in detail – though the memory may be associated with a mother's comforting presence:

Int You mentioned I think sometimes going with your parents to films. Is that right?

TA I only went once. And it was a film. A silent film about the sea. And these waves were making this ship go, it was a sailing ship. And I was so frightened I got on the floor to hide my face in my mother's lap. I was scared stiff. I don't know why. It wasn't very frightening but I was frightened.[17]

JH My remembrances are very slight. One is, being taken by my mother to watch a film about a werewolf and I was terrified; hiding my face in my mother's shoulder and peeping, from time to time, through my fingers.[18]

In telling their stories of early terrors at the pictures, informants will sometimes acknowledge that their behaviour might have been inappropriate or excessive. Certainly among the frightening films mentioned by name there are some which would not normally be regarded as 'horrific':

IL I [couldn't?] have been very old because I definitely remember going one time and being absolutely petrified by something I saw. And I can still see this thing now. And it was in a sort of laboratory and a horrible sort of creature came out of the wall. Now I don't think it was a horror film cause everybody was in fits of laughter.

BL [*Laughs*] Yes.

IL D'you know, I was frightened to go to bed for weeks after that [*amused voice*] in case this thing came out of the wall. So I don't think I could've been very old.[19]

Many informants link their memories of 1930s horror films with recollections of Boris Karloff, who starred in many, including *Frankenstein* (James Whale, 1931); *The Old Dark House* (James Whale, 1931); *The Mask of Fu Manchu* (Charles Brabin, 1932); *The Mummy* (Karl Freund, 1932); *The Bride of Frankenstein* (James Whale, 1935); and *Son of Frankenstein* (Rowland V. Lee, 1939). Some recall that Karloff was a 'great source for impersonations'. Interviewee Thomas McGoran, for example, describes how children would be 'carted away to another world' by the pictures, and shows the interviewer how this magic world could be brought back into their lives outside the cinema: 'of course, if we'd seen a Boris Karloff picture, you would walk down the road like *this* [*stiff and glum mime*], like *monsters*![20]

The actions accompanying Mr McGoran's memory-talk, and indeed the story itself, serve as a reminder that there can be a performative element in children's use of frightening images and scary stories. Children take delight in terrifying each other with imitations of monsters and other frightening creatures or by telling each other frightening stories, with much emphasis on the scariest moments. At the age of 84, interviewee Nancy Carrington slips readily into this mode, entertaining her co-interviewees and the interviewer with a gory rundown of the 1933 film *Mystery of the Wax Museum*:

NC Oh now, mind you, I did like Boris Karloff. And another one I saw was, em, it was called *The Mystery of the Wax Museum*.

NP Oh, I've heard of that. The name rings a bell.

NC Well this man, he'd been in a fire. And his face got *absolutely*, *dreadfully* burnt. And so he wore a mask.

Int Mm.

NC He wanted revenge.

EH I'm goin upstairs, if it's all right.

NC You know, the waxwork thing. And eh…

EH I'm all right. Leave me alone. Let me get up.

NC What he used to do was to steal the bodies from the mortuary and, eh [*pause: 2 seconds*] Glynis, now what was that girl's name? Glynis Farrell [sic: Glenda Farrell] was it? I think her name was. She was a reporter in it. Film star. And, eh, he got somebody and this person was alive and he got her on this slab. And all the wax was boiling and it was getting, nearly boiling over, you know.

NP Oh yeah.

NC And, eh, she reported it or something. And just before the wax before to kill the girl [sic] em, she scratched her leg and found it was human. That she was alive.

Int Oh-h.

NC But you saw him take all the bodies out the mortuaries.

Int [*Laughs*]

NP Ooh.

NC And put 'em through a window.

NP Ooooh! [*Screams*]

NC And lay 'em on the slab and he'd, eh, cover them with wax. And then sometimes there used to be eyes watchin' you.

NP [*Screaming*] Oooh! [*Laughs*]

Int Aw-w, that's horrible. [*Laughs*]

NC It used to be [*laughs*]. I liked that.

NP Oooh! [*Screams with laughter*]

Int [*Laughs*]

NC Because that person was alive, ye see.

NP Oh-h, dear.

NC He had a lovely face, this man. But when the hero came and then found out that he was stealing the bodies, and making 'em into a wax museum. But they were the real bodies, you see.

Int Eugh! [*Laughs*]

NC And this girl, she wasn't dead. And he had revenge on her for some reason or other. And I think she clawed him, an' the mask came off.

NP Oh-h!

NC An' he was *hideous*. He was almost burnt to a cinder, his face.

NP Oh-ooh!

NC Course they caught him and he was done away with. It all came all right in the end, you know, in the end.[21]

A number of informants associate memories of frightening films with the ruses they concocted for getting into the cinema in the face of prohibitions of one sort or another. Two sets of obstacles to seeing 'horrific' films are remembered: vetoes laid down by parents and other authority figures; and the British Board of Film Censors' 'A' certificate which was sometimes enforced with rigour where 'horrific' films were concerned. One film in particular stands out in memories of both sorts of prohibition. Zena Jesney was forbidden by her father to see the 1933 feature *King Kong*, because, he told her, 'you will never sleep'. Fred Curnick remembers having to be taken to the film by an older cousin, because 'You had to be over a certain age or go with an adult... there were quite a lot of films that came in that category, weren't there? That you couldn't go and see unless you'd got somebody with you'.[22] *King Kong* was among the films Beatrice Cooper's mother disapproved of, but Beatrice got around the veto on horror films by bunking off school to see them on her own:

BC That was, they were good films. I loved those. *King Kong* and things like that.

Int [*Gasps*] Oh yes.

BC Mmm. They were the ones I used to, em, you know, skip school for.

Int Really? [*Laughs*]

BC Yeah, because my mother wouldn't have let me go to see them. [*Laughs*]

Int Ah I see.

BC *King Kong*. I went to see it on my own. And *Frankenstein*. And the *Bride of Frankenstein*![23]

On the other hand, as noted above, Jessie Boyd's mother colluded with her daughter in circumventing the 'A' film rule when Jessie wanted to see *Dracula*, pleading with the doorman: 'My little girl has been *so* looking forward to this'. And Emily Soper's memory of having to wait until 'I came of an age when I was allowed in alone' to see the horror films with Boris Karloff and Bela Lugosi that she enjoyed shows how much this generation was affected by official prohibitions on certain sorts of films. Reaching 16, the age at which the 'A' films rule no longer applied, was clearly regarded as an important step towards adulthood.[24]

By far the majority of 1930s cinemagoers' memories of frightening films, then, are of the films themselves and of the responses and reactions they evoked. Discursively speaking, the most striking feature of these memories is their predominantly anecdotal quality: Annie Wright's memory of *The Mummy*, in which the informant sets herself up as central protagonist of a story narrated in the first person, is a case in point. Repetitive memory discourse, which suggests repeated actions is considerably less prominent. There are also a few instances of impersonal memory discourse, in which the narrator distances herself or himself from the narration.

The primacy of anecdotal discourse in memories of frightening films is in marked contrast to informants' memory-talk in general, in which the anecdotal is rather rare. Here, too, anecdotal discourse embraces a relatively wide range of enunciative positions, with varying degrees of closeness between the narration and the events recounted and differing degrees to which the 'child's voice' is apparent. The strongest form of anecdotal discourse involves the narrator's self-construction as central protagonist reliving an experience, with full scene-setting and specific details of the occasion recollected, and a memory-story that has a beginning, a middle and an end. 'Frightening films' stories embodying such strong forms of anecdotal discourse include Tom Affleck's memories of his phobic reaction to *The Werewolf of London*; Hilda Moss's account of coming out of *Dr Jekyll and Mr Hyde* into thick fog; and Lois Basnett's memory of taking a cab home after seeing *Night Must Fall*.

At the other extreme, the weakest form of anecdotal discourse still implies a particular event or occasion in which the narrator is involved, but the involvement is implicit, details of the scene may be vague or absent, and the story itself may lack beginning or closure. There is one distinctive type of weak anecdotal discourse in memory-stories of frightening films: here, a description of a scene from a film may suggest that this might not be a direct memory from childhood but one 'implanted' since, perhaps as an image which has acquired a culturally iconic status over the years. The famous scene from *King Kong* in which the monster grasps in his hand a tiny, struggling Fay Wray is a case in point. Several informants produce 'memories' involving this scene:

EC You'll never believe this! Broke my heart crying in bed about *King Kong*!

Int [*Gasps*]

EC *King Kong*! D'you know with the end where all the planes were going round. And he's firing at 'em an' he's grabbing the planes, you know. And, eh, the one that was with him, Fay Wray. Oh my God! I was! Although, there was sick in it with her screaming. They called 'er the queen of the screamers.

Int [*Laughs*]

EC [*High voice*]. *They called her the queen of the screamers.* She was *screaming* out when he had her in his hand ye know. Waaaaaaaaa! [*Screams*]

Int A-ah.

EC Screaming! Screaming! Screaming! [*High voice*][25]

NC And I remember *King Kong*. Remember *King Kong*, the gorilla. They made a big film of it.

Int With Fay Wray.

NC Yeah.

Int Yeah.

NC And the girl who was in it. Now who was it? [*Pause: 3 seconds*] Oh, she was a lovely girl. He got hold of her in his hand. Cause it was made up of, it was all electrical. It was a wonderful film. And he loved this girl. But he picks her up, she was *screaming* [*said with animation*] *shouting* and *screaming* and this ape was as big as this house.[26]

OS And Fay Wray. In *King Kong*.

Int Mm.

OS I didn't like that. I never liked anything that was at all *horrific*.

You got this great big animal on the top of the building, holding her in his hand. No.[27]

Repetitive memory discourse, which is usually associated with memories of responses and reactions to frightening films rather than of the films themselves, may also embrace varying levels of self-implication on the narrator's part. This can be indicated by the choice of personal pronoun – 'I', 'we', or 'you', and on occasion 'they'. Variations here are sometimes expressions of informants' idiosyncratic storytelling styles, however. East Anglian native Jim Godbold's highly distinctive style, for instance, is informed by the local Suffolk idiom. His memory, quoted above, of girls cuddling up to boys at screenings of 'horrific' films, is an example of repetitive memory discourse. In response to the interviewer's invitation to talk about his own memories of horror films, he distances himself somewhat by using the second-person pronoun in its collective sense ('specially if you was with a girl'), then proceeds – perhaps in deference to the interviewer – to move on from these potentially embarrassing revelations to comment on the unsophisticated responses of other audience members: 'You got people call out, look out, he's behind you! [*laughs*] and all that. Cause they thought it was real. Course a lot of people sort of come from country districts and that, you know. They couldn't realise that was only a film. [*Laughs*]'[28]

In a frequently observable collective variant of repetitive memory discourse, the narrator implicates himself or herself fully in the story as a peer group member. For example, in his memory of impersonating Boris Karloff, Thomas McGoran shifts between 'we' and the collective 'you'. Collective/repetitive memory discourse characterises accounts of the subterfuges employed for getting into cinemas to see 'horrific' films. Olive Johnson remembers that 'If the film was really gripping, it would be natural to sit through all the "other rubbish" in order to be frightened again… [T]hese so-called chillers were restricted to adults [and] we had to implore older folk in the queue to "take us in" with them!'[29] Finally, in the strongest type of repetitive memory discourse, the narrator places herself or himself firmly at the centre of repeated actions, as in Beatrice Cooper's memory of *King Kong*: '['Horrific' films] were the ones I used to… skip school for… because my mother wouldn't have let me go to see them'.[30]

Again, individual storytelling styles can be deceptive. Ellen Casey's is distinctive in that her apparently repetitive memory-discourse is actually closer to anecdotal. This is evident in her story, quoted above, of the lighted candle that rolled down the stairs; and also in her remembered response to the Fu Manchu films:

EC   Oh Charlie Chan! [*Spooked voice*] Used to be terrified of him.

Int   [*Laughs*]

EC   Charlie Chan in *Fu Manchu*. Ho! Used to have nails right out here! Oh *Fu Manchu*! Used to see it once and you'd say, 'Oh I'm not gonna see that again!'[31]

In impersonal memory discourse, the narrator remains fully in the present moment of narration, speaking all the time from an adult standpoint, eschewing immersion in the past and assuming a distanced stance towards the contents of her or his account. Gloria Gooch, for example, whose father was a cinema entrepreneur, comments that 'horrific' films were 'far-fetched', and says that although they would terrify some people, 'you couldn't fully believe in all that'.[32]

Other accounts shuttle between impersonal and more self-implicated modes. Raphael Hart's talk, for instance, segues from his own youthful memories of seeing frightening films to a more impersonal critical commentary. In discussing *King Kong*, he is explicit about the difference between his boyish response to the film and his more distanced adult evaluation:

Int   *King Kong*. Em, as you say, 1933.

RH   1933!

Int   With Fay Wray of course.

RH   I went down to the Grand to see it myself. I enjoyed it to the nth degree!

Int   [*Laughs*]

RH   I was not in any way frightened whatsoever! *King Kong* did not frighten *me*! I've seen it so often, I know the bloody story!

Int   [*Laughs*]

RH   Fay Wray and Robert Armstrong and Bruce Cabot. Oh, I can tell you. I know it! I've seen it and seen it and seen it over and over again!

Int   Mm.

RH   Didn't realise the full implication of it. That it was in fact

Beauty and the Beast. Fay Wray. Fay Wray brought about [*amused voice*] King Kong's downfall. But that was *not* part of my category. What I enjoyed seeing was the dinosaurs and King Kong.[33]

Memory-talk about frightening films, then, embodies a highly distinctive mix of contents and discursive registers, typically taking the form of strong anecdotal accounts of isolated scenes or images in films and of narrators' responses to these. This is in marked contrast with cinema memory in general, in which such vividly detailed anecdotes are most unusual, and it suggests there is something culturally distinctive about the 'distress and delight'[34] of cinema terrors. It certainly suggests that the fear element has a particularly strong purchase in the individual psyche and the collective imagination; for in reaching back to retrieve their memories of terrors in the cinema, informants demonstrate an extraordinary capacity to access the voices of the children they once were.

As children, though, these cinemagoers of the 1930s could scarcely have been aware of the extent to which their experiences of frightening films were the subject of public concern, and it is instructive to set their memories alongside official and other inquiries into children and the cinema conducted in the 1930s. During these years an evolving set of constructions of the child audience at the cinema was produced through these inquiries and the debates surrounding them, as well as through certain practices of regulation and exhibition of films.

In the UK, the early 1930s saw a rise in the visibility of the activities of the British Board of Film Censors (BBFC) and its system of film classification, and of film exhibitors' policing of children's access to certain types of films. These pressures centred on a cycle of Hollywood films, which came to acquire the label 'horrific', and an unprecedented set of events involving the BBFC, the government, a series of pressure groups and the film industry itself was to unfold around these films.

From the earliest years of cinema, the effects of moving pictures on children had been a subject of considerable public concern. This was centred at first on cinema's supposed physical effects – damage to eyesight, fatigue and so on – as much as on its potential for 'demoralising' children and the working class.[35] The early 1930s, however, saw a new focus for anxieties about young people's cinemagoing. This was directed less at cinema's negative effects on children than on what was held to be good for them, and at the ways in which cinema could detract from child welfare or make a positive contribution to it. In the period from around 1930 to 1934, the government was subjected to pressures from numerous quarters to reform the system of film censorship and children's cinemagoing practices. These arose largely as a result of concerns about frightening films.[36]

A category label for these films – 'horrific' – emerged towards the end of 1932 in response to a cycle of Hollywood talkies released in Britain in the early 1930s, including *Frankenstein* (1931) and *Dr Jekyll and Mr Hyde* (1932). Interestingly, the genre is defined not in terms of the films' contents – plots, characters, iconographies – but in relation to their audiences and to audiences' responses: the standard definition of a 'horrific' film was one 'likely to frighten or horrify children under the age of 16 years'.[37] In fact, the 'horrific' film was a discursive product of a debate about the meaning of the BBFC's 'A' and 'U' classifications in relation to the child audience. This debate touches on the question of parental rights and responsibilities in choosing the films children will see, the problem of non *bona fide* guardians taking children into 'A' films, and the issue of what is and is not a film suitable for children.

As the 'fear element' moved to the forefront of public concern, the emphasis had shifted away from unsuitable contents ('sordid themes', mainly around sex and crime), towards responses and effects (terrors, nightmares and so on). Later in the 1930s, concern with the child audience and its 'problematic' reactions to 'unsuitable' films shades into a more positive advocacy of films suitable for young audiences, and the British Film Institute assumed a proactive role in promoting the commercial exhibition of films suitable for, or produced especially for, children.[38]

This shift is part of a series of changes, beginning in the early decades of the twentieth century, in how children and childhood were understood. At the start of the century a new construction of childhood had emerged in Britain in tandem with three sets of historical changes: the separation of the child from the world of employment and the child's coming to be regarded as a non-worker; the rise of compulsory mass schooling, with childhood being seen as a period of learning and socialisation outside the home; and a set of institutions designed to regulate the moral behaviour of the young in which the child is regarded as peculiarly vulnerable to moral corruption.

It is largely the last of these views which informs the regulation of cinema in the years between its beginnings in the early 1900s and the mid to late 1920s.[39] However, by the early 1930s the child in the cinema is decreasingly seen as physically at risk, morally corruptible or criminally susceptible, and increasingly regarded as psychologically vulnerable. In consequence, the problem is no longer viewed as one of public morality or public order, but of the moral or – increasingly – the psychological welfare of the child.

The 1930s saw the institutionalisation of child-centredness and adult advocacy on the child's behalf. In the discourse of child-centredness, the child's difference from the adult lies in the fact that it requires guidance and protection by those who, as parents or professionals, assume responsibility for its psychological welfare. Harry Hendricks contends that in the interwar years approaches to childhood were increasingly informed by the 'new psychology', whose components include the nursery school movement, educational psychology, psychoanalysis and child guidance. The Child Guidance Council was founded in 1927, and the first child guidance clinic in London opened at around the same time. The Children and Young Persons Act of 1933 made the welfare of the child (as neglected, or in care, or delinquent) a central concern.[40] These new institutions and discourses, says Hendricks, were to become 'the centre of a web of *preventative and therapeutic* child *welfare* embracing the nursery, the home, the school, the playground, and the courts'.[41] As a place where the children of the 1930s spent a considerable amount of time, the cinema might with justification be added to this list.

Indeed, surveys of children's cinemagoing conducted during the 1930s increasingly take a child-centred approach. For example, an investigation conducted in 1930 and 1931 by a pressure group called the Birmingham Cinema Inquiry Committee (BCIC) adopted the then groundbreaking tactic of asking children themselves, through questionnaires and interviews, about their cinemagoing habits: how often they went to the pictures, what sorts of films they liked and disliked, why they went to the cinema. Concern for psychological welfare is apparent in the investigators' interest in children's views on and responses to 'frightening pictures'. Also in 1930 and 1931, an inquiry by the Sheffield Social Survey into children's cinema matinees in the city revealed that most programmes supposedly for children were in fact identical to ordinary cinema programmes for the week, which often included 'A' films. The researchers concluded that much of the entertainment available for children in cinemas was 'unsuitable' for them.

The Birmingham and Sheffield inquiries were followed by a series of similar investigations whose indebtedness to child psychology is evident. The most influential of these was undoubtedly the London County Council's 1932 study of schoolchildren and the cinema, which looked at the 'effect of attendance at cinema on the *minds* of children', with data gathered from 21,280 children between three and 14 years of age from 29 London schools. The conclusion was that there was no great cause for alarm over films' moral effects on children, but that their being frightened in the cinema was certainly a cause for concern.[42]

As the decade wore on, research into children's cinemagoing increasingly approached the subject from an educational and a psychological point of view, and from the standpoint of children's specific needs.[43] At the same time, pressure group activity around film censorship was increasingly justifying itself in terms of concern about the harmful effects on children's minds of seeing 'unsuitable' films.

Historians of cinema have noted a shift in attitudes towards the medium from around the mid-1930s, when 'the pictures' became more widely acceptable and a certain embourgeoisement of filmgoing took place as luxuriously-appointed new supercinemas were built, many of them in middle-class suburbs.[44] It is perhaps worth noting in this regard that public concern about children seeing 'frightening' films peaked in the early 1930s. The 'horrific' films debate may perhaps be regarded as marking a moment of transition in constructions of the child cinema audience. It bridges on one side pre-embourgeoisement negative notions about cinema's harmfulness to children or the unsuitability of certain sorts of films, and on the other more positive, post-embourgeoisement, ideas about and campaigns for films suitable for children.

Richard Ford's book, *Children in the Cinema*, published in 1939, embodies the latter position to perfection. Articulating the end-of-decade orthodoxy on children and cinema, Ford refers to the outbreak of interest in children's 'welfare' with the coming of talkies, and argues that too many films had been and still, in 1939, remained unsuitable for children, pointing to the 'difference between children and adults in the cinema'. The solution to the problem of suitability is not to prohibit or to censor, he contends, but rather to recognise children's special needs, and to cater for them.[45] For Ford, the key aspect of the child audience's distinctiveness lies in 'the intensity of child experience in seeing films'.[46] This, he says, applies especially to fear and consequent disturbed sleep, bad dreams and so on. It is very common, he says, for children to be frightened at the pictures, and this should perhaps be regarded as 'an inevitable baptism to regular film-going'.[47]

When research on children's cinemagoing conducted during the 1930s is set alongside memories of 1930s cinemagoers gathered many years later, a surprising degree of consensus emerges on what exactly was frightening about 'frightening' films. For example, the young people who took part in the Birmingham inquiry in 1930 and 1931 mention being scared by scenes of violence, decapitation and ghosts, and by images of Chinese people. Similar observations emerge elsewhere. Citing the Payne Fund studies in the USA, published in 1933, alongside the findings of surveys of child and adolescent filmgoers in Britain and of his own survey of cinema managers, Richard Ford concludes that the types of films containing incidents likely to provoke nightmares are 'Mystery, Ghost, Murder, War and Fighting, with an especial emphasis on films with Chinese or Oriental faces'.[48] Frightening items in children's matinee programmes include: various scenes from *Flash Gordon*, including prehistoric monsters and 'the Clayman coming out of the wall'; 'an apparently disembodied hand appearing from the wall in *The Clutching Hand*'; 'ugly Chinese characters'; torture, cruelty and characters in danger; closeups, especially of 'evil-faced villains'.[49]

In their recollections of being frightened at the pictures, 1930s cinemagoers refer to a similar corpus of terrifying images: huge gorillas, werewolves and other monsters; decapitated heads and other kinds of dismemberment; 'a horrible sort of creature [coming] out of the wall'; the dead coming to life (as, for example, in *The Mummy*, or in the form of a half-remembered 'mechanical man').

What many of these frightening images have in common is that they betoken aversion to things which are neither dead nor living, or which shift between the two states. Film has the capacity precisely to animate what is not actually there, to bring shadows to life and indeed to separate parts of bodies from the whole and magnify them in huge close-ups. The combination of abject subject matter with cinema's distinctive expressive qualities could certainly explain the affective salience attaching to informants' earliest cinemagoing memories. This is especially so where these reawaken the terror brought on by barely-remembered images, or by scenes which to the rest of the audience were unperturbing or even amusing. The untutored cinema spectator is highly susceptible to the uncanniness of those huge disembodied faces, those ghostly shadows on the screen. At the same time, if cinema terrors are medium-specific to a degree, they also reference the culturally pervasive stuff of tales of the supernatural – stories and images whose frightening qualities certainly predate cinema.[50]

There is a category of frightening things for the 1930s generation which is both peculiarly insistent and, in not obviously belonging to the cultural repertoire of the frightening or the uncanny, curiously anomalous. Richard Ford more than once mentions children's unanimous abhorrence of oriental characters, particularly 'Chinese or oriental faces'.[51] Virtually every inquiry into children's cinemagoing undertaken during the 1930s includes references to fears of all things Oriental, and cinemagoers of the 1930s still remember their terror of the 'oriental scheming villain', Fu Manchu.

Fu Manchu, Sax Rohmer's infamous literary creation, was the subject of a number of serials and feature films from the 1920s on, and Fu's reign of terror in the cinema reached its peak in the interwar years.[52] In his various cinematic manifestations, Fu was always constructed, by means of make-up, framing and lighting, as the ultimate 'evil-faced villain'. In the 1932 feature *The Mask of Fu Manchu*, for example, the eponymous villain makes his entrance seven minutes into the film, after a substantial buildup: 'There's a fanatic in the East… Dr Fu Manchu'; 'They have ways in the East of shattering the strongest courage'. The evil doctor, played by Boris Karloff, appears on the screen with no introductory establishing shot and in huge closeup, his exaggeratedly oriental physiognomy eerily lit from below and reflected and enlarged in a distorting mirror. Only after this lingering closeup is the setting established, as the camera tracks back to reveal Fu in his laboratory surrounded by the familiar accoutrements of the deranged scientist (smoking retorts, scientific instruments, sparking electricity) and a *memento mori* in the conventional form of a skull. Fu's trademark long fingernail – deployed later in the film as a magic wand – is visible throughout.

The villain's power, it transpires, lies in a lethal combination of western learning (he reminds his first victim that he holds degrees from Edinburgh, Cambridge and Harvard) and mastery of the mysterious and supra-rational 'ways of the East'. The film's plot involves a hunt for 'the lost tomb of Genghis Khan' by a group of scientist-explorers working on behalf of the British Museum. The party includes the daughter of another explorer believed to have been captured by Fu Manchu. Their mission is to reach the tomb before their adversary gets

Boris Karloff in *The Mask of Fu Manchu*

there, and bring its 'priceless' contents back to the British Museum. The explorers eventually return alive but without the treasure, having tangled with Fu Manchu and undergone terrible tortures at his hands: earsplitting bells, whippings, injections of lethal serum, a crocodile pit and an unspecified 'sacrifice' from which the heroine makes a narrow escape.

Significantly, the story is set in train by the West's incursion into the Orient rather than vice versa. The terror and torture, in other words, are set loose by the white man stirring up things he does not understand and which are, we infer, best left alone. Matters are not utterly straight-forward, however, for East and West are in several respects combined in the figure of Fu Manchu. Not only do his extraordinary powers derive from a command of both the arcane arts of the East and 'rational' western science, the trouble that sets the plot in motion arises from the interpenetration of East and West. Orientalism is not, then, constructed as incontrovertibly Other. In this, perhaps, lies its uncanny quality: the terror lies within, and thus cannot be abjected. At the end of the film, Genghis Khan's sword, the 'priceless treasure', is thrown into the sea. But the problems set up by this narrative are not so easily resolved: 'There may be other Fu Manchus in the future', hints one of the westerners, darkly.

This open ending recalls Fu Manchu's earliest cinematic outings, which took the form of silent serials, among them *The Mystery of Dr Fu Manchu*, produced in Britain in 1923 and starring Harry Agar Lyons in the title role. Each episode is a more-or-less self-contained story featuring the same main characters, in which the villain, though thwarted in the previous episode, always returns. Among the serial's main characters is a young woman named Karamaneh (Joan Clarkson) who functions as both (unwitting) femme fatale and woman in peril. One of Fu's antagonists, Petrie (Humberstone Wright), is attracted to Karamaneh, who in various ways falls victim to Fu's evil powers and repeatedly has to be rescued. Part Asian and part Europen, Karamaneh figures as a key narrative motivator in some episodes of *The Mystery of Dr Fu Manchu*, for she is both dangerous and in danger.

A woman of mixed race who combines the attributes of the femme fatale and the woman in peril is pivotal also in the 1933 feature *The Mummy*, whose story also bears certain resemblances to that of *The Mask of Fu Manchu*. *The Mummy*'s opening sequence shows archaeologists with the 'British Museum Field Expedition' at work in Egypt in 1921. They are inspecting a recently unearthed Mummy, Imhotep. Buried alongside Imhotep is a casket whose hieroglyphic inscription contains a curse of death on anyone who opens it. Ignoring the warning, one of the archaeologists opens the box and starts translating the scroll within. Meanwhile, in the film's first and most memorable frightening moment, the mummy (Boris Karloff) comes to life.

We see its bandaged face in closeup;

and its eyes slowly open.

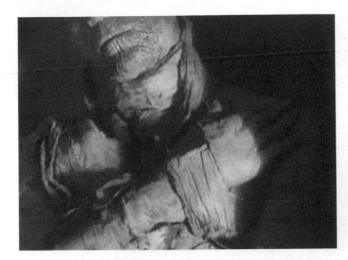

There is a slow tilt down to a closeup of the Mummy's bandaged arms folded across its chest.

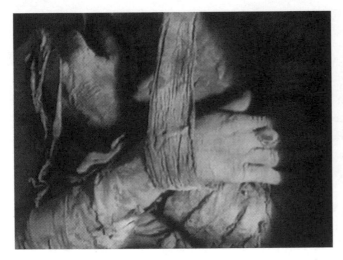

The right hand moves slightly;

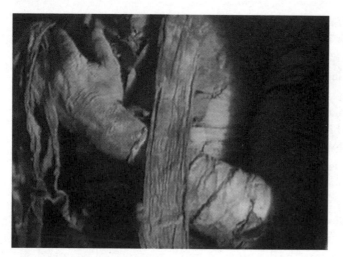

and then the left.

Eleven years on, Imhotep reappears in disguise as Ardath Bey, an Egyptian scholar who helps the British Museum's 1932 expedition find the tomb of 'an ancient princess'. It emerges that in life Imhotep had loved the princess, but that she had suffered an untimely death. His resort to forbidden knowledge to try to bring her back to life had been punished by execution. Imhotep's quest in the present is to make another attempt to resurrect his lost love. For this, he needs the co-operation of a living woman. He chooses Helen Grosvenor, daughter of an English father and an Egyptian mother. The rest of the film details Ardath Bey's/ Imhotep's repeated attempts to entrance and take possession of Helen, and the woman's increasingly vain attempts to resist him.[53] Helen's mix of Englishness and Egyptianness, of West and East, renders her at once susceptible to Imhotep's mesmeric powers and capable, but only up to a point, of resisting them. In the end, the lure of the East almost wins the day, as the living Helen narrowly avoids being embalmed and turned into a dead thing. Again, the film's ending fails to deliver a complete resolution, and the 'victory' of the powers of western enlightenment remains somewhat unconvincing.

As in *The Mask of Fu Manchu*, the white man's curiosity about the Orient stirs up things better left alone. Western scholarly endeavour and western acquisitiveness together unleash the ancient and recondite arts and knowlege of the East. These threaten the white man not with extinction but with something far worse: incorporation. It is not coincidental that the white men in these stories are British: both *The Mummy* and the Fu Manchu films at some level reference the British Empire, mapping imperial power and subject empire respectively onto Europe and Asia, West and East, and proposing a relationship between the two grounded in a mix of fear and desire.

The Mummy's topical references are apparent: the fictional 1921 field expedition which opens the film is an obvious allusion to the unearthing of the tomb of Tutankhamun in February 1923, an event which took place a year almost to the day after Egypt's declaration of independence from the British Empire. Significantly in this regard, the film contains a scene in which the ownership of the 1932 archaeological finds are discussed. On discovering that these have been kept by the Egyptian government, the expedition leader defends his country against the implications of this declaration of ownership: 'The British Museum works for science, not for loot'. The terrifying resurrection of the buried arts of an earlier Egyptian civilisation takes place, in both fact and fiction, at the very moment of the secession of a contemporary Egypt from the rational and 'civilising' powers of the Empire and the West, and of its embarkation on a new quest for national identity. *The Mummy* at least constructs this quest as a return to the dangerous glamour of ancient Egypt.[54]

Both the fact and the manner of interwar popular cinema's production of an Oriental Uncanny betray an ambivalence at the heart of the West's relationship with the East. A powerful combination of fear and desire is embodied in the figures of the monsters Imhotep and Fu Manchu, as well as in the compellingly attractive and unwittingly dangerous hybrid ethnicity of the female characters Helen and Karamaneh. Monsters and women figure here as embodiments of Europe's ambivalent fascination with the the East, of an Empire soon to be lost. The uncanniness of both types of creature – monsters and women – lies, psychically and culturally, in the liminal qualities they embody. They dissolve and transgress boundaries between life and death, between West and East. The male monsters Fu Manchu and Imhotep also derive their power from knowledge not available to the mortal, white male; knowledge corrupted and misused in the pursuit of their, the monsters', desires.

The perversion of arcane knowledge also underlies the complicated plot of the 1933 film *The Mystery of the Wax Museum*. As in *The Mummy*, this film's opening scene is set in 1921, in this case in London. A museum of waxworks whose owner, Ivan Igor (Lionel Atwill), is obsessed by his model of Marie Antoinette, is destroyed by fire. The rest of the film's action is set in New York in 1933 where, amidst a mystery involving unexplained deaths and missing bodies, the wax museum is about to reopen. Intrepid girl reporter Florence (Glenda Farrell) discovers that Igor has been embalming the missing corpses and mummifying them for the museum. He has met a young woman, Charlotte (Fay Wray), who resembles 'his' Marie Antoinette and decided to add her to his waxwork collection.

The Mystery of the Wax Museum's most memorable frightening moment occurs in the penultimate scene, when Charlotte and Igor come face-to-face in his huge basement laboratory, and he tells her she is about to be embalmed, offering the consolation of immortality.

1. In a track right, MLS to MS, Igor pursues Charlotte as she retreats in terror. He reaches out to grab her.

2. Brief closer
two-shot
from the
same angle.

3. Charlotte
beats Igor
with her fists:
'Let me go!'

4. Close two-shot from behind Charlotte, with Igor's face partially visible. As she continues hitting him, his face cracks open.

5. Brief CU of Charlotte, aghast.

6. Two-shot as 4. Charlotte tears off the rest of the mask.

Like Imhotep, Igor is driven by desire to bring the past into the present by resurrecting or recreating a lost love object, a process which entails killing and embalming a living woman. *Mystery of the Wax Museum*, however, presents a doubled past: firstly, eighteenth-century France, where the historical queen Marie Antoinette was beheaded during the bloody creation of a new republic; and secondly, a much more recent England, site of Igor's loving creation of a waxwork of the executed queen. As a piece of human artifice, a simulacrum of a once living woman, the monster's object of desire was already 'dead' when destroyed by fire 12 years earlier on another continent. Moreover, Igor's quest rests not only on the perversion of rational knowledge, but also on the passage of his corrupted science westwards from Europe to America.

If the Fu Manchu films and *The Mummy* are about the seductive threat posed to Europe by the ancient and mysterious arts of the East, *Mystery of the Wax Museum* posits Europe itself as a site of darkness, corruption and bloody history, and the New World as vulnerable to infection by the virus of a retrograde past. In the unmasking of the monster, the ugly, repulsive face of Europe is exposed. In this story, Europe figures as America's Orient, except that the relationship between the two worlds is far less ambivalent and mutually dependent than that between Europe and Asia: the ending of *Mystery of the Wax Museum* can propose that America may abject the horrors of Europe.

If young cinemagoers of the 1930s were frightened by films of the Oriental Uncanny, they appear not to have been especially sensitive to their plots, their historical and contemporary references or their discursive constructions of race, gender, knowledge and Empire. And yet the phenomenon of the Oriental Uncanny certainly appears to be historically specific. These films constitute a subgenre of the 'horrific' film which draws the social and the historical into its formal conventions in specific ways. They are frightening because they embed cultural signifiers of Orientalism in broader iconographies of the Uncanny, and do so in a manner peculiar to the medium of cinema.

In all the 'horrific' films of the 1930s, concepts and images held to be uncanny or frightening *per se* – disfigured faces, tortures, 'undead' figures, decapitation and the like – make an appearance. Moreover, the moments in these films which were experienced as especially frightening are the ones which are particularly cinematic. These draw on cinema's own conventions of mise en scene, framing, lighting and editing to produce highly memorable 'attractions', moments of cinematic spectacle which interrupt the flow of the narrative.[55] The ways in which these frightening moments are described and remembered by filmgoers who were children in the 1930s certainly suggest that the impression they made has as much to do with their cinematic presentation as with their content.

The debates of the 1930s about the child cinema audience and its exposure to frightening films were focused largely on children's responses to the films rather than on their contents: this view, in-terestingly, was also taken by Freud in his definition of the 'Uncanny'. As far as the memories of the 1930s generation are concerned, the ex-perience of being frightened was what impressed itself most forcefully on the young cinemagoer, and the emotion – fear – is expressed and remembered non-verbally, somatically: inside the cinema you cower under the seat or cover your eyes; afterwards you are troubled by waking fears and nightmares. There are many constants here: in the attributes of terror-inspiring moments in films, in immediate responses to the fear, in coping strategies. This, along with the peculiar salience of cinema terrors in memories of filmgoing, confirms what observers have noted over the years about the intensity of the child's experience in the cinema, and sheds new light on the question of how the child looks.[56]

Notes

1. T95-32, Annie Wright, Manchester, 26 May 1995.

2. In *The Interpretation of Dreams* and elsewhere, Freud discusses secondary revision as one of the functions of the dreamwork, a process through which waking accounts of dreams are structured and through which order, intelligibility and narrative coherence are provided.

3. 95-87-1, Joan Donaghue, Cardiff, to Annette Kuhn and Valentina Bold, 11 February 1995; 95-135-1, Hilda Moss, mid Glamorgan, to Annette Kuhn and Valentina Bold, n. d. 1995.

4. T95-12, Molly Stevenson and Margaret Young, Glasgow, 20 February 1995. *I Was A Fugitive From A Chain Gang* (Mervyn Leroy, 1932).

5. T95-53, Norman Wild (Vee Entwistle interpreting), Bolton, 13 June 1995.

6. T95-113, E. J. Godbold, Suffolk, 17 October 1995.

7. T95-35, Lois Basnett and Herbert Partington, Manchester, 30 May 1995. On the censorship of *Night Must Fall* (Richard Thorpe, 1937) see BFI Special Collections, BBFC Scenario Reports, 19 July 1935.

8. T95-37, Ellen Casey, Manchester, 31 May 1995. Mrs Casey is referring to *The Mummy*, not *The Mummy's Hand*, which was released in 1940.

9. 95-93-1, Jessie Boyd, Gwent, to Annette Kuhn and Valentina Bold, 5 February 1995.

10. T95-27, Dorris Braithwaite, Vee Entwistle and Kath Browne, Bolton, 11 May 1995.

11. 95-135-1, Hilda Moss, mid Glamorgan, to Annette Kuhn, n. d. 1995.

12. 92-16-1, 'Horror Films', Tom Affleck, Glasgow, November 1992.

13. 95-121-1, James F. Barton, Lincolnshire, to Annette Kuhn and Valentina Bold, 27 February 1995 (two versions of *Seven Keys to Baldpate* were made by RKO in the 1930s, one in 1930, directed by Reginald Barker, and one in 1935, directed by William Hamilton); 92-33-1, Rose Mint, Edinburgh, to Annette Kuhn, 11 May 1992; 95-29-1, Mary Cecil Pook, Sussex, to Annette Kuhn, 15 October 1992; 95-137-1, Reg Ireland, Gloucestershire, to Annette Kuhn and Valentina Bold, 16 February 1995; 95-149-1, Trevor Hillyer, Wiltshire, to Annette Kuhn and Valentina Bold, 12 February 1995.

14. T95-15, Helen Donaghy, Sarah Irvine and Davy Paterson, Glasgow, 3 March 1995.

15. T95-35, Lois Basnett and Herbert Partington, Manchester, 30 May 1995.

16. T95-27, Dorris Braithwaite, Vee Entwistle and Kath Browne, Bolton, 11 May 1995.

17. T95-158, Tessa Amelan, Manchester, 28 May 1996.

18. 95-91-1, Joan Howarth, Wiltshire, to Annette Kuhn and Valentina Bold, 3 February 1995.

19. T95-97, Irene and Bernard Letchet, Harrow, 21 July 1995.

20. 92-34-1, 'Films 1930s: some random thoughts', David Moore, Hampshire, October 1991; T94-12, Thomas McGoran, Glasgow, 30 November 1994.

21. T95-101, Nancy Carrington, Nancy Prudhoe and Elsie Horne, Harrow, 25 July 1995. For a similar present-day example, see David Buckingham, *Moving Images: Understanding Children's Emotional Responses to Television* (Manchester: Manchester University Press, 1996), pp. 117–24.

22. 95-325-1, Zena Jesney, Lincolnshire, to Cinema Culture in 1930s Britain, 15 January 1996; T95-75, Fred and Gwen Curnick, Harrow, 5 July 1995; T95-95, Fred and Gwen Curnick, Harrow, 19 July 1995.

23. T95-153, Beatrice Cooper, Harrow, 27 November 1995.

24. 95-93-1, Jessie Boyd, Gwent, to Annette Kuhn and Valentina Bold, 5 February 1995; 95-146-1, Emily Soper, Hampshire, to Annette Kuhn and Valentina Bold, 13 February 1995.

25. T95-37, Ellen Casey, Manchester, 31 May 1995.

26. T95-82, Nancy Carrington, Harrow, 7 July 1995.

27. T95-89, Olga Scowen, Harrow, 18 June 1995.

28. T95-113, E. J. Godbold, Suffolk, 17 October 1995.

29. 95-60-1, Olive Johnson, West Midlands, to Annette Kuhn and Valentina Bold, 14 February 1995.

30. T95-153, Beatrice Cooper, Harrow, 27 November 1995.

31. T95-38, Ellen Casey, Manchester, 31 May 1995. Mrs Casey is confusing the character Charlie Chan with the actor who played him, Warner Oland, who also played Fu Manchu in a number of films.

32. T95-141, Gloria Gooch, Norfolk, 16 November 1995.

33. T95-151, Raphael Hart, Harrow, 27 November 1995.

34. This is the title of a chapter in David Buckingham, *Moving Images*.

35. Annette Kuhn, *Cinema, Censorship and Sexuality, 1909–1925* (London: Routledge and Kegan Paul, 1988), pp. 120–2.

36. Tom Johnson, *Censored Screams: The British Ban on Hollywood Horror in the 1930s* (Jefferson, NC: McFarland, 1997). See also Annette Kuhn, 'Children, "horrific" films, and censorship in 1930s Britain', *Historical Journal of Film, Radio and Television*, vol. 22, no. 2 (2002).

37. Public Record Office, HO45/17036/58, London County Council, Entertainments Committee, minutes, 20 June 1933.

38. See, for example, William Farr, 'Films for children – plea for co-operation', *Cinematograph Times*, 12 September 1936. Farr was at this time Assistant General Manager of the BFI.

39. See Kuhn, *Cinema, Censorship and Sexuality*.

40. Harry Hendricks, *Children, Childhood and English Society, 1880–1990* (Cambridge: Cambridge Univrsity Press, 1997), p. 30; p. 51.

41. Ibid., p. 53. Emphasis added.

42. Birmingham Cinema Inquiry Committee, 'Report of Investigations, April 1930– May 1931', 1931; Public Record Office, HO45/14731/91, report of inquiry by Sheffield Social Survey Committee on films shown at children's matinees, July 1931; London County Council, Education Committee, 'School Children and the Cinema', 1932. Similar inquiries were also conducted in Birkenhead (Birkenhead Vigilance Committee, 'A Report of Investigations, June–October 1931'); and Edinburgh (John MacKie, 'The Edinburgh Cinema Enquiry', 1933).

43. Bath Children's Cinema Council, 'Report on Questionnaire Drawn Up by the British Film Institute as Applied to Seven Bath Schools', 1936; William Farr, 'Analysis of Questionnaire to Adolescents 14–18 Years', British Film Institute, (1939); A. Maxwell Lewis, 'The Theory and Practice of Film Observation: An Experimental Investigation

into the Child's Attitude to Educational and Entertainment Films', MA Thesis, University of London, 1938; J. Struthers, 'Leisure Activities of Schoolchildren in a Middlesex Secondary (Mixed) School', MA thesis, University of London, 1939.

44. Annette Kuhn, 'Cinema culture and femininity in the 1930s', in Christine Gledhill and Gillian Swanson (eds), *Nationalising Femininity* (Manchester: Manchester University Press, 1996); Nicholas Hiley '"Let's go to the pictures": the British cinema audience in the 1920s and 1930s', *Journal of Popular British Cinema*, vol. 2 (1999), pp. 39–53.

45. Richard Ford, *Children in the Cinema* (London: Allen and Unwin, 1939), p. 47.

46. Ibid.

47. Ibid., p. 51.

48. Ibid., p. 61.

49. Ibid., pp. 57–60; Public Record Office, HO45/2118/22, Odeon Theatres, Report on Children and the Cinema, October 1938.

50. Freud lists 'the return of the dead', 'spirits and ghosts', 'dismembered limbs, a severed head, a hand cut off at the wrist' among things which inspire a sensation of uncanniness: 'The "Uncanny"', *Pelican Freud Library*, vol. 14 (Harmondsworth: Penguin, 1985), pp. 364, 366.

51. Ford, *Children in the Cinema*, p. 130; p. 61.

52. Feature film and film serial versions of Fu Manchu stories include: *The Mystery of Dr Fu Manchu* (Stoll Film Co, 1923); *The Further Mysteries of Dr Fu Manchu* (Stoll Film Co, 1924); *The Mysterious Dr Fu Manchu* (Paramount, 1929); *The Return of Dr Fu Manchu* (Paramount, 1930); *Daughter of the Dragon* (Paramount, 1931); *The Mask of Fu Manchu* (1932); *Drums of Fu Manchu* (Republic, 1940). Studies of representations of China and Chinese characters in films include Richard A. Oehling, 'Hollywood and the image of the Oriental', *Film and History*, vol. 8, no. 2 (1978), pp. 33–41; Gina Marchetti, *Romance and the 'Yellow Peril': Race, Sex and Discursive Strategies in Hollywood Fiction* (Berkeley: University of California Press, 1993).

53. On the hypnotised heroine in horror films, see Rhona J. Berenstein, *Attack of the Leading Ladies: Gender, Sexuality and Spectatorship in Classic Horror Cinema* (New York: Columbia University Press, 1995), chapter 4.

54. On cinema's fascination with Egyptiana, see Antonia Lant, 'The curse of the pharaoh', in Matthew Bernstein and Gaylyn Studlar (eds), *Visions of the East: Orientalism in Film* (New Brunswick, NJ: Rutgers University Press, 1997).

55. See Tom Gunning, 'The cinema of attractions', in Thomas Elsaesser (ed.), *Early Cinema: Space, Frame, Narrative* (London: British Film Institute, 1990).

56. This is an allusion to Linda Williams's essay 'When the woman looks', in Mary Ann Doane et al (eds), *Re-Vision: Essays in Feminist Film Criticism* (Los Angeles: American Film Institute, 1984).

5

Growing Up With Cinema

FOR the 1930s generation, cinemagoing is associated almost exclusively with childhood and adolescence and remembered as an important part of their lives as they were growing up. Yet while they formed ideas about their favourite stars and types of film early in life, few cinemagoers of the 1930s confess to having been cinephiles or devoted fans of particular stars. About a quarter of those interviewed remember regularly reading the popular film weeklies, collecting cigarette cards bearing star portraits and potted biographies, or keeping film scrapbooks. But only a handful recall writing fan letters to stars, and just two had contact with film societies.[1]

For the majority, going to the pictures is remembered as being less about films and stars than about daily and weekly routines, neighbourhood comings and goings and organising spare time. Cinemagoing is remembered, that is, as part of the fabric of daily life, and 1930s cinemagoers paint a lively picture of cinema's role in their young lives. But if everyone has something to say about how they grew up with cinema, they all have different stories to tell and different ways of telling them.

The most striking differences in 'growing up' memories are between men and women. Male informants, generally speaking, offer memories from childhood rather than from adolescence, and they emphasise how, as boys, they drew on what they saw in the cinema to provide imaginative raw material for make-believe and play. Women, on the other hand, have relatively little to say about their preadolescent cinemagoing, but overall offer more 'growing up' memories and explore a wider range of themes in them. Discursively, too, women's memory-talk is more varied than men's, and suggests deeper and perhaps more complex individual and group investments in cinema culture on their part. Barbara Mack offers an apt summation of gender differences: 'The boys in their younger years would play at cowboys and indians... and imitate their cowboy "heroes"; the girls would dream of becoming famous film stars and fantasise in a dream world'.[2]

Men do indeed recall being particularly inspired by film westerns as boys. William Ward is one of many who remember how he and his friends acted out the plots of films they had seen, taking on the parts of their screen heroes: 'One would be Tom Mix and one the baddie or some other hero or villain of the time,' he writes. There was a certain amount of vying for the best parts, it seems: Mrs A. Close is unusual among female informants in recollecting playing 'cowboys and indians' with the boys. Girls, she writes, were tolerated on condition that they accepted the parts the boys shunned: 'You could always tell when we had seen an exciting Western film, for, on leaving, the boys became cowboy heroes, whilst we poor girls had to be the downtrodden Indians – as we all galloped home!!'[3] In general, there are three main themes in men's memories of play, imitation and make-believe inspired by 'the pictures': an emphasis on 'making do', memories of bodily movement and recollections of the outdoor spaces where the make-believe was carried out.

Some of the men remember making do by improvising toys and props for boyhood play from whatever came to hand. Ashley Bird and Jimmy Murray, for example, talk about boys making their own wooden swords for their games of swashbuckling:

AB I remember [*pause: 3 seconds*] when you were eight or nine. Once again the children of today wouldn't do it but we made our swords. From bits of wood with a piece of crossbar and we'd do *Mutiny on the Bounty*, you know.[4]

JM Mind, the very early ones, you always came home then and made a, eh, got two pieces of wood. A small one for the cross. And then everybody had a sword then when they came out. When you were about [*chuckles*] ten year old and everybody had to have a sword fight. Somebody'd get cracked over the head going home. [*Laughs*]

Int　[*Laughs*]

JM　Douglas Fairbanks.

Int　I mean, did you do it because I mean, when you think of kids today or, you know, they're playing football and they're the stars.

JM　Oh yeah.

Int　I mean were you being Douglas Fairbanks versus Errol Flynn? [*Laughs*]

JM　Oh yeah. As I say, when you were younger like, you'd come home and you'd make this, eh, sword out of two piece of wood. And then you'd be going out, fighting each other.

Evoking the crazes that swept through children's playgrounds, Mr Murray continues his story by explaining how boys could just as easily enter into the make-believe with an improvised prop as with a shop-bought one:

JM　Well, after a week, two days and then it'd be gone. Yeah. You'd go back to your skipping rope or something.

Int　Then you'd see a cowboy film and...

JM　Oh you'd have your gun with your caps.

Int　Ah.

JM　You used to have that little roll of, roll of caps. And eh, if you had one of them you were *rich*. You had to either use a piece of wood or your fingers. But you had, eh, oh everybody was a cowboy.

Int　And was it the same sort of thing? Were you being sort of Tom Mix or something? [*Amused voice*]

JM　Yes! Yeah, the same thing.[5]

Pretend horseback riding is remembered as an indispensible part of 'cowboys and indians'. Mrs Close recalls that she and her friends 'galloped home'; and Arthur Orrell demonstrates the action involved:

AO　And, eh, we had a particular run. You could run a particular way. You did that with your hands, as if you were on a horse [*amused voice*], you see. So...

Int　[*Laughs*]

AO It, eh, yeah. I always wanted to be either a cowboy or a mounted police. [*Laughs*][6]

Many of these descriptions and re-enactments re-evoke boyhood sensations of physical energy and release. Lewis Howells, for example, recalls how the dreary landscape of his South Wales home was transformed, in boys' imaginations, into the Wild West: 'with wide open hillsides sensationally dotted with small hills and ravines left by earlier surface coal mining, we gloried in "cowboys and indians"'.[7]

Men's memories of their adolescent engagements with cinema culture further extend these themes of entering into the part and imaginatively becoming one's screen hero, and the emphasis on improvisation also remains. At the same time, a more self-conscious sense of performance and display emerges. Several male informants talk about being prompted by films to try out dance routines, while others recall attempts to imitate the gestures, mannerisms, and occasionally the dress styles, of characters in films.

All the men who mention dancing claim to have been inspired by Fred Astaire's example, and Astaire's 'invitation to dance' is discussed in detail in Chapter 7. Bernard Letchet, for example, describes how Astaire's films made you want to dance:

Oh I think you entered right into the film, you know. I used to see a lot of them, Fred Astaire. And on the way home we used to dance along the pavement [*laughs*] like this. But you know, you *really* got into it. Didn't you?[8]

One of Jim Godbold's hobbies was tap dancing; and sometimes when out with friends he would be called on to show off his skills:

Int What was it about Astaire and Rogers that attracted you?

JG That was the tap dancing. I go so I could tap dance a bit in them days.

Int A-ah.

JG Yeah, I used to be out with the boys and they'd say, give us a tap dance, Jim.

[…]

JG Sometimes at a dance and the…

Int Thank you [*to someone else*].

JG … band would stop and say we have Jim Godbold here tonight. And I'd say, o-oh no!

Int [*Laughs*]

JG I would say. Give a demonstration.⁹

Jimmy Murray paints an amusing picture of young men at the local *palais de danse* trying, with varying degrees of success, to imitate Fred Astaire:

And eh, ooh yeah. After you'd seen it, you'd go there and think, ooh ah. Be a bit of Fred like kinda thing. You *couldn't* but you felt like getting on the dance floor. That's how you associated yourself with, eh, Fred and Ginger kind of thing.¹⁰

Less demanding, perhaps, than trying to copy Fred Astaire were impersonations of the mannerisms of actors and characters in films. Favourite subjects of imitation include James Cagney ('Course, everybody did Cagney, if you know what I mean'¹¹), Douglas Fairbanks Jr, Ronald Colman and Boris Karloff. John and Marion Cooper remember a friend's Charlie Chaplin impression:

MC I just remembered, my brother's friend [*amused voice*], he was quite a clown. And, eh, he [*laughs*] cut a piece out of his mother's black fur coat and made a little moustache.

Int [*Laughs*]

MC And he had a little [*inaudible*]. Do you remember?

A Yes, I remember that [*amused voice*].

JC Who was this, Marion?

MC Bill [B?].

JC Oh. A friend of yours.

MC A friend of Jim's. A friend of Jim.

JC That's right.

MC And he'd put it on and he had a little cane.

A Yes.

MC He had a cane and he would come in an whirl it round.

Int [*Laughs*]

MC Be Charlie Chaplin, wouldn't he?

MC Yes.

JC Yes. [*Laughs*]

A So *that* made you laugh.

MC Yeah.[12]

Ashley Bird liked to imitate Jackie Cooper:

AB I went as Jackie Cooper. Used to wear his cap, his black cap, on one side.

Int Mm.

AB I don't know whether you've got any pictures of him here.

Int I think I know the chap you mean. But I mean, was that your idea or your mother's idea?

AB I don't know. Mine I should think.

Int Yeah.

AB 'Cos we used to wear these flat caps. My friend now has got [*rest inaudible*].

Int It's interesting. He must've caught your imagination…

AB Yes, yes.

Int At that sort of age.

AB Well, I was a bit of little devil.[13]

Bert Partington's memory of honing his impersonation of George Raft is one of many references by men to the allure of the gangster figure:

LB Who was it who tossed the money?

BP Oh that's George Raft [*amused voice*]! He used to put the coins [*laughing*] in his…

LB And all the boys [*laughing; inaudible*]!

BP No. No [*laughs*] they didn't. Cause it took a lot of skill to do that.

LB [*Laughs*]

BP I could do that. It was the only thing I could do. I could flip a coin…

LB [*Whoops with laughter*]

BP Without looking at it. Like George Raft in *Scarface*.

[...]

BP   But that was when I was younger.

Int   [*Laughs*]

BP   That was when I was at school.[14]

Affectations of the mannerisms of Hollywood gangsters sometimes extended to trying out a particular style of dress or manner of wearing clothes:

> I know my friend used to wear a dark shirt and tie like the gangsters. And when he come out the cinema, he used to strike a match under his fingernail just like they did. [*Laughs*] He was holding the door once for somebody and soon as they got there, he let it go, you know. The sort of thing like a gangster [*laughs*] would do. It impressed him.[15]

Nancy Prudhoe, recalling how girls would sometimes make fun of boys who got themselves up as gangsters, performs a mocking impression of a young man swaggering about with his belt tied over his raincoat.[16] Tom Walsh talks about the allure of the private eye in films of the 1940s, and of Hollywood's version of the American way of dressing:

> *TW*   Aye well eh, Raymond Chandler's heroes are, you know, Philip Marlowe, that's the hero. Well he wears the kind of drape model suits and the big hat, the fedora hat. And I mean Willie Glen said to me, 'Have you been to the States?' This was just at the end of the war. I says, 'No.' He says, 'Because I'm just back from the States and you're wearing the exact same dress.' And I remember just laughing. I says, 'Well it's a pal of mine from whom I got this clobber.' Well he hadn't been at the States yet but he was very States conscious. So maybe there was an element of...
>
> *MW*   Oh aye.
>
> *Int*   Mm.
>
> *TW*   Copycat.[17]

Jimmy Murray elaborates on the daydreams and feelings that lay behind such 'copycat' behaviour:

> *Int*   I mean what about when you saw someone like Edward G. Robinson or, eh, Cagney? How did that make you feel?

JM Well, sometime it did brush off a little bit. Because it was the way your wore your trilby. Or had your cigarette. Just, just jotted one down here. Eh, trilbys, macs and cigarettes. And this was the, eh, this was the American type. You take Bogart, Edward G., eh, any of them. It'd be the trilby at one side. And the cigarette in the hand or in the mouth or something like that like. [...]

Int [*Laughs*]

JM You'd be doing a Bing Crosby, holding the pipe, in the corner of the mouth, or wearing a trilby like Edward G. on the side of the head. Bogart or something. Bogart. That's how you *associated* with them. In a way. But in your coat, you had your hand in your pocket like. A little [*pause: 2 seconds*], no way to shoot anybody like but still [*laughs*]. You did little things what they, eh, what *they* did.

Int So their sort of style you admired.

JM Yeah. Yeah.

Int The way they carried themselves.

JM The little things what they...

Int Yeah.

JM You felt a little bit *tougher* like. And the dancing, you tried it at palais and, eh, you felt *better*. You know. You'd *brace* yourself a bit more.[18]

George Turner, on the other hand, suggests that copying styles of dress from the films was merely the sensible thing to do if one wanted to be fashionable:

Int Yeah. I mean do you think that the, 'cause you were talking about learning things from the films. Do you think that the way people behaved in films affected them. I mean did you learn things from that as well?

GT Well yeah. I suppose so, really. Eh, dressing up and things like that, you know. I suppose, you used to. I mean, eh, fashion-wise, I suppose you used to try and sort of take a pattern more or less of what the people wear.

Int Mm.

GT And what you could afford. You used to try and make yourself look smart in other words.[19]

While there is evidence of identificatory fantasy in some of these adolescent memories ('you *associated* with them'), the feeling of wanting to 'be' one's film hero emerges more forcefully in men's recollections of their boyhood cinemagoing; and the name of Tom Mix arises repeatedly in this context. The archetypal popular hero of his day, Mix enjoyed a long career in films, but is best remembered for the pictures he made in the 1920s, with their spectacular physical exploits, fast-moving adventure and 'prevailing spirit... of fun and boyish enthusiasm'.[20] The star's physical presence is a key element in the success of Mix's films, publicity for which emphasised his athletic prowess: he was widely (and not entirely accurately) reputed to perform all his own stunts. The American West provided Mix with a vast stage for action and adventure, and the oath of the Tom Mix Fan Club, 'I promise to be a straight shooter with my Mom and Dad', 'I promise to be a straight shooter at school', and so on, appealed strongly to young boys, to whom Mix offered a model of masculinity centred around physical activity and moral rectitude.[21]

Hollywood stars are the favourites, too, in men's memories of their adolescent picturegoing and, as already noted, there is a particular fascination with the figure of the gangster. In the USA, gangster pictures were at the centre of a moral panic which was instrumental in tightening up Hollywood's system of self-censorship; and on both sides of the Atlantic, the 'problem' posed by the figure of the gangster was clearly its attraction to young working-class men. The Hollywood gangster arguably represents social mobility and success through non-sanctioned means, as opposed to the more acceptable routes of education, thrift and hard work. In the British context, there is a particular social class issue here. The insouciance, the absence of deference, which characterises these figures of identification hint at a rebellion, at least in imagination, against the middle-class, patriarchal values which dominated Britain in the 1930s.

The sartorial side of this nascent class rebellion prefigures subsequent developments in British working-class culture. Reporting in 1934 on some young men frequenting a cafe in Islington, London, a journalist remarks: 'Nearly every youth, with a very long overcoat and a round black hat on the rear of his head, was to himself a "Chicago nut".'[22] While the gangster lookalikes of the 1930s were not members of a youth subculture, they were very likely the forerunners of postwar clothes-based, marginally delinquent, working-class male subcultures like the zoot suit wearers of the 1940s and the Teddy Boys of the 1950s. These identifications and behaviours signal if not a rejection, then certainly a potentially troubled negotiation, of the acceptable modes of masculinity available to British working-class boys and young men in the interwar years.

From the shared imaginative worlds of boyhood games of cowboys and indians to the male-to-male displays of dancing prowess and gangster impersonations, male bonding is clearly a key component of masculine identification here. Jim Godbold remembers his displays of dancing as being performed at the behest of 'the boys' he went out with; while Bert Partington's trick of tossing a coin *à la* George Raft was done for the benefit of his schoolmates. The transition from boyhood to young manhood does not appear to be straightforward, however, nor does an unambiguous relation to masculinity emerge in these men's testimonies. In retrospect, this is perhaps rendered more complex for this generation by the fact that most of them subsequently saw war service in the armed forces.

The emphasis on physical action noted by Pat Kirkham and Janet Thumim[23] in cinematic representations of masculinity is echoed here to a certain extent. It also sits well with the repeated finding in investigations of children's and young people's cinemagoing conducted during the 1930s that the boys and young men of the day preferred action pictures to all other types of film. Men's memories, too, foreground the body at the level of content and also, where gestures and body movements are deployed to illustrate a point, through the narration itself. And yet unlike boyhood memories of cowboys and indians and of running about in open spaces, men's recollections of their adolescent engagements with cinema culture centre on dancing more often than on combat or sport. Moreover, the behaviours associated with gangster imitation are, beyond a certain amount of strutting and swaggering, virtually devoid of physical action. On the contrary, they have a somewhat static and, in both senses of the word, posing character. There is an 'indoor' quality, too, to all these memories of performances and displays.

Significantly, both dancing displays and gangster impersonations are remembered as being directed largely at the male peer group. The homo-sociality at the level of outward behaviour which emerges from these memories sits alongside feelings of identification ('living the part', in Jim Godbold's words) at the level of daydream and imagination. The kinetic qualities of discourses around space and freedom of movement are perhaps significant in relation to the question of masculinity and its organisation of subjects' inner and outer worlds.

However, all these accounts are marked by a particular interaction between the world of the imagination and that of the informant's everyday surroundings: Lewis Howells situates his remembered boyhood games of cowboys and indians in the hills and the coalfields of his neighbourhood, Jim Godbold talks of nights out with the boys, Jimmy Murray stresses the impossibility of successfully acting out one's daydreams in the real world. In Chapter 3 it was noted that young filmgoers took the familiar worlds of home and neighbourhood with them when they went to the cinema. These men, it appears, brought the dream worlds opened up on the cinema screen back into their own worlds, domesticated them, and made them part of their daily lives.

Women of the 1930s generation domesticated the world of the pictures, too, in their own ways. Looked at in historical and social context, the differences between men's and women's engagements with cinema culture suggest that during the 1930s cinema was a more potent force in women's lives than in men's. Cinema, for this generation of women, extended imaginings of what a woman could be, and proffered modes of feminine identity unavailable to previous generations. By comparison with men, women offer few recollections of childhood play and make-believe inspired by films, and their accounts rarely include memories suggesting freedom of movement in open spaces. Women's memories of growing up with cinema, in fact, are usually about adolescence rather than girlhood, and suggest a gender-specific relationship with cinema culture as a site of identifications or a template for imitations.

For example, by far the most prominent theme of women's 'growing up' memories is copying the appearance of female stars – usually their hairstyles, sometimes their makeup, occasionally their clothes:

Int   Mm. I mean did you model the way you dressed yourself on the stars then?

HB   Oh yes. You used to copy the hairdos and everything like that. Us girls did you know. I mean you used to go there, you know. Yeah. [*Pause: 2 seconds*]

Int   Certainly looking at a page like that, I see exactly what you mean.

HB   Mm.

Int   The beautiful hairstyles.

HB Ye-es. And you used to go for the makeup, you see, as well. How they used to makeup.[24]

Some informants give accounts of great length involving detailed descriptions of certain styles and how these were achieved, and generally giving the impression that considerable time and effort was devoted to these activities. Rosemary Skinner, for example, writes that she 'spent ages in front of the mirror trying to make my hair cascade down my back and over my shoulders at once'. Interviewee Eileen Scott wore her hair in a pageboy style ('I think we all had this craze for a pageboy'), influenced by Ginger Rogers, 'who had such go-orgeous hair'.[25]

Ginger Rogers is remembered as the most popular model for hairstyles and makeup. Hazel Pickess, demonstrating the style with a gesture of the hand, describes how she liked to copy Ginger's hair:

Int Cause you were telling me about how much you liked Ginger Rogers. I mean that explains…

WP Oh yeah.

HP There's a [*inaudible*] and she used to copy them. Yeah. Yes we had some lovely things then, didn't we?

WP Mm.

Int Did you do your hair?

HP My hair was more, I always had a fringe. Always had a fringe. But I used to do the stuff where you rolled it up and that come up here like this and like this. And like this.[26]

Ellen Casey, however, preferred the brunette Kay Francis:

EC Kay Francis. Oh-h! I thought she was *beautiful* [*hushed voice*] Kay Francis. Oh! She was lovely, her! Funny I've not seen her, I've not seen her in, em, in a film for, I don't think she made a lot a films. But she was gorgeous, Kay Francis. I used to love her. I used to try and have my hair like her.

Int Ah.

EC And some of the kids used to say, 'Aw, you're trying to be like Kay Francis!' [*Laughs*]'Aw, you're trying to be like Kay Francis aren't you?' You know.[27]

Some of the women remember experimenting with hairstyles and cosmetics as a rather daring activity, risking adult disapproval. As far as many women of their mothers' generation were concerned, only prostitutes wore makeup, and a number of informants tell stories about being ordered to remove all traces of the stuff before being allowed out of the house:

SI   When you got a wee bit older you put a wee tip powder on your face, see, when ye were going up the stairs?

HD Aw, I [*with emphasis*] got a row for that.

SI   Oh my God!

HD I told ye about that the last time, I got a row for that.

SI   Ye'd get battered!

HD Aye, my mother says.

DP   'What's that ye've got on your face!'[28]

Peggy Kent and her friends Hilda Green and Hilda Catchpol worked together in a laundry in Lowestoft, Suffolk in the 1930s. Their laughter-filled recollections of doing each others' hair during working hours emphasise the enjoyably subversive quality of this activity:

PK   We used to start doing our hair in the afternoon so we'd look nice for the evening.

HG How many times did we have our hair done during the day, I wonder?

HC   I can't think, knocking about.

HG Fiddling about.

PK   Having curlers, you know these long piece curlers stacked up [along our hair?]

HC   That's right.

HG Daren't let the manageress see it though.

PK   Who was it they went, somebody had this, I remember going to the pictures she had this big blonde streak so we had a saucer of hydrogen proxide.

HC   Yeh! [*Laughs*] That's right.

PK   And we all had a blonde streak, didn't we!

All   [*Laugh*]

PK   We put a bit of cotton wool in it and any time I went by I picked up the cotton wool and went like this! [*Indicates pulling wool through hair*] You see?

HG [*Laughs*]

PK   So I was getting my blonde streak! My mother said to me, 'Your hair has gone a funny colour.'

HG [*Laughs*]

PK   I said, 'That's the sun, mother!'

All [*Laugh*]

PK   And then we had, who was it, the film star that had this row of kiss curls? So we mixed up sugar and water.

HG That sticky.

[*Unintelligible: overtalking*]

PK   That was all, it went all sticky and then.

HC I know.

HG Yes.

PK   And you can get the curls you see and twist them round and when the wind blew it'd lift them up and put them down again! [*Laughs raucously*]

Peggy Kent (third from left) with friends

PC   I remember I dyed my hair once and that went blonde like that and we got.

PK   Dyed hair! We used to dye our hair.

HG   We had every colour under the sun!

PK   I think that's why I'm white now! [*Laughs*]

HC   Is that natural white or have you dyed it!

Int   [*Laughs*]

PC   No that *is* natural, that *is* natural that, that *is* natural.[29]

Copying film stars' clothes called for a certain amount of cash, or at least some dressmaking skills, hence perhaps the relatively few memories involving clothes. Here too, though, Ginger Rogers is remembered as a favourite role model. Myra Schneidermann writes about an aunt of hers who improvised one of the star's styles by 'sewing lace collars onto every dress she had, as she had seen Ginger Rogers wear a lace-collared dress in a film'. Hazel Pickess, too, remembers copying Ginger's clothes as well as her hairstyles:

Int   And I wondered what it was that particularly appealed to you in the stars that you did like.

HP   Well the fashions really. I liked about Ginger Rogers. Liked her fashions and dancing.

WP   Used to copy her clothes, didn't you?

HP   I used to copy her clothes.

Int   Mm. So it was the way she looked...

HP   The way she looked and dressed.[30]

When juvenile singing star Deanna Durbin appeared on the scene in the late 1930s, she was the first major Hollywood player to wear outfits designed with girls of her own age in mind. Durbin enjoyed an enthusiastic following, and Beatrice Cooper was among her admirers:

BC   Course Deanna Durbin was one that I was keen on.

Int   Mmm.

BC   Because, em, because [*laughs*] funny! There she is. Because she was the same age as me and we both sang. And, of course I sang all the songs she sang [*laughs*]. As her films came out, I got the songs. And, em, sang them. Eh, and eh, you know, and I dressed like her. I think a lot of kids of that age...

Int   Mmm.

BC   You know, around 15, 16. Eh, because there were no fashions for children of that age. No teenagers. You either dressed as a very small child. Or you dressed as an adult. Sophisticated clothes. You know, there were no teenage clothes at that time. And she brought a new fashion.[31]

Sisters Margaret Young and Molly Stevenson also liked Durbin ('she was such a bright personality and she was a lovely singer... And then again her clothes appealed to us'[32]) and Molly bought a hat like one of Deanna Durbin's:

MS   I had a Deanna Durbin hat. Remember I got it in Watt Brothers.

MY   Uhuh.

Int   What was that like?

MS   Eh, it had a turned up brim. It was very like, eh, the kind of hats that, eh, the Austrian people wear when they went shooting.

Int   Right.

MS   That kind of, you know a felt hat that had a wee feather.

MY   Feather, uhuh.

MS   At the side.

MY   Was that similar to the Joan Crawford hat that Dad always liked?

MS   It was a bigger brim. This was a small brim.[33]

In a group interview in Glasgow, Sarah Louise Gale treats her fellow interviewees to a description of her own Deanna Durbin hat:

SLG I used to wear Dee, Deanna Durbin hats, they're nice.

Int   What are they like?

SLG Deanna Durbin?

Int   No, the hats?

SLG Aw, something like that [*indicates shape*], we used to, something like a soft hat. [*Pause: 1 second*] It slipped down.

PMcC	A wee round hat, it sorta crowns on their head.
SLG	A wee round one.
PMcC	Quite nice.[34]

Women's 'growing up' memories are just as likely as men's to emphasise the centrality of the same-sex peer group in engagements with cinema culture. But women's accounts foreground the sharing and mutual assistance involved in creating the looks they wanted over against the public display of the results. Often, as in the testimony of Peggy Kent and her friends quoted above, there is enormously detailed description of styles and the methods used to achieve them.

The theme of 'making do' – making the best of your appearance on limited means – surfaces again and again in women's stories. Even those who lacked the cash or the skills to try out fashions, hairstyles and makeup could still share their dreams with friends. When still at school, Ellen Casey admired and longed for the beautiful, smart clothes she saw in the films. But her family was large and poor, and these things were far beyond her reach. Nevertheless, she says:

[W]e'd talk with girls in the school yard. We used to sit, sit down in the school yard, in a group, talk. They were all as bad as me, you know. All as bad as me. Wanting to know. Who. If I didn't go the night before, somebody did. Talked about it all the time. And that's how our life was there. In the thirties. I lie in bed sometimes now of a night thinking how *thrilled* I used to be. And how *envious*, when I seen all these lovely things and all that. And I thought, I wonder if I ever, you know. I wonder if I ever will get better and sorted out.[35]

The memory stories of Peggy Kent and her friends are essentially performances, in the present, of exactly this kind of 'girl talk'. Rehearsing the topics of their adolescent conversations, they re-enact, for each other and for the interviewer, the style of those exchanges. Topics of conversation touch on cinema culture in different ways, from hairstyle and makeup ideas to talk about films recently seen and the pros and cons of different stars. The women's mode of interaction serves to demonstrate how cinema-related topics could constitute a taken-for-granted component of girl talk, and how gossip about the cinema could be interwoven with other, non-film related, topics. Performances of girl talk take place in other interviews involving pairs or groups of women, particularly if those involved knew each other during adolescence.

Girl talk does sometimes arise outside all-female couple or group interview settings, however. A number of women giving solo interviews slip into reinhabiting their past selves, addressing the interviewer 'as if you were the same age'.[36] In such cases, interviewees often rapidly correct themselves and re-enter the present moment. Occasionally, however, interviewer and interviewee enter together into the spirit of a conversation between two young women:

ES   You see, she's another beautiful [*pause: 2 seconds*]. Lovely, beautiful. But even, yes, I mean. Now to me, *there*…

Int   Uhuh.

ES   Greta Garbo is even better proportioned than she is.

Int   Than Madeleine Carroll. Yes.

ES   Because she's a little bit. I'm awful, aren't I? I do pick them to pieces.

Int   Why not?

ES   The most *bea-utiful* eyes!

Int   Mm.

ES   But she's a little bit squashed. Where Greta Garbo's face was absolutely in proportion.

Int   Yes. She's not got that, the bone structure either, has she?[37]

One interview was conducted almost entirely in 'girl talk' mode. After Phyllis Bennett's interview at her home in Norwich one nasty November afternoon, the interviewer noted that the pair had entered 'a sort of cosy time zone' together. Mrs Bennett produced her impressive collection of albums of neatly cut out and lovingly arranged pictures of stars and snippets of star biographies from *Picturegoer* and *Film Weekly*, and the two women sat 'hugging our knees and really looking quite eager and teen-y' as they leafed through the albums and chatted, very much as adolescent girls might.[38]

The content and style of women's growing up memories suggest that venues for the activities described in them were usually private or intimate: conversations between girls in a school playground, say, or skiving at work to try out a new hairstyle on workmates. They suggest, too, that young women's efforts to transform themselves with hairdos, makeup and clothes inspired by 'the pictures' were directed primarily at each other. Indeed, in women's memory-talk the weight of emphasis lies so unequivocally on the side of trying things out that it might with justification be concluded that this was the real point of the exercise and that the public display of the results was merely a coda. It is as if these young women experimented with femininity in the safety and security of each other's company and mutual support, and that making the new images public was slightly risky. The distinctive quality of these memories hinges in part on how talk about honing cultural competences around cinema ties in with negotiations of femininity. It is as if cinema was always present as a participant in the girls' conversations.

This is especially apparent in women's accounts of imitating female stars. Here the names of Ginger Rogers and Deanna Durbin arise repeatedly. These two stars offer interestingly contrasting modes of feminine identification for the adolescent of the 1930s. Durbin, who was about 13 when her first film, *Three Smart Girls*, was released, stands for the predilection of the British audience of the 1930s for juvenile stars and for the 'good taste' increasingly demanded after the mid 1930s.[39] Significantly, when Beatrice Cooper and the sisters Margaret Young and Molly Stevenson mention Durbin and the fashions of hers that took their fancy, it is in the context of comments on the star's entire persona: 'she was such a bright personality and she was lovely singer'. References to Ginger Rogers are rather different in that Rogers' image is often talked about in isolation from her talents as an actress and dancer. While Durbin is constructed as a whole person, Rogers is an almost depersonalised purveyor of a (desired) image.

While this quality of blankness perhaps makes Ginger Rogers a readier object of identification, there seems to be a class issue here as well. Durbin's admirers are middle class and metropolitan, and those who talk about Rogers are overwhelmingly working class or from rural areas. Moreover, talk about Ginger Rogers, even by those who claim to have admired her, is rarely entirely complimentary. Her skills as a dancer are repeatedly compared unfavourably with Fred Astaire's, and she is often characterised as lacking the latter's 'class' and even on occasion as 'common'. Because Rogers died during the fieldwork period, her name crops up frequently in interviews, and many informants make a point of mentioning how overweight she became in her later years. Ginger Rogers' glamorous but slightly vulgar persona, it seems, renders her, in retrospect at least, the object of some ambivalence.

The more highbrow, asexual quality of Deanna Durbin's star persona is underscored by the attention devoted to her in the popular film press of the late 1930s. She is characterised very much as a normal girl with a magic gift

Deanna Durbin (centre) in *Three Smart Girls*

that lifts her out of the ordinary.[40] The obsession with Durbin's first screen kiss and the arch titles of her films of this period (*That Certain Age* (1938), *Three Smart Girls Grow Up* (1939), *First Love* (1939)) are revealing. *First Love* was the film in which Durbin's long-awaited 'screen encounter with sex' (which, as *Picturegoer* put it, 'rises above the polluting influence of Hollywood's diseased mind'[41]) took place. But while Durbin was much hyped, she appears to have genuinely caught the imaginations of enormous numbers of youngsters, boys as well as girls, for whom she figured as a very positive role model, 'a powerful symbol of youthful optimism'.[42] For some, Durbin represented the highest values and offered a glimpse of the best person they could be.[43] And yet while Deanna Durbin is always remembered in a positive light, few have much to say about her, and there is little affect attaching to these memories.[44]

There are a number of possible explanations for this, prominent among which must be the ways in which 1930s cinema figures in popular memory. For example, while both films garnered equal critical acclaim and box-office success in Britain during the 1930s, a Ginger Rogers vehicle like *Top Hat* has become part of the 1930s canon, while, other than by her still devoted fans, Deanna Durbin's *Three Smart Girls* is largely forgotten.[45] Perhaps, too, the Ginger Rogers persona sits more comfortably than Durbin's alongside the wave of consumerism that was to sweep Britain after the Second World War, but which was barely nascent in the 1930s. Hollywood cinema might have been a force in the rise of consumerism in 1930s USA,[46] but in Britain there remained a considerable gap between the lifestyles on display in Hollywood pictures and those to which most of the population could realistically aspire.

In the 1930s, young female cinemagoers could organise their engagement with Hollywood consumerism in one of three ways: they could buy, they could improvise, or they could go without. Of these, improvisation appears to have been the favoured strategy. Beatrice Cooper and Molly Stevenson, who talk about buying clothes like Deanna Durbin's, are in a minority. Aside from the problem of money, the notion of seeing something you liked on the cinema screen or in a magazine and then going out and buying it was simply foreign to most people at this period, as Olga Scowen points out:

> But I did like to see the Americans because they, well they got so much money. Or apparently, according to the films, you know. The women were always dressed in furs and fancy hats and, em, lived in lovely homes and got *refrigerators*! I mean we hadn't got a refrigerator! [*Laughs*]. You saw things that, you know, we, I mean you probably wouldn't remember a time when people didn't have refrigerators. But where I used to live down the road we had, em,

a very nice larder that was on the back of the house away from the
sun. With marble slabs and a stone floor and a walk-in larder, you
didn't really need a refrigerator. Except we used to have something
to keep the milk cool. We used to have a special thing over the
milk. But, em, I mean I didn't have a refrigerator until [*pause: 2
seconds*], well, after I was married. But we didn't even have electricity down at that house. Until 1938. [...] So I was brought up in
a house full of gaslight and, em, oil lamps and things. We had an oil
lamp in the kitchen. We lived with my grandparents and they
weren't going to spend money having electricity put in. We had it
done in the end. But, em, when we went to the cinema and people
switching lights on and opening fridges and hoovering, it was a
different world. I think it made us all a bit more ambitious. I think
we all tried to dress a bit better and tried to do our hair a bit better.
As far as we were able to do it.[47]

If consumer durables like refrigerators and vacuum cleaners are
remembered as being completely out of reach in the 1930s, memories
about the accessibility of Hollywood-inspired 'looks' for women are
more ambiguous. Asked how she felt when seeing elegant stars like
Joan Crawford on the screen, Sheila McWhinnie, who worked as a
cinema usherette, replies: 'You just accepted it, I mean, you didn't say,
"Oh look at them, and look at me" kind of thing'. Mary McCusker
draws a distinction between buying clothes like those in films, which
cost money, and imitating hairstyles, which cost little or nothing: 'You
copied the hairstyles. There was no way you could copy their *clothes*!
Same as just now. *No way*. No way. Your financial situation did not
allow you to do that.' But then both informants immediately modify
their statements:

SM You just accepted it, and as I say, I started to like wearing
black a lot, and it was somewhere I was about 17 when I went into
that cinema, the Star, and as I say, the main article, 'Have you got a
black dress?' I'd only a navy blue one but I did get a black one. I
got a black dress, well, and started wearing it, and got a collar from
Woolworths, and we all got the same collar out of Woolworths.
And, I would never have thought, from the Gorbals, of wearing a
black dress, then I began to think, 'Uhuh, it's very smart.' Ever
afterwards [*laughs*] I began to think it was very smart and then
you swan about in it! You know? But, eh, it was funny that, they

Sheila McWhinnie (far left), wearing the collar from Woolworths

did influence a lot of what you wore and things like that. Both working and watching the screen, you know?

Int   I mean, did you, were you conscious of imitating the styles of the stars?

SM   You weren't conscious of it, but subconsciously, now, when you look back, you say… [*pause*]

Int   Yeh.

SM   You know? I think everybody did, I think everybody did. And then this, the shops started turning out what they did see on the screen too, the style.[48]

MM Your financial situation did not allow you to do that. But, em, [*pause: 3 seconds*]. Maybe after a big picture had been showing around a town, if you went to dancing, you'd see a girl and maybe somebody had *made* her a dress like that, you know.[49]

While many informants, male and female, stress the poverty of the 1930s as compared with today, they are also keen to proclaim their generation's ability to 'make do' on limited means. Looked at in this light, Mrs

McWhinnie's and Mrs McCusker's statements are by no means self-contradictory.

They may also be read as testament to the earliest stirrings of consumerist ways of thinking. A sea change in culturally normative modes of femininity took place in Britain in the mid to late 1930s,[50] and these accounts may be read as statements about the lived experience of this process of change. For at some point, in Mrs McWhinnie's words, women became aware that 'the shops started turning out what they did see on the screen, too, the style'. It was perhaps at this moment that the idea of being able, if not yet entitled, to acquire something you had seen and wanted in the cinema began to enter the consciousness of some young women.

For most women, though, making do was the practicable and achievable solution, a step between being content to go without on the one hand and feeling sufficiently affluent or entitled to buy on the other. Making do is an essentially creative activity, which Michel de Certeau defines as a form of counter-hegemonic production, an art of 'using' by 'poaching' from the 'rationalized, expansionist, centralized, spectacular and clamorous production' with which people are faced.[51] In this sense, making do is a kind of seizure of power in small, everyday acts. Making do can also create its own institutions and discourses. For example, parts of the popular press of the 1930s attempted to buy into filmgoers' improvisations of the fashions and styles they saw in the cinema.

There is a distinctive type of popular periodical, a hybrid of film magazine and woman's magazine, which is peculiar to the 1930s. *Film Fashionland*, with a broad emphasis on lifestyle, fashion and leisure, was published monthly between March 1934 and April 1935, with the mission to 'bring all the charm and romance, all the beauty and intelligence, of the Film World into every woman's life'. A dress pattern was given away with each issue, 'chosen and designed from the wardrobe of one of Screenland's smartest stars'. Alternatively, readers could send away for readymade 'film fashions' based on stars' outfits. *Woman's Filmfair*, which appeared monthly between 1935 and 1941, offered similar material. Its first issue included knitting and embroidery patterns and offered featured dresses by mail order or as paper patterns.

Towards the close of the 1930s, the popular woman's press too began to run features on films and stars and instructions for making clothes modelled on those in the films. In 1937, *Woman* published instructions for making a Deanna Durbin-style hat for a shilling (5p).[52] Around the time Durbin's film *Three Smart Girls Grow Up* was released in 1939, *Woman* ran a knitting pattern for a hat and scarf under the punning title 'Two Smart Bits of Fluff!' and a cosmetic ad with the slogan 'Three Smart Girls'.[53] Even the more traditionalist *Woman's Weekly* added a touch of film glamour to its down-to-earth fare by running offers of patterns for dresses with stars' names ('Merle', 'Greta' and so on).

The film weeklies, too, carried features on fashion and makeup. *Film Pictorial*, for example, included a regular feature in the mid-1930s called 'Learn Style from the Stars'. Throughout the 1930s, *Picturegoer* ran a column, 'Leave it to Anne', directed at women readers who wanted to model their appearance on the stars'; and in the early 1930s, it occasionally featured instructions for making clothes modelled by film personalities.[54] A prominent feature of all the film weeklies during the 1930s was the numerous advertisements for cosmetics and other products aimed at young women: long-running campaigns for Lux soap and Max Factor makeup, for example, used endorsements by female stars.

Helen Smeaton recalls her avid consumption of the magazines, and her quest for a particular feminine image:

> You all wanted to be as thin as they were. I never thought of ever looking like them in a facial manner. Eh, and I liked to [look] smart or decent. But we all wanted to be thin. And they were all thin. I mean, even looking at them now, they're as thin as the other ones were nowadays and you used to read all these magazines, the *Filmgoer* [sic] magazine, what was the other one, oh, there was umpteen. And all my pocket money went on buying and reading all about these film stars. My mum used to say if I knew as much about my school work as I knew about the film stars, I would pass every exam with flying colours. 'Cos I never forgot it. I'd read it, and read it and read it.[55]

Other female informants describe items of clothing which they remember improvising from fashions seen in films. One of Molly Stevenson's hobbies was knitting, and she made a cardigan 'which was a copy of one that Jane Wyman wore. I had no pattern, but must have got a number of stitches from a similar pattern as it turned out a success.'[56] She provides a highly detailed description of this home-made garment:

> *MS*   Yes, I did. The Jane Wyman. Jane Wyman's cardigan.
>
> *Int*   What was that actually like?

Film Fashionland, March 1934

From *Woman,* July 1939

Beauty feature, *Picturegoer,* April 1930

MS It eh'm, it had a band, round here and it had buttons and the collar.

Int Ah.

MS What else? And then the sleeves came down to the same kind of double knit band.

Int Right.

MS There was a double knit band down here and the cuffs ended up in a double knit band as well.

Int What colour was it?

MS Eh, it was grey, grey wool that I got for it. And it had wee imitation pockets here with a button in the middle of it. So you had buttons down there, buttons here.

Int It sounds very smart actually with the...

MS It was smart. Because most cardigans just came down in a V but this actually came up to here [*pointing*] with the collar outside.[57]

As a girl, Mary McCusker thought the clothes she saw in the pictures were so 'lovely' that her mother improvised a copy of a fur-trimmed

From *Film Weekly*, November 1933

coat for her daughter by thriftily customising an outgrown old one. Mrs McCusker's description of this coat has an almost tactile quality:

> So, I was growing out of this coat. And, eh, my mother thought she'd be very practical. And they had come out in this picture with *beautiful* pale-blue coats with fur. Grey fur muffs, grey fur hats and a big band of grey fur on the bottom of their coat. So here I had this wine-coloured coat and it had black fur on the collar, black fur on the cuffs. And my mother thought, practically, to get another month or two out of the coat, she would buy black fur and put it on the bottom. And I felt like, whoa! [*Laughs*]. Felt good! You know.[58]

Memories of hairstyles, too, sometimes have this tactile quality, with informants miming the gesture of creating a wave or of patting the hair into place. Nancy Carrington and Nancy Prudhoe, born respectively in 1911 and 1913, remember the very short hairstyles sported by female stars of the 1920s:

> *NC* I was going to say we used to copy the film stars, 'cause they used to have a shingle length, the very *short* hair.
>
> *NP* Short hair and then they had the semishingle.
>
> *Int* Ooh?
>
> *NC* Yeh.
>
> *NP* Then it came the *long* hair again.
>
> *NC* Yeh.
>
> *NP* And then it came the semishingle *again.*
>
> *NC* That's right.
>
> *Int* What, what, I don't know the term a semishingle, what was that like? The semi...
>
> *NC* Well, it was taken in to the neck, [*demonstrates with hand at the back and top of the neck*] like a boy, wasn't it more...
>
> *NP* Yes it was cut in close to the back.
>
> *NC* And taken in to the neck at the back.
>
> *NP* Yeh, yes.
>
> *Int* Aah.
>
> *NC* Similar to what they've got now, some of the short styles.
>
> *Int* Yeh, I think I know what you mean.[59]

The loving detail with which clothes and hairstyles are described, and the often anecdotal manner of their description (a particular garment, say, is remembered in conjunction with a specific occasion or event), suggest a high degree of affective and imaginative investment in these memories. Often, too, memories of making and wearing a particular garment have a sensual quality: informants evoke in their telling the sensation of touching the knitting wool or the fabric, or the feel of the garment when it was worn ('And I felt like, whoa! Felt good! You know.') And so if memories of making or buying copies of clothes seen on the cinema screen may be fewer in number than recollections of creating hairstyles and trying out makeup, memory-talk about clothes, with its enormous attention to detail and its reliving, in the telling, of what they felt like, appears to be particularly highly invested.

The profundity of this investment is most apparent when memories involving clothes have a social class dimension, and particularly so when women from poorer backgrounds talk about clothes. A scarcity trope characterises their stories, betraying acute consciousness of relative deprivation as they contrast their own situation with that of contemporaries who seemed able to afford to buy the clothes they wanted. Underlying these stories is a powerful and abiding yearning for things which you know are out of reach, and a sense that knowing and even accepting this fact does nothing to assuage the longing. This is sometimes expressed as a kind of existential wish, a diffuse desire for life to be better, as in Ellen Casey's forceful testimony to her yearnings: 'I thought, I wonder if I ever, you know. I wonder if I ever will get better and sorted out.'

Such an urgency of desire combines with a sense of unattainable abundance in sensuous evocations of images of plenteous quantities of fabulously luxurious cloth. Ellen Casey remembers *42nd Street*:

> That was a *beautiful*, that was a *beautiful* musical. Dick Powell and Ruby Keeler. And, em, oh, I used to be, eh, oh, I admired those dresses. They seemed to be all furs [*delighted voice*] and *fluffy*, you know. And there'd be *yards and yards* of material. Gosh! So that was it.[60]

This memory calls to mind Carolyn Steedman's account of how clothes and fabrics figured in her own mother's longings. Like Steedman's mother, Mrs Casey is a Lancastrian and a worker in the clothing trade:

a skilled machinist for her entire working life, she shares with Steedman's mother 'a heightened awareness of fabric and weave'.[61]

Mickie Rivers' evocation of a 'subterranean culture of longing for that which one can never have'[62] also centres on a story about clothes. Mrs Rivers was born in Suffolk in 1922, a labourer's daughter and one of five children. She left school at 14 and worked at a number of jobs, first in factories and later as a cinema usherette. Towards the end of her second interview, Mrs Rivers' thoughts turn towards clothes:

MR Because we had so *little*. I think I had *two* dresses. Maybe two or three skirts, no more and that was about everything. I know I didn't have very much compared to a lot of people but I was one of five. They couldn't afford it. I had to be taken away from grammar school because my mum couldn't afford a replacement uniform. Which was wrong. These days [*pause: 2 seconds*] I don't know what would've happened. They would have to have done it because everybody wears school uniform. But in those days you only wore uniform when you went to school after you'd passed your scholarship.

Int Mm.

MR Or if you went to a private school. But *clothing* aspect, oh-h-h, you used to drool and think, I wonder if I could do that to my old dress. I could do that. You'd see them [in] their dark dress and different coloured [*inaudible*]. And you'd got about half a yard of [taffeta?]. And spend all night making a [sack?]. But, I mean, do a little bit a trimming somewhere else on the clothes. You'd pick it up. You know. […]

Int [*Laughs*] So even then you were good at making clothes and…

MR Oh yes.

Int Ah.

MR My mum used to go to jumble sales and come home with a dress, *outsize* dress and fit me out of it. *Had* to. Hadn't got the money. I used to earn, when I first went to work, I earned seven and sixpence. I had to pay my mother seven shillings a week and buy my stockings out of the sixpence. The cheapest stockings you could buy were *ninepence a pair*. And they were lisle stockings with an artificial silk covering. And of course you wanted a pair of *silk* stockings. You went up to one and nine, one and elevenpence.[63]

This poignant testimony to making do might seem to have nothing at all to do with the cinema. It begins with a story often heard from working-class women and men of her generation: Mrs Rivers was unable to take advantage of a scholarship for secondary education because the uniform required by the 'good' school was beyond the family's means. This apparent divagation is set in train by pictures of stars in a 1930s film annual, and turns out not to be a divagation at all but a train of thought prompted by, and leading back to, the remembered feeling of earnestly desiring something you know you cannot have.

In Mrs Rivers' account, cinema was more accommodating than the education system where clothes (and in this train of thought, aspirations) were concerned, for the former at least allowed for a certain amount of successful 'making do': you could create something desirable and even 'smart' for yourself from the limited materials to hand – jumble sale cast-offs, a piece of taffeta. The vividly remembered detail of the cost of a pair of stockings is extraordinarily revealing of the depth of emotional investment in this yearning for something which is out of reach.[64] A sense of missed opportunity saturates this story with almost tangible affect, a feeling of lack which has never gone away and which is brought to life once again in the remembering.

Women who entered adolescence between the mid 1930s and the start of the Second World War were very different from previous generations; and cinema culture, figuring prominently as it does in their formation as women, plays a large part in this difference. Regardless of social background, this generation of women enthusiastically embraced aspirations for lives very different from those of their mothers, and Alison Light points to 'the buoyant sense of excitement and release which animates so many of the more broadly cultural activities which different groups of women enjoyed in the period'.[65] These women's aspirations are informed by their dreams of a better, more beautiful self, dreams nourished and given expression through cinema culture. For cinema, above all, offered new models of femininity. These women's growing up is imbued, in memory, with dreams of a different sort of womanhood, represented not just in the personae of the various film stars they chose to emulate – from the girlish tastefulness of Deanna Durbin to the adult and risqué glamour of Ginger Rogers – but in the more generalised desires and wishes embodied in films and cinema culture.

For these women, wishes and aspirations are condensed in the nexus of personal appearance and clothes. Through work on her appearance, a young woman could enjoy 'an imaginary identification with a graceful or beautiful self which both anticipated the woman she would like to become, and transcended the hard work and poverty around her'.[66] In the memories of 1930s cinemagoers, this identity-work emerges above all as collective and homosocial. Their embrace of cinema culture at once sets these women apart from the older generation and, while cementing their relationships with their peers, holds out the prospect of entirely new ways of being a woman.

But although the new young woman of the mid to late 1930s represents a genuine shift in normative modes of femininity, this shift is not without ambiguity and contradiction. Girls' experiments with their appearance could still attract censure, ridicule or even danger if taken into the public domain. It is significant that it is the intimate, private, homosocial aspects of these experiments which are now remembered most vividly and with greatest affect by those involved. This suggests that aspiration perhaps outstripped opportunity for this generation of women.

There remained, too, marked differences between women in life chances and opportunities, and these were, and often still are, keenly felt by those who regard themselves as held back in their youth by material poverty, lack of opportunity, or by limitations on aspiration set by the consciousness of being an outsider in class terms. Such memories are often coloured by a sense of lack or disappointment, and this is expressed most fully in memories centred on clothes. You only owned one dress. You coveted luxurious dress fabrics. You had to give up a longed-for secondary education because there was no money to buy the school uniform. And yet, proudly rising above these limitations, you and your friends improvised a smart appearance on the most limited of means.

But if many young women's dreams outstripped their life chances, the dreams themselves remain in memory, powerful and pleasurable. In the 1930s, cinema culture provided a space in which young women could at least imagine themselves just as beautiful, interesting and adventurous as film stars.

In the 1930s, cinema culture – films and the cultural competences associated with them – was an accepted and quite ordinary part of daily life, and even those who never went to the pictures could hardly escape the cultural pervasiveness of the medium. Cinema culture played an especially important role in the lives of men and women who were children and adolescents at the time, inspiring their games, providing topics of conversation with friends and family, and animating hobbies, and activities shared with peers. In these ways, young people brought into their daily lives something of the otherworldliness, the magic, of what they saw on the cinema screen. For some of them, bringing home the magic meant bringing it into their inner lives, into their dreams of what life could be like.

The dreams of adolescence may be powerful, and their feeling tone is tangibly present in the testimonies of the 1930s generation. But few, it seems, abandoned themselves to the dream. Both in the remembered past and in the discursive present of its narration there is invariably a return to earth. As Jimmy Murray matter-of-factly says of people's attempts to imitate Fred Astaire's dancing prowess, 'you couldn't'. The imitation fell short, or hindsight judges that the attempt was foolhardy. At the same time, few informants dismiss outright the dreams of their younger selves: a sense of a lost perfection colours many accounts, usually expressed through a past/present trope as regretful comparisons between films and stars then and now. Films today are violent and too preoccupied with the seamier side of life; films were more innocent then, more romantic, more magical. The stars of the 1930s were smarter and more elegant than those of today. Memories of adolescence, as Sally Alexander points out, bear the weight of possibility. What is lost with age is precisely that space of possibility, those dreams of a better life, of a more beautiful self, that pervade the adolescent's 'intense wondering what might become'.[67] For this first movie-made generation, the dreams were saturated with cinema; today 'their' cinema is gone. But the dreams are not forgotten.

Notes

1. Sheila McWhinnie wrote to Bing Crosby (T94-19, Sheila McWhinnie, Glasgow, 12 December, 1994); Denis Houlston wrote to Anna Neagle and other British stars (T95-19, A.D. Houlston, Manchester, 26 April 1995); Beatrice Cooper wrote to Francis Lederer (T95-153, Beatrice Cooper, Harrow, 27 November 1995); Dorris Braithwaite had some correspondence with Nelson Eddy (95-38-1, Dorris Braithwaite, Bolton, to Annette Kuhn, 17 February 1995). Denis Houlston was a member of a film society in Manchester (T95-20, A.D. Houlston, Manchester, 26 April 1995), and Douglas Rendell attended screenings of the London Film Society (T95-48, Douglas Rendell, Manchester, 8 June

1995). For details of fan club membership, see Chapter 8; and Annette Kuhn, 'Cinemagoing in Britain in the 1930s: report of a questionnaire survey', *Historical Journal of Film, Radio and Television*, vol. 19, no. 4 (1999), pp. 531–543.

2. Barbara Mack, Irvine, to Annette Kuhn, 11 May 1992.

3. William Ward, Cheshire, to Annette Kuhn and Valentina Bold, 9 February 1995; 95-324, Questionnaire, Mrs A. Close, Lincolnshire, December 1995.

4. T95-105, Ashley Bird, Harrow, 26 July 1995.

5. T95-57, Jimmy Murray, Manchester, 15 June 1995.

6. T95-68, Arthur Orrell, Bolton, 12 May 1995.

7. Lewis Howells, Gwent, to Annette Kuhn and Valentina Bold, 9 February 1995.

8. T95-97, Irene and Bernard Letchet, Harrow, 21 July 1995.

9. T95-113, E.J. Godbold, Suffolk, 17 October 1995.

10. T95-56, Jimmy Murray, Manchester, 15 June 1995.

11. T95-104, Ashley Bird, Harrow, 26 July 1995.

12. T95-55, John and Marion Cooper, Bolton, 14 June 1995 (also present Mrs Cooper's sister Alice).

13. T95-104, Ashley Bird, Harrow, 26 July 1995.

14. T95-35, Lois Basnett and Herbert Partington, Manchester, 30 May 1995.

15. T95-129, E.J. Godbold, Suffolk, 27 November, 1995.

16. T95-156, Interviewer's fieldnotes, Nancy Carrington and Nancy Prudhoe, Harrow, 30 April 1996.

17. T95-5, Tom and Margaret Walsh, Glasgow, 27 January 1995.

18. T95-56, Jimmy Murray, Manchester, 15 June 1995.

19. T95-133, George Turner, Suffolk, 10 November 1995.

20. William E. Tydeman, 'Tom Mix: king of the Hollywood cowboys', in Gary A Yoggy (ed.), *Back in the Saddle: Essays on Western Film and Television Actors* (Jefferson, NC: McFarland & Co, 1998), p. 30.

21. See *Film Dope*, March 1990, p. 10; also Jeffrey Richards, 'Boy's own Empire: feature films and imperialism in the 1930s', in John M. MacKenzie (ed.), *Imperialism and Popular Culture* (Manchester: Manchester University Press, 1986), pp. 140–64.

22. J. White, 'The worst street in North London', cited by Andrew Davies in 'Cinema and broadcasting', in Paul Johnson (ed.), *Twentieth-Century Britain: Economic, Social and Cultural Change* (London: Longman, 1994), p. 271. Richard Ford notes that in Britain in the early 1930s gangster films were held responsible for juvenile crime, but says there was no evidence to support this: Ford, *Children in the Cinema* (London: Allen & Unwin, 1939), pp. 73–5.

23. Pat Kirkham and Janet Thumim, 'You Tarzan', in *You Tarzan: Masculinity, Movies and Men* (London: Lawrence and Wishart, 1993), pp. 11–18.

24. T95-145, Hilda Bennett, Norfolk, 21 November 1995. Jackie Stacey addresses this topic in *Star Gazing: Hollywood Cinema and Female Spectatorship* (London: Routledge, 1994), Chapter 5.

25. Rosemary Skinner, Sussex, to Annette Kuhn and Valentina Bold, 21 February 1995; T95-111, Eileen Scott, Suffolk, 16 November 1995.

26. T95-117, Hazel and William Pickess, Suffolk, 20 October 1995.

27. T95-38, Ellen Casey, Manchester, 31 May 1995.

28. T95-15, Helen Donaghy, Sarah Irvine and Davy Paterson, Glasgow, 3 March 1995.

29. T95-114, Peggy Kent, Hilda Green, Hilda Catchpol, Barbara Harvey and Gladys Kent, Suffolk, 18 October 1995.

30. Myra Schneidermann, Cardiff, to Annette Kuhn and Valentina Bold, 10 February 1995; T95-138, Hazel and William Pickess, Suffolk, 14 November 1995.

31. T95-153, Beatrice Cooper, Harrow, 27 November 1995.

32. T94-17, Margaret Young and Molly Stevenson, Glasgow, 5 December 1994.

33. T95-12, Margaret Young and Molly Stevenson, Glasgow, 20 February 1995.

34. T95-8, Patrick McCambridge, Tommy Dunn, Tommy Adams, Sarah Louise Gale and Nancy Keyte, Glasgow, 13 February 1995.

35. T95-37, Ellen Casey, Manchester, 31 May 1995.

36. T95-96, Interviewer's field notes, Beatrice Cooper, Harrow, 20 July 1995.

37. T95-132, Eileen Scott, Suffolk, 9 November 1995.

38. T95-144 Interviewer's field notes, Phyllis Bennett, Norwich, 17 November 1995.

39. Annette Kuhn, 'Cinema culture and femininity in the 1930s', in Christine Gledhill and Gillian Swanson (eds), *Nationalising Femininity* (Manchester: Manchester University Press, 1996), pp. 186–91.

40. 'Fair, famous – and fourteen', *Picturegoer*, 6 March 1937; 'Schoolgirl star', *Film Weekly*, 29 May 1937; 'Going to school with Deanna', *Picturegoer*, 11 June 1938; 'Bringing up a breadwinner', *Picturegoer*, 4 February 1939.

41. 'Deanna's first kiss', *Picturegoer*, 30 December 1939.

42. Georganne Scheiner, *Signifying Female Adolescence: Film Representations and Fans, 1920–1950* (Westport, CT: Praeger, 2000), p. 126.

43. William Farr, 'Analysis of questionnaire to adolescents 14–18 years', (London: British Film Institute, [1939]); Mass-Observation Archive, Topic Collection: Films, Boxes 5 and 6, Letters to *Picturegoer*, passim; J.P. Mayer, *Sociology of Film: Studies and Documents* (London: Faber and Faber, 1946), pp. 182, 237 and 188; J.P. Mayer, *British Cinemas and Their Audiences: Sociological Studies* (London: Dennis Dobson Ltd, 1948), pp. 60, 90, 83, and 42.

44. Memories of Durbin invariably refer to her 'sweet', 'beautiful' or 'thrilling' voice: 95-143, Questionnaire, Lily Harper, Clwyd, February 1995; 95-110, Questionnaire, Mrs B. M. Verdant, West Midlands, February 1995; 95-60, Questionnaire, Olive Johnson, West Midlands, February 1995.

45. The Deanna Durbin Society is still active; and at the time of writing there were at least three Durbin fan internet sites, including *The Deanna Durbin Page*, http://www.geocities.com/Hollywood/Academy/5228/ddpage.html [7 April 2001].

46. *Quarterly Review of Film and Video*, special issue on Female Representation and Consumer Culture, vol. 11, no. 1 (1989).

47. T95-89, Olga Scowen, Harrow, 18 June 1995.

48. T94-20, Sheila McWhinnie, Glasgow, 12 December 1994.

49. T94-5, Mary McCusker, Glasgow, 22 November 1994.

50. Kuhn, 'Cinema culture and femininity in the 1930s'.

51. Michel de Certeau, *The Practice of Everyday Life*, trans. Steven Rendall (Berkeley: University of California Press, 1984), p. 31.

52. *Woman*, 6 November 1937.

53. *Woman*, 27 May 1939; *Woman*, 29 July 1939.

54. For example, 'Evelyn's loveliest jumper for the Spring', *Picturegoer*, 18 March 1933, includes an interview with British stage and screen star Evelyn Laye along with instructions for knitting her jumper.

55. T95-72, Helen Smeaton, Glasgow, 28 June 1995.

56. Molly Stevenson, Glasgow, to Annette Kuhn, 15 November 1992.

57. T95-12, Margaret Young and Molly Stevenson, Glasgow, 20 February 1995.

58. T94-5, Mary McCusker, Glasgow, 22 November 1994.

59. T95-156, Nancy Carrington and Nancy Prudhoe, Harrow, 30 April 1995.

60. T95-38, Ellen Casey, Manchester, 31 May 1995.

61. Carolyn Steedman, *Landscape for a Good Woman* (London: Virago, 1986), p. 31.

62. Ibid., p. 8.

63. T95-130, Mickie Rivers, Suffolk, 8 November 1995.

64. On the significance of clothes in working-class women's memories of cinema, see Joanne Lacey, 'Seeing through happiness: Hollywood musicals and the construction of the American Dream in Liverpool in the 1950s', *Journal of Popular British Cinema*, no. 2 (1999). In her essay 'Becoming a woman in London in the 1920s and 1930s', in David Feldman and Gareth Stedman Jones (eds), *Metropolis-London: Histories and Representations* (London: Routledge, 1989), Sally Alexander notes: 'via the high street or the sewing machine, the mantle of glamour passed from the aristocrat and courtesan to the shop, office or factory girl via the film star' (p. 264).

65. Alison Light, *Forever England: Femininity, Literature and Conservatism between the Wars* (London: Routledge, 1991), p. 9. For a contemporary account of young working-class women's lives and leisure, see A.P. Jephcott, *Girls Growing Up* (London: Faber and Faber, 1942).

66. Sally Alexander, 'Becoming a woman', p. 257.

67. Ibid., p. 249.

6

This Loving Darkness

TRYING out hairstyles, practising makeup techniques and swaggering about like Hollywood gangsters are behaviours that bear all the hallmarks of courtship rituals, and yet they are never remembered as such. And while the back row of the cinema and the 'courting' that took place there are legendary in popular memory, romance and sex do not figure very prominently in 1930s cinemagoers' memories of their adolescence. Times shared with friends of the same sex, for example, are far more often and more vividly recollected. At the same time, some refer to portrayals of romance in films, and others offer memories of how cinema figured in their own love lives. There are some gender differences here, however. Men rarely raise the topics of sex, romance and courtship at all, and only one does so at any length. And while women are more likely than men to volunteer details of their own courting activities at the pictures, memories of spying on courting couples in the back row of the stalls are exclusively male. For a small minority of female informants, cinemagoing is more strongly associated in memory with courtship than with female friendship; and these women seem particularly happy to talk about their own love stories, often making explicit connections between their courting days and the 'romantic' pictures they saw at the cinema.

Overall, three sets of themes emerge in memories of romance, sex and courtship, each associated with particular discursive registers. First, some informants talk about cinemagoing and courting as self-evidently linked activities, and this approach is associated with repetitive, and occasionally with anecdotal, memory discourse. Second, there is a distinct set of memories about courtship activity inside the cinema, and these are associated with place memory and embodied memory. Third, some accounts make implicit or explicit associations between courtship, romance and sex and the contents of films or the spectatorial engagements evoked by what was on the screen. These references to the 'cinematic apparatus' often embody a past/present trope.

Many 1930s cinemagoers, men and women alike, record that for their generation an invitation to the pictures was the accepted way for a boy to express romantic interest in a girl. As letter-writer Margaret Houlgate recalls: 'A visit to the pictures was often the venue for a "first date"'. It was the boy's part to make the first move, says Margaret Ward: 'If a boy wanted to take you out it was always would you like to go to the pictures'. Courtship norms of the day, adds Mrs Houlgate, ensured that a girl 'never allowed a kiss in the first or even the second date, of course'.[1]

Freda McFarland was not, she says, particularly interested in the pictures *per se*, but remembers her cinemagoing heyday as coincident with her courtship. The man she later married took her to the same cinema every Wednesday night until the couple were parted by the war in 1941.[2] Ashley Bird talks in similar vein about regular visits to the cinema during the long years of his courtship. He met his wife when both were only 15 years old, and the couple married as soon as they could do so without parental consent, in 1938 when they turned 21. Bert Partington's memories underline how taken-for-granted the cinema-courtship association was for his generation, as he recollects his picturegoing habit in the context of the routines of his working week:

> Before the war, I was a shop boy. And my girlfriends, or particularly the woman I married worked with me. So as, what we call courting in those days, you tend to go to the cinema. You see we worked till eight o'clock at night. Nine o'clock on Saturdays. So one went to the cinema probably Mondays and Wednesdays. Eh, because you'd go to the second house. Half past eight.[3]

In the 1930s, an evening at the dance hall was almost as popular a leisure activity as an outing to the cinema. As Helen Smeaton says, 'You either went dancing on a Friday or a Saturday or to the cinema'.[4] For some informants, courting is associated with dancing as much as with the pictures, and indeed dancing is often remembered as more grown up and daring, and more firmly associated with courtship, than the pictures. Mrs Smeaton, who 'liked the dancing as well as the pictures – especially when courting',[5] is one of several informants who draw this distinction. For those like Nancy Prudhoe, who says she stopped going to the cinema once she started going dancing, the two activities are remembered as separated in time.[6]

The dance styles of the 1930s favoured male-female pairing and called for close physical contact between partners. To this extent, the dance hall was an excellent venue for seeking, meeting, or showing off a girl-friend or boyfriend. As a public place it provided the reassurance of safety in numbers, and as a place where looking at and being looked at by members of the opposite sex was positively *de rigueur*, it offered an opportunity for displays of prowess in dancing and of self-presentation in general. Peggy Kent and her friends recall spending hours on Saturday afternoons getting ready to go out together in the evening: they would go first to the pictures and then on to the dance hall. They exchange rather elliptical anecdotes as they step into, and then retreat from, potentially sensitive territory:

HG We only used to go because Hilda was sweet on a man up there and we…

All [*Laugh; protest; overtalking*]

PK Yes but the thing that we're not going to talk about is…

HG Yes.

PK That he was courting.

HG Yeh.

PK And she used to make him *after* he took the other one home! [*Giggles*]

HC I [*with emphasis*] wasn't going to talk about that!

All [*Laugh*]

HC It couldn't have been like that! [*Unintelligible for laughter*]

PK I thought *everybody*'d known about that!

[*Laughter*].[7]

Cinemas are remembered as places where courting could be conducted in relative comfort and privacy. But for the 1930s generation memories of courtship and romance are associated exclusively with one kind of cinema: the sumptuous new picture palace as opposed to the modest local picture houses of childhood picturegoing discussed in Chapter 3. If both types of cinema are recalled with pleasure, each has very different associations.[8] The luxurious, spacious, modern picture palaces are associated with treats and special occasions and remembered as in every way a far cry from home. These cinemas are the heterotopias of courtship.

Heterotopias, according to Michel Foucault, are unlike utopias (utopia translates as 'nowhere') in being real places, spaces 'outlined in the very institution of society, but... in which all the real arrangements, all the other real arrangements that can be found within society, are at one and the same time represented, challenged and overturned; a sort of place that lies outside all places and yet is actually localizable'.[9] One of the principles of the heterotopia, moreover, is that it 'has the power of juxtaposing in a single real place different spaces and locations that are incompatible with each other'.[10] Cinemas, as physical spaces – as *places* – embody all these qualities of liminality and heterogeneity: they are very much part of the built environment, and yet they conjoin the mundanity and materiality of bricks and mortar with the worlds of fantasy and the imagination. Cinemas differ in the degree to which they balance other-worldly as against localisable everyday space; and the supercinema, representing as it does for 1930s cinemagoers the passage from adolescence to adulthood, lies beyond the worlds of home and neighbourhood while still remaining part of a real and accessible world.

Muriel Peck offers a vivid description of one such supercinema, the Astoria in Finsbury Park, London, which opened in 1930.[11] Her words convey the feelings of awe and wonder inspired by these cinemas when they first appeared on the scene:

> To go to the Astoria was like going to wonderland. One passed from the ticket office into the foyer which had a marble type floor and in the centre was a fountain and I think there may also have been fish. From there we passed the ticket collector into a carpeted area leading down into a sunken auditorium. The air was faintly perfumed...
>
> The decor was Moorish. Overhead one could see what appeared to be a night sky with stars twinkling. High up there were doors and balconies which were illuminated during the interval and one fully expected a beautiful princess to emerge with her prince.[12]

The Astoria, Finsbury Park

According to 1930s courtship codes, the boy's duty was to impress the girl. So much the better if he could afford to treat her to a good seat in a luxuriously-appointed modern cinema. Several female informants note that the very first time they entered a supercinema or sat in an expensive seat was when they started courting.[13] Alex Mawer says that as soon as he could afford it, he would do what 'pretty well everybody did' and take his girlfriend to one of the plush cinemas in Glasgow's city centre on an outing that was in every way a special occasion:

> This was the highlight of the week. There was a bit of luxury about these cinemas. Tastefully decorated, well heated, comfortable seats and of course the latest film releases. For such outings both sexes would put on their best outfits… The girls would make the best of their appearance, often copying the hair style of a favourite actress.[14]

As a young man in employment, Bert Partington also took it for granted that he would pay for his girlfriend when he took her to the pictures, and that he would buy her chocolates, too: 'And of course, best seats were a shilling, 5p that is. A quarter box of chocolates was the same. So was that. You see.' Mrs D.E. Cowles recalls that the chocolates she was given depended on how well-off her boyfriend was feeling: 'If the boyfriend was flush I would have a 6d box of Rowntrees Dairy Milk chocolates, if he was hard up I would get a 2d chocolate bar'.[15] The association between the pictures, courtship, and giving or receiving sweets or chocolates evokes the sense of plenty and generosity that, as noted in Chapter 3, characterises memories of childhood cinemagoing. In all these accounts, there is an implied contrast between the abundance associated with picturegoing and the 'getting by' of everyday life.

Nancy Carrington was born in 1911, and her courting days predated the supercinema era. Nonetheless, when asked if she ever went to the cinema with her husband before they married, she embarks on a train of thought which links the memory of being in the back row of the stalls with her boyfriend's romantic proposal of marriage, which did not actually take place in the cinema. Significantly, the link in this series of associations is sweets:

Int When you were courting your husband, did you go to the cinema with him?

NC Oh, I went with him.

Int Yes.

NC Oh, yes, yes. [*Very definite*].

SN Did you used to sit on the back row?

NC Yes. [*Laughs*]. Yes we did if we could get there.

SN [*Laughs*]

Int [*Laughs*] Yes.

NC Yes, it used to be very good then, you know, very romantic. *very* romantic. When my husband and I were courting, we used to get, used to be sweets called fairy whispers. They were all colours. And we used to sit, when I lost my mother, we used to sit in the kitchen with dad. And it got on it, 'Do you love me?'. And I'd pass one and say, 'Yes'. 'Will you marry me?'. 'Yes'.[16]

The flip side of these courtship mores was that young men who for whatever reason – being still at school perhaps, or unemployed, or in a poorly-paid job – lacked the cash to take girls to the pictures could feel left out of things. Denying having taken part in the courting that went on in the cinema, Jimmy Murray makes light of how hard up he was as a young man:

Int   Did you ever [use the back row for courting] yourself when you got a bit older?

JM   Eh, I never bothered. Well, I couldn't take anybody in't cinema. [*Laughs*]

Int   [*Laughs*]

JM   Never had *enough* for two! [*Laughs*].

Int   Ah, I see.[17]

Nancy Carrington, whose wistful memories of adolescent picture-going involve gallant and courtly young men and generous treats of sweets and ice creams, is repeatedly called to order by her friend and co-interviewee Nancy Prudhoe, who reminds her that the boys they knew were far too poverty-stricken to take girls to the pictures: 'The boys were all out of work!' she insists, 'They used to wait for us girls to pay them in'.[18]

As cinemagoers of the 1930s remember it, sexual activity never figured in romantic attachments between young men and women. Insisting on the innocence of boy-girl relationships in her youth, Mrs Carrington maintains that 'you never let a boy kiss you the first time. *No way!* You'd give him a clout if he did!'[19] Such coyness looks rather different, however, when the story is told from the male point of view. Ashley Bird recalls that he would on occasion agree to take a girlfriend to see the sorts of romantic or melodramatic pictures women liked. He had ulterior motives, though:

AB   And when we had girlfriends, we had to go and see the, what we would call, sloppy films.

Int   Yes. [*Laughs*]

AB   Ye-ah. Stupid teenagers.

Int   Were you sitting through these gritting your teeth? [*Laughs*]

AB   That's right. Yes. [*Laughs*] Trying to get [*laughing*] to grips with the girlfriend, that's a fact.

Int   [*Laughs*]

AB   Stop it, or else, Stop it. [*Laughs*] Yes. You could hear it going on. [*Laughs*] Yes.[20]

Mr E. Harvey remembers one film in particular. When he took his girlfriend to see Al Jolson in *The Singing Fool*, she was so moved by the film that she clung on to him tightly: 'it was so sad when he sang "Sonny Boy"... I had on a white mac... and during that scene she twiddled a button off'.[21]

Others note that the entire ambience of the cinema auditorium was conducive to courtship. The 'loving darkness'[22] is taken as given, but decor, design and seating arrangements are sometimes described. For example, several informants mention that in some cinemas seats in the back row of the stalls were designed expressly for courting couples:

[O]ur cinemagoing was great way of courting... [One cinema] had double seats on the back row and we used to go and queue early to procure one of these back row 'seats for two' where we could cuddle up together to watch the programme.[23]

Helen Smeaton offers a detailed account of similar seating arrangements in a cinema in her native Glasgow:

We moved from that part of Maryhill, then off Great Western Road and there was a cinema called the Gem. And, by this stage I was what, I was getting up to, I must have been 16, yes, em, and in the Gem, you had, it was very comfortable and nice. And if you went up to the balcony they had the chummy seats. You just sat two each but it had the high, high back and it went straight around, and then it curved round the side. That's where all the [laughing] courting couples went, who weren't really interested in the cinema. So every time after I met, ended up with my husband, eh, and then we started going out, we always used to go [laughing] to the Gem...[24]

While Mrs Shaw and Mrs Smeaton recall their own courting in the back row, other informants, most of them men, remember the back row as the object of intense voyeuristic fascination. Jimmy Murray gleefully recalls the activities of courting couples in the double seats at the back of a Manchester cinema:

JM   One cinema had special, eh, special seats. The Scala, there. They were way out like, you know. And they had the back row. They'd took arm rest off so it made one seat for the couples, you know. They could do a bit of *snogging* on the back seat kinda thing. [Amused voice]

Int   [Laughs]

JM   Instead of having arms sticking into the other. Aye.[25]

Sometimes the goings-on in the back row proved more interesting than what was happening on the screen, as Brigadier J.B. Ryall recalls:

> When a youngster could sneak into the back row of the cinema he sometimes got more pleasure out of the corner of his eye at the 'fumbling' and 'squeaks' that sometimes went on.[26]

There is a clear association in informants' memory-talk between courtship and romance on the one hand and the supercinema's heterotopic qualities on the other. Bob Surtees writes:

> Later in the 30s an evening at the cinema with your girl friend. The comfort! warmth! the nearness and love, the dreamland atmosphere. What a lovely world it was! Until '39![27]

This memory has a sensual quality, conveying the experience of bodily ease and release induced by the cinema's all-encompassing warmth and comfort, and associating this with the memory of physical closeness with his girlfriend. It conveys, too, a palpable sense of missing that 'lovely world' of adolescence with its leisures and pleasures, a world doubly lost: first when war broke out in 1939 and now, in the moment of writing, with old age.

The picture palaces of the 1930s are remembered as heterotopias in a number of respects. They are located at some distance from home; their architecture and interiors are exotic or avant-garde; and they provide amenities of unaccustomed splendour – wall-to-wall carpeting, heating, plush seats. For cinemagoers of the 1930s, these things were clearly enjoyable in their own right. But they are also the point of entry to a further set of 'other' spaces, the worlds of fiction and the imagination offered up on the cinema screen. Location, architecture, interior design, and finally the cinematic apparatus itself: all are of a piece.

Many informants observe that the pictures took them into a different world, an observation none the less apt for being conventional. Indeed, commentators who would frown on cliches about escapism have noted that cinema buildings work exactly like machines that transport users away from the everyday, the 'localizable', and deliver them into the other world opened up by the cinema screen.[28] Moreover, theorists who conceive of cinema as a machine of another kind – an apparatus in which the spectator is caught up in a set of psychical processes centred around vision – are pointing to a key component of the relationship between cinema and its users. Though not as universally explanatory a feature of the spectator-screen relationship as its proponents suggest, the concept of the cinematic apparatus sits well with the particular combination of the supercinema-heterotopia and the classical Hollywood film which distinguishes popular cinema culture of the 1930s. But while the apparatus model gives centre stage to vision and looking, it is apparent from the memories of cinemagoers of these years that the pleasure of looking at the cinema screen is but a small part of an all-encompassing somatic, sensuous and affective involvement in the cinema experience.

Cinema's engagement of body, senses and feelings has particular resonance where romance, sex and courtship are concerned. For example, it is sometimes assumed that the warmth and comfort of the darkened cinema auditorium may induce a lowering of the defences imposed by the external authority of the adult world or by the internal authority of the superego. If this is so, under what conditions might this process be channelled into erotic reverie or fantasy, or even into sexual activity? In many minds, certainly, sex and the cinema are irrevocably linked, a view succinctly expressed by the cinema reformer of the early 1930s who argues that film dramas 'affect the nerves, and above all, the sexual instincts... In that lies the mysterious secret of the astounding success of the cinemas'.[29] Films' capacity to activate 'sexual instincts', it was felt, could readily promote sexually promiscuous behaviour, both inside and outside cinemas.[30]

The cinema-sex conjunction begs many questions, however. Do different sorts of films channel desires differently? How precisely might the portrayal on screen of heterosexual romance, a prevalent theme of films in the 1930s, engage cinemagoers 'sexual instincts'? While it may well be true that there is an analogy between the psychological processes involved in falling in love (projection, idealisation) and the operations of cinematic identification and star worship,[31] these processes will always be modified in practice by sociocultural factors. Mores surrounding courtship behaviour and patterns of courtship and marriage, as well as demographic factors such as class, age and gender, are all key features of, in Foucault's term, the 'localizable'.

For example, male informants are forthright about their youthful scorn for romantic pictures and for all forms of 'sloppiness' on the screen:

Well, see now, when you're young, if ye, if ye got, eh, men and girls *slabbering* over each other, you know when you're sitting, they would have catcalls, '*Aw, get them off!*' [*Shouts*] '*Get them off!*' That didn't appeal to us. There had to be something happening in a picture. Gangster pictures, there were a lot of gangster pictures. I liked them, because there was a lot of shooting in them.[32]

Research on cinema audiences conducted during the 1930s confirms that there was a clear gender split in film preferences, with boys and young men going out of their way to deride the sorts of 'sloppy' pictures that appealed to girls and women.[33] And yet, as noted above, young men were prepared to endure romantic films if they thought this would help them, in Ashley Bird's words, 'get to grips with the girlfriend'. The assumptions are that a boy's agreeing to his girlfriend's choice of film might make her more favourably disposed towards him, or that a romantic picture might put her in an erotically receptive frame of mind.

Women, on the other hand, expatiate on their enjoyment of romantic films and stars and make the connection between these and their own adolescent romantic longings. These are invariably recalled as innocently romantic rather than erotic or sexual. 'It was a romantic era, as far as I was concerned', says Annie Wright. 'And there were weepies and romantic films. And, as I said, at that age, 17 and you're going out with a boy, there was nothing else. And of course, you was in love and of course, that enhanced the feeling. All these films were sort of made for you. You know you could see yourself in. Well I did anyway.' Mrs Wright's conclusion – 'It was *lovely*'[34] – echoes other female informants' talk about romantic pictures.

Fans of the film romance invariably emphasise the innocence of the love stories portrayed in the films they saw in their youth, and by implication the innocence of their own adolescent love lives as well. Nancy Carrington makes this point in several ways:

> *Int*   Did you have any particular favourite kinds of films? You were saying that you liked the romance. Was it the romantic films you liked?
>
> *NC*   Well, we used to have lovely romances. [*Said warmly*] They were so *beautiful*, you know. Clean romances. You know. Like they'd never show you a couple in bed together. They always had separate beds. You used a lot of your imagination but it was really all clean, beautiful.
>
> *Int*   Mm.

NC You know, it was real romantic. And of course if we could get at the back seat, then course [*laughs; remembering*] we used to have a good time, you know. Used to get ice creams in the interval, you know. And, eh, oh used to be great. [*Said nostalgically*][35]

I remember I went to, em, it was the Harrow Coliseum, em, picture place, you know. And we went to see *Ramona*. Aw, that was beautiful. I think that was Bebe Daniels and Ben Lyon. And eh, it was really romantic. Really lovely. And then we'd walk all the way over the hill at the back by the cenotaph, all the way home. You know. Really lovely. [*Said nostalgically*][36]

Many informants, male as well as female, take pains to distinguish between past and present, between the films of their youth and the films and television programmes of today, invariably insisting that the latter are too sexually explicit. Beatrice Cooper, for example, recalls that 'films were never that *risqué* that they are [*sic*] anything like they are today! You know there was a limit on the number of seconds they could kiss each other'. Doreen Lyell notes that 'nobody was shown, no man and woman was shown in bed together... And there was no actual scenes of sex or anything like that'. Jim Godbold complains about films 'where everybody's jumping in bed and that sort of thing... You didn't want to see all this writhing about on the bed and all this'.[37] As Mrs Carrington implies, films of the 1930s left a lot to the imagination, and this was exactly what made them so 'lovely'.

Helen Smeaton, though, tells a story which, while drawing a distinction between love and romance in films past and present, eschews nostalgia and makes fun of her own youthful naivete:

To me, when I was young, I believed all the romantic stuff. I could think of seeing a film, *Seventh Heaven*, I think it was called or something. Somebody called Simone Simone and James Stewart. They were in an attic away up somewhere in Paris and it was all so romantic. And I sat there and I took all that in. I thought that was what love was like. I never bothered about what happened afterwards. I can remember going on thinking about that film for *countless* years. And then when my younger son, the one in America, was about 17, and I was always telling him about the great films that we had when I was young. How ours were so much better. Sometimes they would come on on the telly and I remember saying, 'This *Seventh Heaven*'s coming on now.' And I said, 'Aw Alan. If you're staying in, look at this, look at this film.' [*Laughs*] And we sat down to look at it and I remember thinking, 'Oh, my gosh! Did I really think that was *good*?' And when it was finished, Alan nearly fell about laughing. He said, 'You're right, mother. They don't make films like that any more nowadays.' And I couldn't understand how my whole attitude had changed in about what, about 20, 30 years from I was 16, 17 when I saw it and it was all just so romantic and wonderful. Once you've lived a bit and you see it again. [*Laughs*] Oh dear, oh dear![38]

The testimonies of 1930s cinemagoers suggest that interactions between the pictures and their own adolescent romantic dreams, desires and courtship behaviour could take a number of forms. These might range from romantic and erotic daydreams fuelled and shaped by films and film stars, through projections of fantasies onto individuals in their everyday worlds, to more diffuse memories in which cinemas figure as venues for their own courtship, and finally to anecdotal memory-stories in which 'the pictures' becomes a protagonist in informants' own love stories.

The imitative activities described in Chapter 5 all contain an element of cinema-fuelled fantasy, and some are expressions of wishes of a specifically romantic or erotic nature. Emily Soper's memory of her and her friends' feelings towards their favourite female stars captures the urgency of the desire lying behind such identifications: 'We had our special heroines, too, whom we admired and our great desire was to be as beautiful as they and as successful in catching the man of our dreams!'[39]

Others remember adolescent longings provoked by stars of the opposite sex. Ellen Casey's screen idol was Ross Alexander, who appeared in a number of Warner Bros pictures during the 1930s (he died in 1937). So obsessed with Alexander was the 15-year old Ellen that she developed a crush on a young man she thought resembled him. The boy, who – significantly – remains nameless in Mrs Casey's anecdote, was in a good job and could afford to take her to a 'posh' cinema and treat her to a seat in the circle. She is carried away not only by the presence at her side of the companion who in her mind has become her idol ('I was so thrilled being with this Ross Alexander') but also by the magical 'other' world opened up by the musical on the screen:

EC   Anyway when I got to about 15 I seen this lad. Well I think he was 19 at the time. I was about 15. And he resembled Ross Alexander. Aw did I chase him!

Int   [*Laughs*]

EC   Oh I did. Honestly. He was. He had the same jet black hair. Brushed back as they used to have it. And the same sort of, you know wave. And he *did* resemble. Aw [*swooning voice*]. I was mad on him... *Finally* I got for him to take me out... [It was a] Fred Astaire, Ginger Rogers musical. And it was that one where they were singing. Oh I still remember the song. Even now. Em, 'Cheek to Cheek'.

Int   Oh, *Top Hat*.

EC   Yeah. Em, how did it start, 'Cheek'. [*Sings*] 'When we're both together dancing cheek to cheek.' And I thought, oh-h-h. Going upstairs on the balcony! Aa was so *thrilled* being with this Ross Alexander![40]

Bert Partington recollects that as a schoolboy he and a group of friends cultivated an obsession with a local girl they thought looked like Marlene Dietrich. In this case, however, the admiration was from afar, the fantasy acted out in peer group activity:

BP   I can remember the same group at school. We thought Marlene Dietrich was *terrific* you see. And there was a young woman. We were in Bolton then. And we had Wednesday afternoon off school. And on Wednesday lunchtime we used to *race* to the cloakroom. Wash our hands and face. And three of us used to *hurtle* out to the town centre. Because there was a young woman who worked at the gown shop who we thought was like Marlene Dietrich. And we used to sort of stare at her and follow her. [*Laughs*]

LB   [*Laughs*]

BP   And we were normal! [*Laughs*] There was nothing sinister about it.

LB   No. Just admiring.

BP   I mean, she wouldn't have been frightened of us. I mean it wasn't that kind of following.

LB   Mm.

BP   We just thought she was Wow! She was *absolutely* marvellous, you know.[41]

A few informants, all women, offer highly personal, and obviously treasured, memories of the part played by cinema in their own love lives. These are stories about the transition from courtship to marriage, about how women met their spouses, and about how cinema figured in their courtships. Mrs K. Scott writes: 'when we were courting my husband and I went regularly to the pictures... he belonged to the St Johns Ambulance Brigade [and] would be on duty in his uniform, he had to stand at the back of the stalls and I would sit in the front stalls. Our family think it was a funny way to do our courting!' Olive Johnson adds a postscript to her letter: 'My first proposal of marriage came in the back row of the Odeon!'[42]

Other memories are of husbands now deceased. Mrs M.W. Spicer relates that she went to the pictures with the boyfriend she 'courted for 7 years until married for 42 years, and then he died 12 years ago'. Clarice Squires, in a story which itself exhibits many of the formal conventions of popular romantic fiction – destiny, coincidence, the 'meet cute' – writes about the first time she met her husband:

It was in a cinema queue where I was destined to meet my future husband. He was home on leave and 'The Bells of St Mary's' with Bing Crosby was showing at the Coliseum. My mum went early to save me a place in what seemed like a mile long queue, and I joined her straight from my work. Who should be beside her but handsome Ken. They chatted and Mum explained she was keeping a place for me.

We didn't sit near each other, but seemed to come out the same time...

Now I think this is where fate lends a helping hand. Mum had to catch the bus home as my Dad was on the night shift and being my Mum she couldn't possibly let him go without seeing to his supper. I on the other hand had a card to post in the General P. O. it being my brother's birthday the next day, so say no more that's where it all started and after we got to know each other we were happily married for just over 30 years when he died of cancer 17 years [ago] on 2nd April.[43]

The themes and styles of narration of these accounts of courtship, romance and sex, and their particular combination of memories of courtship with memories of cinemagoing, are peculiar to the 1930s generation. For this generation, the 1930s is a time that stands out very clearly in memory. The majority of informants were born in the early to middle 1920s, which means that the heyday of Hollywood glamour and the era of the new supercinemas coincided with a formative period of their lives. At the same time, their adolescence was curtailed at the close of the decade by the outbreak of the Second World War, an event remembered by many as a personal watershed, a time of dramatic life changes. Isolated in memory, the 1930s are recollected all the more distinctly from other times in informants' lives. Perhaps, too, because the war brought such profound social changes, not least in sexual attitudes and behaviour, the years preceding it seem all the more innocent to those who were young at the time. Their insistence on how different attitudes to and behaviour around courtship were then may be understood in this light.

As noted earlier, informants rarely address themselves to more than one of the key themes and discourses that characterise memories around courtship, romance and sex. However, one informant's testimony not only interweaves all the themes, but also ties them in with memories of his own sexual awakening and situates them in their social and historical context. In the process, this account throws into relief the specific meanings of coming into masculinity for men of his generation, and the role played in it by cinema culture.

Denis (A.D.) Houlston was born in Levenshulme, Manchester in 1917; and aside from war service has lived there all his life. On leaving school at 17, he went into clerical work, first as an office boy and later as a cost clerk and cashier. Mr Houlston's two lengthy interviews reveal a strong feeling for his locality and a detailed memory of the many picture houses that were once in his neighbourhood. His recollections of the exterior and interior features of his favourite cinemas are exceptionally vivid, as is his memory of cinema programmes and of images, shots and sequences in his favourite films. He joined the *Picturegoer* postcard club in the early 1930s, and his collection of postcard portraits of film stars remains intact, along with a number of letters from and signed photographs of film stars and some film-related publications of the 1930s.[44] Obviously a cinephile, he later became a member of a film society in Manchester.

Mr Houlston's testimony is unusual for the fluidity with which it moves between talk about erotic moments on screen, the sexiness of his favourite leading ladies, courtship activities in the back row of the cinema, and adolescent sexual feelings more generally. Like other informants, he regards the 1930s as a bounded period characterised by a strict and widely-observed set of codes of behaviour around courtship and sex. Unlike other informants, though, he constructs himself as actively involved in the sexual preoccupations of adolescence. In a period marked by sexual innocence and restraint, he contends, the cinema was for him – and indeed for others – a source of education in sexual matters as well as of pleasurable looking.

Mr Houlston reminds the interviewer that during the 1930s he passed from boyhood to young manhood: 'in those days, [19]30, I would be 13, and in 1939 I'd be 22!' In these nine years, memorable for him as a time of considerable intellectual and psychosexual development, Mr Houlston's taste in films and stars underwent some sea changes:

> So the, the early impressions were Cowboys and Indians and then, we got farther on to romantic comedies. I'd love to see them again to see how they were but, of course, I don't suppose they'd put them on film now, because. Oh and the musicals, we loved the musicals.

A few years older than most other informants, he entered adolescence before Hollywood films were subjected to the rigorous regulation of the Production Code. Many films of the late 1920s and early 1930s were quite racy, and Mr Houlston remembers well the changes wrought by the Hays Office. It was in the pre-Code years that as a 'romantic school-boy' he began to cultivate an interest in the opposite sex:

> *DH* And of course by that time, with becoming more conscious of, eh, of girls being different from boys, so I started getting my favourite female stars, like Madeleine Carroll.

> *Int* Right!

> *DH* Was the quintessential English star. Blonde naturally! We didn't have colour so I can't remember if she was blue-eyed or not but I mean Madeleine Carroll! [*said slowly and lovingly*] The first one I ever liked was a silent filmstar, American, Evelyn Brent, who was a brunette and I can't even remember why I fell for her now. But Evelyn Brent sticks in my mind, and I saw her years later in a film, when she

was 70, and I saw the name on the cast list and I thought 'That was my first film star lady love, from the silent days!' Then the next one was Thelma Todd who was a blonde, an American blonde, and she was in these B movies and in these short comedies.

He remembers with special affection the romantic comedies of Ernst Lubitsch, films he characterises as frothy, witty, full of gaiety – and *risqué*: 'Cause it was always about, eh, a man endeavouring to get the lady into the bedroom'. The attraction of the Lubitsch films derives, according to Mr Houlston, from their restraint in the portrayal of sex. This restraint fuelled his schoolboy curiosity precisely about what was not shown on the screen:

It was, it was more an age of innocence and one that comes to mind is *The Love Parade* with Maurice Chevalier and Jeanette MacDonald and, em, you got things, hints about the gentlemen going in the ladies' bedroom. Well, we never knew what went on there but, em, they'd show you now, you'd have writhing, naked bodies but those days, they'd go through a door and the door would shut and next thing the door would open and it would be the following morning or something like that. So [*pause*] as curious schoolboys we used to think 'well, what goes on?' Well, when it had a song in that film, and I have a record of it, of Jeanette MacDonald singing it, a song called 'How I would love one hour with you', we gained this impression [*laughs*] that it took an hour that, that this was the sort of height of bliss: one hour with you! We didn't know quite why it was the height of bliss...[45]

Explaining his preference for musicals, Mr Houlston says:

We loved the musicals because there was lots of chorus girls, eh, and Dick Powell sings in one of the musicals about, eh, 'Why do we go, eh, dames' and the song is called 'Dames' and that's why we go to these shows. Eh, well that's why we as schoolboys went.

It later emerges that Mr Houlston's fascination with chorus girls in musicals – he remembers the Busby Berkeley sequences in *Gold Diggers of 1933* and *42nd Street* particularly vividly – has to do with the displays of legs in these films:

DH And the Busby Berkeley. I, I, everybody must say this, of my generation. If only Busby Berkeley had been doing these films when we had colour.

Int   Aah.

DH   Cause they're all black and white.

Int   Mmm.

DH   But I marvel at his routines now. I love his dance routines and, em, they were absolutely and there again, you see, I keep coming back to sex, after, I'll have to have a cold shower!

Int   [*Laughs*]

DH   I think but, there's one in particular where em, a modern film, I can see it *now*, it was on the front cover of *The Picturegoer*, whether it's Ruby Keeler, it might have been, I think it was *42nd Street*, and Ruby Keeler's at one end and she comes through a tunnel and the tunnel is composed of the chorus girls' legs, and it's shot…

Frustratingly, the tape runs out at this point, but the shot referred to could well be from 'I'm Young and Healthy', a number in the backstage musical *42nd Street*. The number ends with one of Busby Berkeley's signature tracking shots through the parted legs of a line of chorines. The track between the legs – 'the semantic unit *par excellence* of the show musical'[46] – engages the spectator's look in a mode of address in which 'the technology of cinema creates a necessary identification

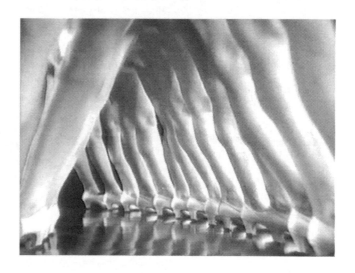

between the spectator and the cinematic apparatus'.[47] Here, the relationship between film text and spectator is grounded in the pleasures of the voyeuristic gaze. Describing how gender spectacle in the Hollywood musical is organised through performances of femininity which 'are most clearly constructed through the convention of the crotch shot (moments where attention is drawn to the female genital area) instead of the heterosexual embrace',[48] Nadine Wills draws a distinction between the musical, which offers the gratifications of display and spectacle, and the romantic comedy, whose pleasures derive from withholding, from not showing.

Withholding rather than showing aptly describes the Lubitsch romantic comedies Mr Houlston enjoyed as a schoolboy. And indeed his account of the sources of his adolescent fascination with certain films and stars suggests that what he found most intriguing was not so much overt display as the tease of the partly revealed female body and the brief glimpse of the forbidden. He eloquently describes the details of costuming, mise en scene and camera angle through which these erotically compelling images are presented cinematically. His account also suggests an understanding of the operation of cinematic point of view, in that many of the shots and sequences he recalls as particularly erotic are exactly those which offer the spectator a peek at the forbidden sight:

> Once again as a schoolboy, with these, like the rest of my schoolboys you got these nice ideas, we loved it because you got plenty of leg shots and the decolletage was quite generous, more generous than later on, eh, so we would see bits of those female bodies which, you know, we'd only dreamed about [laughs] and, eh, there were shots of stocking tops was a favourite thing and always in pictures the leading lady would have to adjust her stockings some time. So up would come her skirt and we'd all be goggle-eyed and, eh, 'Did you see Lili Damita', you know?

This is all the more powerful where the erotic sight is withheld from characters within the film. Mr Houlston describes the famous 'saucy but nice' scene from a picture which enjoyed wide popular and critical acclaim on its release in 1934. In Frank Capra's It Happened One Night, the Clark Gable character, a louche reporter, is in pursuit of a fugitive rich girl (Claudette Colbert).[49] The pair find themselves forced to share a motel room for a night:

I know there's a scene in that where they have to put up at a motel and she insists on hanging a blanket on a string between the two beds but it's a delightful comedy that, and we thought that was, you know, *risqué* with Clark Gable one side undressing and Claudette Colbert the other side undressing and we knew they wouldn't show us anything if anything did develop. Actually I don't think anything did as far as I remember the story but they were saucy if you follow me, saucy but nice.

Taking the interviewer through his collection of *Picturegoer* postcards of film stars, Mr Houlston shows an example of the kind of image he found particularly erotic, this one involving a bare leg peeking from a lacy negligée:

DH Now you see we thought that was [*hands over photo*] out and out naughtiness.

Int [*Sighs*] Lili Damita

DH She's showing her leg there, I mean that was I mean that, that.

Int And a bare shoulder.

DH I'd have to go and take a cold shower after that!

Int [*Laughs*] Yes.

Here, as elsewhere in Mr Houlston's testimony, the point at which exposed flesh meets clothing is recollected as particularly tantalising. He mentions stocking tops several times, and says he found underwear and scanty, translucent garments especially compelling when worn by his favourite stars. These garments are described in detail and in a manner which conveys the tactility, the feel, of their silky fabrics: Thelma Todd in 'quite daring stockings and what the Americans call teddies'; Anna Neagle in a translucent dress, 'sheer as, like a veil really'; Marlene Dietrich's 'frilly knickers in *Blue Angel*! They *sent* us, you know'.

Some particularly tantalising shots involving legs and stocking tops feature in films starring his greatest favourite, Madeleine Carroll:

DH But [Madeleine Carroll] would sweep anybody off their feet, well she did us anyway.

Int Yeh. So that's from *The Kissing Cup's Race* [*reading off photo*].

DH And she'd got nice legs and, and I'll mention this [*laughs*] I hope I don't keep harping back to sex! But she did one film, and I can't even remember the name of it and it was before the Hays Code.

LILI DAMITA   PHOTO. PARAMOUNT

Lili Damita, from Denis Houlston's collection

Madeleine Carroll, from Denis Houlston's collection

Int   Right.

DH   And it was a period piece and it could've been something like Oscar Wilde's *Lady Windermere's Fan*.

Int   Mmm.

DH   But she was getting ready to go out [*laughs*] in the evening with a long period dress and the cameraman shot it from the floor looking all the way up her legs!

Int   Aah!

DH   So you got a, this dress comes down [*indicates*] you know, like a tent [*laughs*] so it was a reversal of striptease really! And it actually, I can remember it now, it was quite beautiful really.

Int   Mmm.

DH   But em I suppose you could call it erotic but, I mean we'd never seen under a lady's dress before! [*Laughs*] As little schoolboys you know, and to get this shot of something, [*pause*] looking like that and then this dress slowly descends.

Madeleine Carroll and, aw I, I thought she was *beautiful*, and I've never forgotten her because she was in *The Thirty Nine Steps* with Robert Donat and she was handcuffed to him and as little schoolboys we, we were thrilled to bits that, at one stage, when they're in this crofter's cottage, bothy, she wants to take her stockings off and she's handcuffed so his hand is inches off her [*pauses*] *bare thigh* and we thought that was the height of daring. We, we went to see that film more than once. And I've seen it since on television [*smiles*] and I've waited for that to see, sort of, what was so exciting about it, but it was whole thing for t'males of course! But, the stocking tops.

Mr Houlston's adolescent fascination with these scenes clearly has a great deal to do with a play of concealment and revelation around the object of desire. The mention of curiosity about what lies beneath a lady's dress invites reference to Freud's essay on fetishism, in which the inquisitive boy's 'peer[ing] at the woman's genitals from below, from her legs up'[50] is linked with his curiosity as to whether or not the woman possesses a penis. The psychical configuration of fetishism, which involves disavowal (simultaneous hanging onto and renouncing the belief that the woman has a penis) is what fuels the fetishist's perpetual fascination with what lies under the woman's skirt. The fetish, significantly, is grounded in looking, and in the conviction that seeing more will satisfy curiosity.

The fetishistic look, along with reverence for the fetish object, are regarded as key elements in the dynamics of various kinds of cinematic fascination, including preoccupation with the technology of cinema[51] and star worship. Mr Houlston's memory of being captivated by Marlene Dietrich in *Blue Angel* ('Oh those frilly knickers! ... we liked the legs of course. Legs Dietrich') calls to mind an iconic image from this 1930 film: a pose in which Dietrich displays naked thighs, stocking tops, suspenders and knickers. As Peter Baxter notes, contemporary commentary on *Blue Angel* (*New York Times* reviewer Bosley Crowther referred to 'the long legs, the bare thighs, the garters, the provocatively ornamented crotch') does indeed suggest that the play of concealment and revelation in the framing and presentation of Dietrich's body throughout the film is exactly what makes it so riveting. Baxter concludes: 'this pose arrests the instant of fetishisation, the instant before the child's glimpse of the female genital organ. Lola's leg tantalises by almost revealing that anatomic feature'.[52]

Mr Houlston's account is testament to one of the key pleasures of cinema, that of looking at the image on screen. As such it gives suggestive

Marlene Dietrich in *The Blue Angel*

ethnographic fleshing out to those theories of the relationship between spectator and screen which give centre stage to scopophilia, the drive to pleasurable looking.[53] At the same time, the fact that his testimony is exceptional, and that accounts implying more diffusely somatic, sensual or affective engagements predominate in the testimonies of 1930s cinemagoers, indicates the limitations of the scope of such theories. So, too, does attention to the cultural and historical embeddedness of these engagements.

Mr Houlston implies that the feelings aroused by cinema were especially powerful in a climate of prohibition which, as in the 1930s, imposed a taboo on the very naming of, let alone action on, sexual feelings. This is particularly apparent in his repeated interjection of comments to the effect that he was at the time entirely innocent of the implications of his feelings: 'we didn't really know quite why it ['one hour with you'] was the height of bliss'; 'I stress it was very innocent'. Throughout his testimony, too, Mr Houlston interweaves memories of films and stars with accounts of the place 'the pictures' occupied in his

own and his contemporaries' daily lives. Punctuated by historical and
sociological observations on courtship behaviour during the 1930s, his
narration shuttles between past and present. His conclusion is that the
cinema was in every respect the best place for courtship: 'Without cars
and without our own flats and all the necessities of post-war youth we
relied on cinemas for our courting parlour – warm, comfortable refuges
from the cold winter elements outside'.[54]

He is at pains to insist on the difference of those times, and on the
importance of understanding the very specific context of the events and
the feelings he describes. In one long passage, he alludes again to the
social significance of the picture house as a venue for courtship, mentioning the romantic atmosphere of the place – its warmth, comfort, cosiness.
He then makes the connection between the 'girl at your side' and the
adolescent boy's reveries about a favourite star. He gives an account of
the heterotopic counterpoint between immersion ('you were lost') and
consciousness of the 'real' world (the girl 'was nothing like Thelma
Todd'). He then returns to the present with some observations on the
sexual mores of the 1930s, and finally rounds things off with a
comparison between past and present:

> But, eh, so we had no money, we'd no car, we'd no groups, we had
> nothing, eh, so all you could ask from a girl, if you'd taken her to
> the pictures, taken to the Farnside and taken her to the balcony
> and that was it, they didn't even allow for Romeo, the balcony at
> the Farnside or the Kingsway or the Regal was the, eh, you know,
> gateway to Paradise as it were, but we'd nothing. So when you
> were courting, in the summer you'd, you went, we went in park
> shelters or something like that, em, you went all over the place but
> your best place, it's a cliche this, I know, and everybody laughs,
> but your main courting area was the back row of the cinema. Not
> for the lewd jokes that you get about it now [*laughs*] nor the
> innuendos but because you went there, you were in the back row
> if you were lucky [*laughs*] if you could beat somebody else to it, it
> was, it, you were seeing your film favourites, Thelma Todd, the
> girl at your side was nothing like Thelma Todd but that didn't
> worry you, you were in the warmth, it was comfortable, you'd got
> sweets, they went round with a tray with ice cream and all the rest
> of it on at the intervals, so it was a cosy atmosphere. So, for two
> hours you were lost with your girlfriend and you did your courting

there. Em, all very innocent of course, well reasonably innocent courting, em, obviously it didn't give you much scope for the greatest intimacy but there you were. I mean that was it, you accepted that, em, apart from which you couldn't indulge in the greatest intimacy anyway, even if you were in those rows, for two reasons. There was a sense of community then, which there isn't now, and if the girl got pregnant that was a disgrace on the community, particularly your street, on her family, on your family so that kept them, kept you both on the straight and narrow. Cause there was shame in those days. Now shame has inverted commas now. But there was shame in those days.

Notes

1. 95-111-1, Margaret Houlgate, Hampshire, to Annette Kuhn and Valentina Bold, 20 February 1995; 95-244-1, Margaret Ward, Buckinghamshire, to Cinema Culture in 1930s Britain, 31 May 1995.

2. T95-46, Freda McFarland, Bolton, 7 June 1995.

3. T95-87, Ashley Bird, Harrow, 12 July 1995; T95-34, Lois Basnett and Herbert Partington, Manchester, 30 May 1995.

4. T95-2, Helen Smeaton, Glasgow, 23 January 1995.

5. 92-36-9, Interviewer's fieldnotes, Helen Smeaton, Glasgow, 23 January 1995.

6. T95-155, Nancy Carrington and Nancy Prudhoe, Harrow, 30 April 1995.

7. T95-114, Peggy Kent, Hilda Green, Hilda Catchpol, Barbara Harvey and Gladys Kent, Suffolk, 18 October 1995.

8. Annette Kuhn, 'Cinemagoing in Britain in the 1930s: report of a questionnaire survey', *Historical Journal of Film, Radio and Television,* vol. 19, no. 4 (1999), pp. 531–543.

9. Michel Foucault, 'Other spaces: the principles of heterotopia', *Lotus,* vol. 48–49 (1986), pp. 9–17. The quotation is on p. 12.

10. Ibid., p. 14.

11. This was the last of a group of four cinemas designed by Edward A. Stone and built for Paramount: see David Atwell, *Cathedrals of the Movies: A History of British Cinemas and Their Audiences* (London: Architectural Press, 1980).

12. 95-164-1, 'The cinema in the thirties', Muriel Peck, Dorset, March 1995.

13. For example, 95-69-1, Mrs Fodden, Cardiff, to Annette Kuhn and Valentina Bold, 9 February 1995; T95-37, Ellen Casey, Manchester, 31 May 1995.

14. 92-32-1, Alex Mawer, Glasgow, to Annette Kuhn, 30 April 1992.

15. T95-34, Lois Basnett and Herbert Partington, Manchester, 30 May 1995; 95-301-1, Mrs D.E. Cowles, Norfolk, to Stephen Peart, 7 September 1995.

16. T95-82, Nancy Carrington, Harrow, 7 July 1995 (also present Sue Nicholls of Harrow Housebound Readers Service).

17. T95-62, Jimmy Murray, Manchester, 9 May 1995.

18. T95-155, Nancy Carrington and Nancy Prudhoe, Harrow, 30 April 1995.

19. T95-148, Nancy Carrington, Harrow, 22 November 1995.

20. T95-104, Ashley Bird, Harrow, 26 July 1995.

21. 95-302-1, Mr E. Harvey, Norfolk, to Stephen Peart, n.d. 1995.

22. This is a quotation from C. Day Lewis's 1938 poem, 'Newsreel': '…this loving/ Darkness a fur you can afford'.

23. 95-74-1, Molly Shaw, Gloucestershire, to Annette Kuhn and Valentina Bold, 15 February 1995.

24. T95-2, Helen Smeaton, Glasgow, 23 January 1995.

25. T95-62, Jimmy Murray, Manchester, 9 May1995.

26. 95-48-1, Brigadier J.B. Ryall, Sussex, to Annette Kuhn and Valentina Bold, 8 February 1995.

27. 95-96-1, Bob Surtees, Gwent, to Annette Kuhn and Valentina Bold, 6 February 1995.

28. Roland Barthes, 'Upon leaving the movie theater', *University Publishing*, no. 6 (1979), p. 3; Jean-Louis Comolli, 'Machines of the visible', in Teresa de Lauretis and Stephen Heath (eds), *The Cinematic Apparatus* (New York: St Martins Press, 1980), pp. 121–142.

29. *Vigilance Record*, November 1931, p. 41.

30. An intriguing piece of participant observation on this subject was conducted by A Mass-Observer in Bolton in 1938: see 'Outing with a girl stranger' in Angus Calder and Dorothy Sheridan (eds) *Speak For Yourself: a Mass-Observation Anthology* (London: Jonathan Cape, 1984), pp. 39–41.

31. Virginia Wright Wexman, *Creating the Couple: Love, Marriage and Hollywood Performance* (Princeton, NJ: Princeton University Press, 1993).

32. T94-12, Thomas McGoran, Glasgow, 30 November 1994.

33. See William Farr, 'Analysis of questionnaire to adolescents 14–18 years', (London: British Film Institute, [1939]) Richard Ford, *Children in the Cinema* (London: Allen & Unwin, 1939).

34. T95-33, Annie Wright, Manchester, 26 May 1995.

35. T95-82, Nancy Carrington, Harrow, 7 July 1995.

36. T95-148, Nancy Carrington, Harrow, 22 November 1995. Mrs Carrington is probably referring to the 1928 version of *Ramona*, directed by Edwin Carewe and starring Dolores del Rio and Warner Baxter. The film tells the story of the tragic romance of a young Indian chief and a 'half-breed' girl.

37. T95-153, Beatrice Cooper, Harrow, 27 November 1995; T95-116, Doreen Lyell, Suffolk, 19 October 1995; T95-113, E.J. Godbold, Suffolk, 17 October 1995.

38. T95-72, Helen Smeaton, Glasgow, 28 June 1995. Mrs Smeaton saw the 1937 remake of the Academy Award-winning 1927 Frank Borzage picture of the same title starring Janet Gaynor and Charles Farrell.

39. 95-146-1, Emily Soper, Hampshire, to Annette Kuhn and Valentina Bold, 13 February 1995. Jackie Stacey discusses similar forms of female identification in *Star Gazing: Hollywood Cinema and Female Spectatorship* (London: Routledge, 1994), Chapter 5.

40. T95-37, Ellen Casey, Manchester, 31 May 1995.

41. T95-35, Lois Basnett and Herbert Partington, Manchester, 30 May 1995.

42. 95-241-1, Mrs K. Scott, Yorskshire, to Cinema Culture in 1930s Britain, 4 June 1995; 95-60-1, Olive Johnson, West Midlands, to Annette Kuhn and Valentina Bold, 14 February 1995.

43. 95-235, Questionnaire, Mrs M.W. Spicer, Sussex; 95-85-1, Clarice Squires, Gwent, to Annette Kuhn and Valentina Bold, n.d. 1995.

44. Mr Houlston was interviewed at his home on 26 April 1995 (transcripts T95-18,

T95-19, T95-20) and on 25 May 1995 (T95-29, T95-30). Interview material quoted here is from T95-18, T95-19 and T95-29. Other extracts from Mr Houlston's interviews are published in Annette Kuhn, 'Memories of cinema-going in the 1930s', *Journal of Popular British Cinema*, no 2 (1999), pp. 100–120; Sarah Street, *British Cinema in Documents* (London: Routledge, 2000). Mr Houlston has donated his film memorabilia to the Cinema Culture in 1930s Britain project: items 95-34-23 to 95-34-32.

45. *The Love Parade* (Lubitsch, Paramount, 1929) stars Jeanette MacDonald in her screen debut, with Maurice Chevalier. It was nominated best film of the year by *Film Weekly* (27 December 1930). *One Hour With You* is the title of another Lubitsch film, released in 1933 and also starring MacDonald and Chevalier.

46. Rick Altman, *The American Film Musical* (Bloomington, IN: Indiana University Press, 1984), p. 223.

47. Ibid., p. 225. Altman here cites Jean-Louis Baudry, 'Ideological effects of the basic cinematographic apparatus', *Film Quarterly*, vol. 28, no. 2 (1974–75), pp. 39–47; and Christian Metz, 'The Imaginary signifier', *Screen*, vol. 16, no. 2 (1975), pp. 14–76. See also Lucy Fischer, 'Shall we dance? women and the musical', in *Shot/Countershot* (Princeton, NJ: Princeton University Press, 1989).

48. Nadine Wills, '"110 per cent woman": the crotch shot in the Hollywood musical', *Screen*, vol. 42, no. 2 (2001), pp. 121-41.

49. In Britain, *It Happened One Night* won Gable the Picturegoer Gold Medal for best performance of 1934, and was among *Picturegoer*'s outstanding films of the year.

50. Sigmund Freud, 'Fetishism' (1927), *The Pelican Freud Library, Volume 7: On Sexuality* (Harmondsworth: Penguin, 1977), p. 354.

51. Metz, 'The Imaginary signifier', pp. 71–2.

52. Peter Baxter, 'On the naked thighs of Miss Dietrich', *Wide Angle*, vol. 2, no. 2 (1978), pp. 19–25. The quotation is on p. 25. Baxter quotes from Bosley Crowther's review of *Blue Angel*, reprinted in *The Great Films: Fifty Golden Years of Motion Pictures* (New York: G.P. Putnam's Sons, 1967).

53. For example, Jacqueline Rose, *Sexuality in the Field of Vision* (London: Verso, 1986), Chapters 7 and 8; Laura Mulvey, 'Visual pleasure and narrative cinema', *Screen*, vol. 16, no. 3 (1975), pp. 6–18.

54. 95-34-1, Denis Houlston, Manchester, to Annette Kuhn and Valentina Bold, 8 February 1995.

7

An Invitation to Dance

B ALLROOM dancing closely rivalled cinemagoing in popularity among the 1930s generation; and as far as spending time with friends, and especially courtship, were concerned, the two activities often went hand-in-hand.[1] The popular film press, too, was full of references to dancing, both on and off screen, with reviews of dance records and instructions on dance steps.[2] As noted in Chapter 6, many of those who went to the cinema in the 1930s remember dancing as something that they added to, rather than substituted for, going to the pictures as they grew older and began to take an interest in the opposite sex.

Dancing and cinema meet in the film musical, and indeed during the 1930s musicals were the top attraction at the British box office. The musical is by nature a heterogeneous genre, and this is especially true of those made in the 1930s, when the worldwide popularity of the Hollywood musical coincided with a period of flux and experiment in the genre following the coming of sound at the turn of the decade and the tightening up of Hollywood's system of self-regulation with the introduction of the Hays Code in 1934.

Perhaps the most important locus of variations within the genre is the relationship between song and/or dance numbers and story or plot. At one end of the spectrum lie musicals where the numbers are entirely irrelevant to the plot, while at the other are 'integrated musicals' in which the plot is advanced by the content of musical numbers. By this definition, popular musicals of the early 1930s like, say, the Warner Bros 'backstage' musicals *42nd Street* and *Gold Diggers of 1933* are not fully integrated, because while in these films the existence of musical numbers is by definition relevant to the plot, their actual content is not.

During song-and-dance numbers in the integrated musical, argues John Mueller, 'something happens which changes the character or the situation, and a test of integration in this sense is whether a number can be left out of the musical without leaving a noticeable gap'.[3] This issue is of some significance because it impacts on the relationship between the 1930s cinema audience, their reception of films, and the part cinema played in their daily lives. Perhaps, for example, the more integrated the musical, the greater becomes the potential for the themes or the address of its numbers to engage with audiences' lives, inner as well as outer, beyond the cinema. In these respects, the films of Fred Astaire and Ginger Rogers, all of them integrated musicals, are of considerable cultural significance.

Between 1933 and 1939, Astaire and Rogers made nine films together, and in the USA they were a huge box-office draw over this period, being among the top ten moneymakers between 1935 and 1938. Their films also enjoyed enormous success in Britain, where in 1936 they were rated second biggest moneymakers in UK cinemas, outstripped only by the unassailable Shirley Temple. In that year, *Top Hat*, Astaire and Rogers's fourth film together and their first custom-tailored vehicle, had just had its British release. It was one of the handful of films nominated by *Picturegoer* as 'outstanding' and one of *Film Pictorial's* select few 'outstandingly brilliant' pictures of the year.[4] It seems reasonable to infer that the spectacular success of Astaire and Rogers with British audiences in this single year is attributable largely to *Top Hat*. *Top Hat* is certainly the Astaire/Rogers picture that figures most prominently in popular memory of 1930s cinemagoing. In fact, Astaire and Rogers and their films appear to be far more widely remembered than the bigger box-office attraction of the time, Shirley Temple.

The reception of Astaire/Rogers films in Britain and cinemagoers' memories of them are usefully looked at in the context of the British cinema audience's distinctive tastes and preferences, and also in relation to the broader youth and leisure cultures of the 1930s. Some two-thirds of the 1930s cinemagoers who gave interviews in the present inquiry make more than passing reference to Astaire and Rogers, who are the only stars mentioned so often and, as a team, with such unanimous appreciation. And yet nobody recalls having done any of the things associated with devoted fandom: joining a fan club, writing to the stars, or getting their autographs. The most avid fan of Astaire and Rogers among the interviewees in fact cultivated her admiration for the pair and their films around her own passion for dancing.

Born in Ipswich, Suffolk, in 1921, Eileen Scott enjoyed many films and stars during the 1930s, but remembers Astaire and Rogers with particular affection. As a small girl, she was taken to see Fred and his sister Adele performing live in London. Born into a musical family – her mother had been a cinema pianist – Mrs Scott took dancing lessons as a child. However, her ambition to be a professional dancer was, in her account, thwarted by her father ('we were always being stopped'). But she did go on to become a dance teacher, and pursued her interest by buying sheet music for the songs in most of the Astaire/Rogers films. She recalls with pleasure playing and singing the songs with her mother and her friends. For this informant, memories of Astaire and Rogers are associated with pleasurable recollections of good times with friends, as well as with her partly fulfilled ambition to be a dancer ('All my life I wanted to do *something* connected with dancing').

Mrs Scott is a great admirer of both Fred Astaire and Ginger Rogers, praising his perfectionism and 'natural' star quality and her hard work and dedication: 'I mean she used to dance until her feet were bleeding. Because he was so fussy about getting things absolutely right'. She remembers modelling her own dancing on theirs ('I had one friend and we used to try and pick their steps up and have a go'), and longed to dance with Astaire:

> ES   Oh, when I was young, all I ever wanted. I wanted to have just *one* dance with Fred Astaire. [*Laughs*]
>
> Int   [*Laughs*]
>
> ES   But eh, that was not to be.
>
> Int   A-ah.
>
> ES   But I wasn't up to the standards that…[5]

Mrs Scott considers Rogers a fine actress as well as an accomplished dancer, and remembers modelling her own hairstyle on the actress's pageboy cut. Twice during her first interview she bursts into song, recalling one occasion when at one of her concert parties she made a mistake with the words of the *Top Hat* number 'Isn't This a Lovely Day (To Be Caught in the Rain)'.[6] The Astaire/Rogers films, she concludes, were always uplifting:

ES   I think I used to come out of Fred and Ginger films and almost be dancing [*laughing*] through…

Int   Ah.

ES   The streets, you know. Very uplifting because I'd enjoyed them so much.

Int   Even if you were a bit down. Or not so happy when you went in.

ES   Yes and I came out and I thought, 'Why have you been feeling so down?' You know, you've got to cheer yourself up. [7]

This informant is unusual in the amount and the detail of what she remembers of Astaire and Rogers and their films, and also in the degree to which she interweaves these memories with elements of her own life story. Nonetheless, it is clear from the tenor of others' accounts that Astaire and Rogers and their films endure strongly in popular memory. This may be in part because the films are often revived on television and are available on video. And yet other regular 1930s revivals (like the films of Joan Crawford, or Bette Davis, say) are by no means so often or so affectionately recollected, and informants talk about many films and stars of the time who have not entered the canon, Jeanette MacDonald and Deanna Durbin being prime examples. Astaire and Rogers's canonical status cannot, then, stand as a sufficient explanation for the stars' and their films' peculiarly memorable qualities. What is it about Astaire and Rogers and their films which makes them so enduringly memorable? How do 1930s cinemagoers talk about Astaire and Rogers, and what does their talk reveal about the workings of cinema memory as a type of cultural memory?

Analysis of interviewees' talk about Astaire and Rogers shows that it addresses itself to a certain set of themes or memory contents, and that these are discursively organised in distinctive ways.[8] The themes, first of all, fall into six categories. These are, in descending order of frequency: professionalism; effects; imitation; real people; romance; 'getting by'.

'Professionalism' denotes comments on the performers' skills and talents. This category also includes references to costumes, sets, production values and techniques in the films. Irene and Bernard Letchet, for example, offer an appreciation of Fred Astaire's skills as choreographer and filmmaker:

Int   Cause I mean you mentioned *Top Hat* there a minute ago.

BL   Mm.

Int   The sort of dance sequences in that.

BL   Oh yes!

IL   Yes. They were very, very clever indeed you know.

Int   Yeah.

IL   And he used to have them all done in one take, didn't he?

BL   Yes.

IL   I mean...

Int   It's incredible.

IL   If you look, he's so...

Int   Yeah.

IL   Whereas, nowadays, eh, you see a bit of this and a bit of that and a bit of that.

Int   Yeah.

IL   But, you know, since I read that, if I see a Fred Astaire film, I really look hard and I think, yes, it *is* one take.

Int   Yeah.

IL   You know, there's no sort of break in there. Which is *fantastic* really.[9]

'Effects' talk includes accounts of affective reactions and behavioural responses induced by the films while the informant was inside the cinema. Annie Wright, for example, recollects the experience of watching Astaire and Rogers on the cinema screen. She enthuses about the joy of seeing Astaire dancing, and about how in that moment she would yearn to be able to dance as beautifully as he: '... Fred Astaire. I used to love to watch him dance. Ooh, I thought, I wish I could dance like that, you know'.[10]

'Imitation', on the other hand, is about the kinds of activities outside the cinema referenced in memories of copying styles of dress, makeup, hairstyles, mannerisms and so on from one or other of the performers, and of imitating dance routines and songs. This category includes performances of songs or dances during the interview itself. Demonstrating a few dance steps for the interviewer, Bernard Letchet recalls that after seeing an Astaire/Rogers film, 'On the way home, we used to dance along the pavement'.[11] Residents of Glenwood Lodge in Glasgow also remember how the impulse to dance like Fred and Ginger carried over into the world outside the cinema:

> *Int*   No, I'm saying did you *like*, did you *like* Astaire and Rogers? Were they...?
>
> *SLG* Oh well, they [*unintelligible*], they were *good*.
>
> *PMcC*   There he is.
>
> *NK* A thing we used to do was tap dancing on the back, at the washing house.
>
> *Int*   Really?
>
> *NK* [Of a night?] Oh aye.
>
> [*Unintelligible overtalking*]
>
> *Int*   Was that you trying to be like them, then?
>
> *NK* Och aye. And if ye, I *tell* ye one or two played with an old fiddle.[12]

As noted in Chapter 5, both Astaire and Rogers inspired many imitations. Male and female informants recall modelling their dance techniques on one or other of the performers, and several men have stories of doing dance floor impressions of Astaire. For a great many women, too, Ginger Rogers was an inspiration for ideas on makeup, hairstyles and clothes.

'Real people' denotes comments on the two stars in real life, and includes observations on their careers after the 1930s. Unlike Fred Astaire, however, Ginger Rogers has detractors as well as admirers. Offering some background details of Astaire's career, Olga Scowen voices an opinion shared by a number of informants that Rogers had less 'class' than her partner, and was even rather 'common':

> *Int*   You mentioned Fred Astaire and Ginger Rogers and a flash came into my mind of a scene in *Top Hat*.
>
> *OS* Yes.
>
> *Int*   Where she wears that feather gown that,
>
> *OS* Oh yes. It was just lovely.
>
> *Int*   Mm.

OS She was another one that, em, she always looked rather common I thought. If that sounds a bit, em, superior. But she wouldn't have passed for a lady I would've thought. And eh, course Fred Astaire was really rather superior. He used to dance with his own sister. And she suddenly gave up. Married into the aristocracy here and Fred went over to America and danced with, well Rita Hayworth at first.[13]

Some interviewees talk about what happened to the stars after the 1930s, often – perhaps with a touch of *Schadenfreude* – mentioning how overweight Ginger Rogers became in her later years. Ethel Cullum, for example, says: 'Ginger Rogers is right fat now. She was in a bath chair…'. Cliff Temple mentions having recently seen her on television: 'You wouldn't recognise her, would you?'[14] Rogers died in April 1995, and this piece of news came up in several interviews conducted around that time.[15] Several months later, Hazel Pickess commented:

HP Yes. Yes. At the dancing and all that. And Ginger Rogers. Used to like her, didn't we?

Int Mm.

HP Well she's eighty odd now, isn't she?

Int Mm.

HP Well didn't she die? She did, didn't she?

Int Yes.

HP A month ago.

WP Went right fat, didn't she?

HP She went all bloatery, didn't she?[16]

'Romance' is the theme of references to the elegant, romantic or charming qualities of the Astaire/Rogers films, as well as of memories of the courtships and romances of informants and their friends. Ellen Casey, as noted in Chapter 6, was taken to see *Top Hat* by the film star lookalike she had a crush on.[17] Olga Scowen has a similarly romantic memory of being taken by her fiance to see Astaire/Rogers films in an expensive London cinema:

Oh yes. We used to see a lot of the them, em, Ginger Rogers and Fred Astaire films. In town very much. Because he lived in, em, Muswell Hill which is north London and I was living here. It was easier very often when we were both working in London. We'd very often go to films up there. Bit expensive. I remember once I was *so* excited. He took me to the cinema. We had nine shilling seats! Now for somebody used to ninepennies, this was wonderful. They were little bucket seats, you know. It was in, em, Lower Regent Street or Pall Mall. I'm not sure which. And em, I *really* thought we'd…! He hadn't got any money. I mean he was only a clerical officer in the Civil Service in those days. So, I don't know how he afforded it. But em, that's what we did.[18]

George Turner recollects that although he normally made every effort to avoid the romantic pictures his girlfriends wanted to see, he would make an exception for Fred Astaire:

GT Taking a lady friend and all that. And of course you used to go and see, we used to sort of say together well, em, what would you like to go and see, you know.

Int That's interesting.

GT Yeah. There used to be Fred Astaire. 'Shall we go to the [*inaudible*] tonight?' Because there used to be about five or six cinemas in Ipswich at that time.

Int So was it a different sort of experience then going when you were, as you say, at the junior stage? Em, and when you went with…

GT Well yes. Oh yes. It used to be, my experience for me cause I mean, em, as I said, you used to have a young lady and you more or less wanted to take her to see [*inaudible*]. Perhaps she didn't mind going to see a cowboy, you see. I mean, I suppose it's like that now. You know, I'm not in that stage now. But em, I mean, if she said, shall we go to so and so tonight, oh, I'd like to see that 'cause I'm very fond of perhaps, Deanna Durbin *or* Fred Astaire if they were particularly on. So that's what we used to do.[19]

Memories of 'getting by' involve various kinds of 'making do' in Michel de Certeau's sense of the term.[20] Several informants offer memories of Astaire and Rogers and their films which are in essence stories about making the best of limited resources. Nancy Carrington and Nancy Prudhoe tried to copy Ginger Rogers's makeup with improvised cosmetics:

Int Did you ever try to look like the film stars?

NP Y-e-es! [*Almost cheering*]

NC Copied the styles. Didn't we? I mean there was no makeup. You know, bit of beetroot, you know. [*Laughs*]

NP Ye-es.

NC Beetroot and the blue you'd get out of a [blue bag?]

NP Ginger Rogers. I used to try and, 'cause she was a dancer and I used to go dancing a lot as you know.

NC Yeah.

NP And I used to try an make myself look like Ginger Rogers. Not that I ever looked like her but, you know.

NC Yeah.

NP You'd think you were. [*Whoops with laughter*][21]

The other 'getting by' memories are anecdotes about various escapades in which Astaire/Rogers films figure in some way. Evoking more subversive variants of the tactic of getting by, these may be regarded as historically and culturally situated expressions of the ancient art of 'putting one over on the adversary on his own turf' practised universally by the powerless.[22] Tom Walsh's story, quoted in Chapter 3, about getting in to a cinema to see *Top Hat* without paying, exemplifies this recurrent theme of 1930s cinemagoers' memories.[23]

Helen Smeaton stole an afternoon off work to go to an Astaire/Rogers film, but unlike Tom Walsh did not get away it:

HS I'm trying to think. There was a Ginger Rogers one [pause: 5 seconds], that I, when I was, just not long started working [*pause: 3 seconds*]. In the Odeon. That's the one in Renfrew Street. The great big one. And I'd gone home for my lunch and coming back for my lunch to go into the office, I worked in, em, [Burns Laird?] shipping lines. I met this young fellow I knew and he was a student. And he said 'What are you doing, Helen?' I said 'I'm going back to the office. What are you?' He says [*in a smug voice*], 'I'm going to the pictures to see Ginger Rogers and Fred Astaire'. And I can't remember what it was. One of these singing and dancing. 'Aw' he said, 'Come on'. 'Oh, no I can't, no, no I couldn't. I've got to get back to the office'. He said, 'Oh, look, look who it is. It'll be great'. And I thought 'Aw, right!' So I went to it. And, oh, I really did enjoy it. I remember it was all singing and dancing and romance and it was just my cup of tea. And when I went home, as we were having tea, my mum said [*pause: 3 seconds*], 'Where were you this afternoon, Helen?' Oh, crivvens! [*Laughs*] I said, 'I was at work, mummy'. And she said, 'Now isn't that odd? Your office just phoned to ask what had happend to you.' And that [was] my lesson for [*laughing*] telling lies.

Int   [*Laughs*]

HS   I had then to burst into tears and say, 'I'm sorry, I didn't mean to tell lies but I couldn't resist when Ian asked me to go to the films [*apologetic, upset voice*]. I couldn't resist it'. [*Laughs*][24]

In discursive terms, memories of Astaire and Rogers and their films deploy across the board all of the four registers of memory discourse outlined in Chapter 1: impersonal, past/present, repetitive, and anecdotal.

In impersonal discourse, the narrator characteristically detaches herself or himself from the narration itself and from the content. In Astaire/Rogers memory-stories, this register is not uncommon, and examples include critical, aesthetic or sociological observations such as the Letchets' comments on Fred Astaire's professionalism quoted above. A lawyer in his working life, Glasgow interviewee Norman MacDonald eschews the more personal discursive modes throughout his interviews. Questioned directly about his feelings about Hollywood films, he hesitates for a moment and then couches an admission of enjoying Astaire and Rogers in observations on the performers' professionalism and the films' production values. He then detaches himself further with a sociological comment on the films' context:

Int   You said, though, that you *did* enjoy some of the Hollywood movies. Em, what were your particular tastes in that area?

NM   Well, em, [*pause: 3 seconds*] you see they were very impressive in the sense that, em, even the musicals, you know there were such brilliant displays of, eh, stage management and, eh, and people like Fred Astaire and Ginger Rogers. They were such brilliant performers, they, you couldn't very well come away from these and not like that sort of thing. It was brilliant in the best sense, there was dancing and singing and behaving and highly professional and it was beautifully executed. And, em, it was impressive. You had the stage and they put on a brilliant show but it was, just a brilliant show, it didn't make you think of anything in particular, I mean the performance of a physical nature, you would say that it didn't do anything for you. I rather have the feeling, looking back on the 1930s, with the American film industry thumping out these wonderful, spectacular films that they did do, that, em, the people were living at the same time under the shadow of the cloud of war.[25]

In the past/present register enunciation may shuttle between past and present; or it may remain fully in the present as past and present are subjected to comparison, as for example in the comments quoted above about Ginger Rogers's ageing. The distinction Irene Letchet draws between the smoothness of the single-take sequences in the Astaire films and the short takes and rapid cutting she considers characteristic of filmmaking today ('nowadays you see a bit of this and a bit of that') also exemplifies this discursive mode. Gloria Gooch, whose father was a cinema manager, makes some observations about the production values of the spectacular Hollywood musicals of the studio era, contrasting these with present-day films which, she implies, no longer put the money on the screen:

> Fred Astaire. Gene Kelly. *Broadway Melody*. Those films, they would be in the 1930s. They were really, really excellent. Of course spent an awful lot of money on them. Metro Goldwyn. Spent *thousands* on them. But, you see, there was a boom in the cinema then. So they could afford it. Now they can't afford to spend that much. You don't get so many *spectacular* films, do you?[26]

In repetitive discourse, the speaker implicates herself or himself in activities which are constructed as repeated or habitual. So, for example, in her second interview Hilda Bennett talks about how the cinema audience reacted to the Astaire/Rogers films:

> *Int* I mean what was it about the films of someone like, em, Ginger Rogers, Fred Astaire, that made them so good do you think?
>
> *HB* Well they were good weren't they? But I couldn't tell you anything else about them but, eh, I used, well we all used to sit there and sigh. You know, when we see them come on. Well you'd hear a pin drop. [*Laughs*][27]

In Mrs Bennett's account, the audience's response to the films is more insistent than any memory of the films themselves. She suggests, too, that this response was collective as well as habitual: 'well *we all used to* sit there and sigh'.

An anecdotal account constructs the narrator as protagonist of a story about a particular event or occasion. Tom Walsh's memory of seeing *Top Hat* without paying is a case in point, as too is Helen Smeaton's story about the afternoon she took off work to see an Astaire/Rogers picture. Ellen Casey's richly-detailed account of the occasion she saw *Top Hat*, with its elaborate scene-setting and characterisation, is an exemplary expression of anecdotal discourse:

EC   Anyway when I got to about 15 I seen this lad. Well I think he was 19 at the time. I was about 15. And he resembled Ross Alexander. Aw did I chase him!

Int   [*Laughs*]

EC   Oh I did. Honestly. He was. He had the same jet black hair. Brushed back as they used to have it. And the same sort of, you know wave. And he *did* resemble. Aw [*swooning voice*]. I was mad on him.

Int   [*Laughs*]

EC   I was mad on him because of this Ross Alexander. If you think about it today and em, so he had a good job actually. In them days. He went in the printing. Which was a good job. And he was dressed nice and smart. *Finally* I got for him to take me out. And he took me to a picture house that was down there. And it hadn't been opened all that long. To me, it was what we call *posh*. It was *posh*. Probably Fred's shown you where it was. It was near Cenotaph. Did he take ye down there? The Cenotaph.

Int   Yes I think so. Yes.

EC   Did he call it the Essoldo or what? At first it was the Rivoli when they took it. It was the Rivoli. Down [L?] Road,

Int   That rings a bell.

EC   Yeah.

Int   Yeah.

EC   And it's just near a cenotaph.

Int   Yeah.

EC   Well that's where it was. And, em, he took me there. And it was really posh. I'd never been there before. Couldn't afford it. And he took me in there and luckily [*quiet voice*] it was Janet Gaynor eh no, no, not Janet Gaynor. Eh Fred Astaire, Ginger Rogers musical. And it was that one where they were singing. Oh I still remember the song. Even now. Em 'Cheek to Cheek'.

Int   Oh, *Top Hat*.

EC   Yeah. Em, how did it start, 'Cheek', [*sings*], 'When we're both together dancing cheek to cheek.' And I thought, oh-h-h. Going upstairs on the balcony! Aa was so *thrilled* being with this Ross Alexander![28]

A key feature of the distinctiveness of memory-talk about Astaire and Rogers and their films is its combination of discursive registers and themes. Taken together, the six themes and four modes of discourse could in theory produce 24 variants of memory-talk. This does not happen in practice, however, for certain themes and discourses cluster together. The table shows the distributions of content/discourse combinations across the interviews.

Contents and discourses in memories of Astaire/Rogers and their films

	Professionalism	Effects	Imitation	Real people	Romance	Getting by	TOTAL
Impersonal	8	3	o	4	o	o	15
Past/present	5	o	o	3	1	o	9
Repetitive	5	9	9	o	1	1	25
Anecdotal	o	o	o	o	2	2	4
TOTAL	18	12	9	7	4	3	53

Though few in number, the anecdotal Astaire/Rogers memories are notable for the vividness and concreteness of the detail with which they are recounted. As a modality of memory-discourse, anecdote clearly has special cultural resonance, suggesting an intersection between cinema memory and life-story material which invites further exploration. Here, all four stories are about either courtship or 'getting by', or both. In essence, these are stories about asserting independence, about growing into adulthood and becoming a man or a woman. They share the latter quality, too, with the imitation stories, all of which are narrated in repetitive mode. As noted in Chapter 5, imitation memories are centrally about explorations of masculinity, femininity, or sexuality. Here, perhaps, we may find a key to the distinctiveness of Astaire/Rogers memories in the testimonies of cinemagoers of the 1930s, and the privileged place of these figures in cinema memory and cultural memory.

It is significant in this regard that the plots of all the Astaire/Rogers films share a single underlying structure, in which, as J.P. Telotte observes, 'forces of confinement, conformity and limitation... initially hold sway and are juxtaposed to the potential energies of the individual'.[29] Telotte rightly links the forces of confinement with the 'stifling influence' of the 1930s Depression; but it is worth reminding ourselves that creation of freedom and creativity within constrained time and space is the very essence of 'making do'.[30] It is also, as noted in Chapter 3, at the root of the child's and the adolescent's struggle towards independence from parental and other forms of adult authority. The song and dance numbers in the Astaire/Rogers films function as 'attractions' which, in the spirit of the integrated musical, are part of, and interact with, this narrative formula, while also highlighting the courtship ritual element of the films' plots.

The fact that these numbers exist as extensions of the thoughts and feelings of the characters, rather than as grandiose spectacles à la Busby Berkeley, is also significant. Rick Altman describes the Astaire/Rogers films as 'fairy tale' musicals as distinct from 'show' (backstage) musicals. The fairy tale musical, he says, derives its appeal from 'a more or less overt display of sexual desire [and] demonstrates, from its earliest presence on film, the extent to which it is driven by the spectator's need for quasi-sexual satisfaction'.[31] Conforming, as they necessarily do, with the strictures of Hollywood's self-censorship, the Astaire/Rogers musicals are quintessentially 'post-Code', in that sexual energy, which can no longer be explicitly acknowledged, is displaced onto a related concern, courtship, which must 'simultaneously stand for, cover over and lead to the sexual source of its energy'.[32] The dance routines in the Astaire/Rogers films have indeed been described as 'rituals of courtship and lovemaking',[33] suggesting that courtship ritual and 'integrated' dance routines operate in tandem at the levels of both narrative and spectacle. In this way, and on a number of levels, the films speak of, and speak to, adolescent impulses towards independence, and adolescent explorations of love, romance and sex.

But integration in musicals is not just about the manner in which numbers are woven into the flow of the narrative. It also figures in the organisation of the films' various spaces, and above all in the relationship between story space and song and dance space. Telotte notes that the backstage musical proposes a dichotomy between the 'stage' and the 'real' world at both these levels. Thus the 'I'm Young and Healthy' number in *42nd Street*, referred to in Chapter 6, is performed in the theatre which is the setting for the show which in turn constitutes the culmination of the story. In this sense, within the terms of the classical realist narrative, the setting offers verisimilitude: the proper place for a song and dance routine is a theatre. Astaire/Rogers films, on the other hand, propose that any venue is suitable for dance, thus 'fashioning an essentially realistic world but making it manifestly open to those coloring musical impulses'.[34] However, while it is true to say that the relationship between narrative space and song and dance space is highly distinctive in Astaire/Rogers films, the suggestion that the latter might be 'realistic' calls for some qualification.

The notion that the characteristic organisation of spaces in the integrated musical proposes particular modes of spectatorial engagement is endorsed by 1930s cinemagoers' recollections of their own responses to Astaire/Rogers films during the act of spectatorship. This group of memories ('effects') is of interest for what it reveals about the distinctiveness of cinema memory as a form of cultural memory, and about the figuration and the productivity of the cinematic in certain sorts of memory-talk. Informants' talk about 'effects' is narrated predominantly in repetitive mode; and it is in the effects-repetitive configuration especially that a connection between cinema memory and the act of spectatorship is proposed in the remembered interaction between narrators/spectators and film spaces. These points of interconnection, and the questions around narrative space and song and dance space in the Astaire/Rogers films, are illuminated by looking at some instances of 'effects-repetitive' memory-talk, and reading these in conjunction with the film *Top Hat*.

Nine instances of 'effects-repetitive' memory-talk emerge from interviews with 1930s cinemagoers. In her first interview, Eileen Scott says she felt uplifted when watching Astaire/Rogers films and 'wanted to have just *one* dance with Fred'; while in her second interview, she adds that if she entered the cinema feeling depressed, she would always come out feeling cheered after seeing Astaire and Rogers.[35] George Turner recollects that watching Ginger Rogers on screen 'used to make you feel great'.[36] Hilda Bennett talks of audiences' remarkable attentiveness during Astaire/Rogers films ('you'd hear a pin drop') and of her own sighs of longing. Annie Wright says that watching the films made her want to dance like Fred. Bernard Letchet tells the interviewer: 'You entered right into the film… You *really* got into it'.[37] All of these remembered responses evoke particular spectatorial engagements with the films: they focus on the speaker's own emotional responses; on the audience's collective response; or on ways in which the films 'hailed' or interpellated the spectator, inviting him or her to enter the space of the film.

'Effects-repetitive' talk marks interviewee Jimmy Murray's entire testimony. Mr Murray was born in 1920 in Bury, Greater Manchester, and aside from seven years in Austria, where he met hs wife, lived there all his life. The son of a railway fireman, he left school at 14 and spent most of his working life as an employee in a dye works. In two interviews conducted in his home, Mr Murray offered vivid memories of local cinemas and of enjoying many and varied films and stars.[38] His lively and engaging recollections of his cinemagoing in the 1930s include memories of the experience of watching Astaire and Rogers on the cinema screen. Indeed, so enthusiastic is he on the subject that at one point he mishears the interviewer's question about *gangster* films as a reference to *dancing* films: an invitation to a symptomatic reading if ever there was one.

Int   What do you think it was about the gangster films that appealed?

JM   Well, *everybody* thought eh. After you'd seen Astaires and that, everybody thought they could *do* this. You went to the palais, and you thought you could do this three point turn or something [*laughs*], whatever.

Int   [*Laughs*]

JM   And eh, ooh yeah. After you'd seen it, you'd go there and think, ooh ah. Be a bit a Fred like kinda thing. You *couldn't* but you felt like getting on the dance floor. That's how you associated yourself with, eh, Fred and Ginger kinda thing.

Int   Yeah.

JM   You know. They made it look that easy. You felt you could do this type of thing, you know. Ah.

Int   So when you saw the *gangsters* did you come out, eh… [*amused voice*]

JM   *Yeah*! You'd, eh, as I say you'd go to t'palais after and, eh, later on in t'week, you'd think, do a bit a Fred here kinda thing.

Int   [*Laughs*]

JM   Never fell over but still. You still did it bad as to what Fred and Ginger did! [*Amused voice*] Or else it was your partner! [*Bursts out laughing*]

Int   We can blame them anyway. [*Laughs*]

JM   Or two left feet.

Mr Murray is talking about how responses inside the cinema carried over into behaviour outside the cinema. His memory is of a kind of bodily involvement in this act of spectatorship, a somatic identification, perhaps ('That's how you associated yourself with eh, Fred and Ginger kinda thing'), which is then taken out of the cinema and onto the dance floor. This move seems to be of a piece with the elision of different kinds of fictional space within the films themselves:

> They'd be sit in a cafe, at a little table, the next minute there'd be a *big stage* there, with flowers all round. They'd be *dancing* away there! Half as big as Bury. The thing. But eh [*laughs*]. Yeah. Ah, big *massive* stage. Where, as I say, there'd be a little fiddling thing for, eh, somebody here, to be dancing on [*amused voice*].

The allusion here is to the opening out of filmic space within a scene (the example of 'a little cafe') into something altogether different ('the next minute there'd be a big stage there'), usually attending a transition between the story and a musical number. This involves a shift from one sort of filmic space, a 'realistic' if fictive one, to a wholly other space, a space of fantasy, a particular kind of heterotopia, 'a space capable of juxtaposing in a single real place several possible incompatible sites as well as times, a site whose system of opening and closing both isolates it and makes it penetrable, as it forms a type of elsewhere/nowhere'.[39] Mr Murray's account conveys at once the wonder of such a magical transformation – the willing suspension of one's disbelief that within the space of the film a cafe could suddenly open up into a space 'half as big as Bury' – and at the same time a selfconscious detachment from the illusion, as he laughs at the unlikeliness of it all:

> It were *marvellous* where they came from like. You know, it'd happen in a little cinema it's supposed to be, next thing it'd be a *big* stage with a thousand musicians behind or something like that. Fred Astaire dancing somewhere. Like a little cafe. Fred's finished, he'd be on a big stage [*laughs*].

The reference to 'a little cinema' may be read either as an allusion to the virtual space of the film (a cinema portrayed on the cinema screen) or as a reference to the 'real' space of the cinema auditorium, in a discourse which elides the 'real' world of the film's plot (as opposed to the other world which opens up beyond this for some of the musical numbers) and the actual space inhabited by the audience in the cinema. This enunciative juxtaposition and conflation of fantasy space with familiar topography ('half as big as Bury'), effectively grounds the fantasy in the mundane. Hence the laughter which, in a characteristic act of disavowal, acknowledges the speaker's simultaneous immersion in and consciousness of the fantasy.[40]

Alongside recollections of the fantasy space of the film is an enunciative conflation of two everyday spaces, the local cinema and the dance hall:

> Oh! They were eh, oh. Well [*pause: 2 seconds*] as I say we had the Bury Palais. It was a cinema but a palais. Well, after you'd watched Fred Astaire and Ginger, you wanted to go to't palais and you thought you could do eh, you could *twirl* about. You couldn't. [*Laughs*]

Both cinema and *palais de danse* are spaces for invitations to dance, the one in the imagination, the other in the world of the everyday; with the latter acknowledged and accepted as in the end a disappointment in relation to the former ('you thought you could do it, eh, you could *twirl* about. You couldn't'). Like 'half as big as Bury', the affectionately self-mocking detachment that acknowledges and speaks engagement conveys the experience of coming down from the fantasy of being an accomplished dancer. Many informants use words to the effect that Astaire made it look so easy, a turn of phrase which captures the wish – and its impossibility – so well.

If the moments in Astaire/Rogers films to which Mr Murray alludes are looked at closely, it transpires that his account offers a good description of the cinematic operations through which the films hail the spectator and invite her or him into their heterotopias. Embodying as it does a peculiarly cinematic way of remembering cinemagoing, Jimmy Murray's testimony produces cinema memory in its purest form.

According to the cultural critic Rene Cutforth, 'There was a time, during the middle thirties, when practically everyone in Britain seemed to be whistling "Cheek to Cheek"'.[41] Indeed when informants remember Astaire/Rogers films, it is always *Top Hat* that is mentioned, and when a song from *Top Hat* is mentioned it is more often than not 'Cheek to Cheek'. The words and tune of this song are so firmly imprinted on informants' memories that some of them even sing a few bars from it during their interviews. The nugatory plot of *Top Hat* centres on an American dancer, Jerry Travers (Astaire), who is in London with his producer preparing for a new show. Jerry falls for fellow American Dale Tremont (Rogers); but Dale mistakenly believes Jerry to be married to her best friend Madge (Helen Broderick), and consequently rebuffs his advances. In the end, of course, love finds a way.[42]

There are good reasons why *Top Hat* and 'Cheek to Cheek' are so memorable. Rick Altman categorises the film as a post-Code fairy tale musical, post-Code in that its romantic story takes the spectator on a 'journey into the forbidden, a detour around the obstacles of censorship'.[43] The mistaken identity plot puts the spectator in a position of superior knowledge *vis-à-vis* the characters in the fiction, and the 'Cheek to Cheek' number marks an important shift in the relationship between the two main characters. It is the moment when the Rogers character, Dale, becomes complicit in what she believes is (but which we, the audience, know is not) a taboo relationship. This is acknowledged firstly and explicitly at the level of story action and dialogue, when Dale decides to stop worrying that she is, as she imagines, dancing with another woman's husband; and secondly when the song duet segues into a *pas-de-deux*, a displaced representation of courtship and the sexual act.

The introductory passage establishes the space of a crowded ballroom in which a conversation between Jerry, Dale and Madge takes place. Dale still believes Jerry – who is pursuing her – is Madge's husband. On Madge's insistence Jerry and Dale get up to dance together. This scene unfolds in some 17 shots, beginning with an establishing shot which shows the entire space of a ballroom crowded with couples dancing, and a crane in to Dale and Madge seated together at a table. The next part of the scene comprises an exchange between the characters in which the prevailing medium two- and three-shots are intercut with reaction closeups of Dale looking shocked. Dale and Jerry get up to dance and their conversation continues, with several cuts from them to an encouraging Madge. The end of the introductory passage is marked by Dale's decision to stop worrying about, as she thinks, dancing with another woman's husband: 'If Madge doesn't care, I certainly don't' – and the cue for a song.

The song and dance number which then follows is in two parts:

I. The song sequence. The transition from the introductory passage to the number is achieved not by a cut (there is none) but by the bridging of the music, the movement of the main characters within the frame, and the beginning of the song. This section is done in a single long take, with shot scale constant at medium two-shot. This single take both effects the shift from conversation to number and also includes the performance of the entire song. Throughout the long take, the couple are half dancing and in general moving screen right with camera following. They are surrounded at first by other dancing couples, but at a certain point in the song the others are

left behind as Dale, Jerry and the camera move into empty space. The song, along with the rightward camera movement and unvarying shot scale, continues until Jerry stops singing and there is a cut on the rightward movement which takes us into

II. The dance sequence. In extreme long shot, the dancers enter a huge empty stage furnished with stairs, pillars, balconies and statues, a space which bears only passing resemblance to the 'real' ballroom of the film's story. This sequence comprises five shots:

i. The dance begins, in ELS, with camera following the dancers:

ii. CUT on the same angle to a closer shot of the dancers as they continue into a tap dance passage, with camera continuing to follow them and with framing more or less constant:

iii. CUT on a leftward movement to very brief wider shot (as at end of shot i):

iv. CUT to medium shot, as in shot ii, as the dance continues and then as the dancers move towards and away from a low wall at rear of set:

v. CUT at slightly different angle to longer shot for the acrobatic climax of the dance; then dancers slow down and come to a stop at rear wall as in shot iv. FADE.

Rick Altman contends that this number derives its intensity from the sense that 'dance and song alike represent the miraculous moment when the search for pleasure has won out over the more conventional respect for morals'.[44] *Top Hat*'s organisation of narrative point of view, and in particular the detachment proposed by the spectator's privileged position, ensures that the spectator's 'need for quasi-sexual satisfaction' is satisfied, while at the same time the demands of Hollywood's self-censorship are met. It might be added that displacement of the culmination of sexual desire onto the dance (as opposed to the song) adds, to the pleasure made possible by this complex enunciation, an embodied and kinetic relation to spectatorship – precisely, that is, a sensation of being set into bodily motion. The 'romance' of 'Cheek to Cheek', then, derives from the film's articulation of narrative space with song and dance space, and a specific embodied engagement with both.

It should be noted first of all that the dance sequence is not (Irene Letchet's recollection notwithstanding) a single shot. John Mueller, who has done detailed breakdowns of all the Astaire/Rogers films, notes that the idea that the dance sequences are single shots is widespread. He demonstrates that this is rarely the case, though the sequences were deliberately constructed so as to appear seamless.[45] This aspect of popular memory of Astaire/Rogers films is symptomatic, however, in that it betokens a desire for seamlessness, wholeness; a wish that is of a piece, perhaps, with the spatial elisions in Astaire/Rogers films noted by Jimmy Murray.

Secondly, the space of the narrative, the diegetic 'real' (the crowded ballroom), gives way to the space of fantasy, to heterotopia (the empty stage) in exactly the manner Jimmy Murray remembers. Interestingly, in this case the transition begins not between shots but within a single shot (the first part of the song and dance number), and with a double kinesis (movement of characters within a mobile frame): the dancers move in step with one another and the camera moves in step with the dancers, as all three escape the other dancing couples. The transition is completed and confirmed, and a triple kinesis effected, in the next cut, the one that links and separates song sequence and dance sequence.

In this elegant and apparently seamless combination of kinesis and heterotopia lies the ultimate dance fantasy: the everyday, the local, the rooted, the communal – for the adolescent of the 1930s, the crowds in the dance hall – all fade from consciousness as, along with the dancers on the screen, you are carried into the space of imagination, that other space where you are utterly graceful and where the dance of courtship proceeds, with never a false step, towards its climax. The sensation imbues your body, and carries you out of your local picture house onto the familiar streets of your neighbourhood, and you are moved to dance along the pavement all the way home.

If space is a key organising feature of cinema memory, what these instances of remembering Fred and Ginger tell us is that their films perfectly present cinema's heterotopia; and that cinema at its most pleasurable can combine the kinetics of the moving image with the kinesis of the moving body in an all-encompassing, embodied cinema memory.

Notes

1. For contemporary research, see C. Cameron, et al, *Disinherited Youth: a Survey, 1936–1939* (Fife: Carnegie United Kingdom Trust, 1943); T.M. Middleton, 'An Enquiry into the Use of Leisure amongst the Working Classes of Liverpool' (MA, University of Liverpool, 1931). For popular memory, see Chapter 6; and Annette Kuhn, 'Cinemagoing in Britain in the 1930s: report of a questionnaire survey', *Historical Journal of Film, Radio and Television*, vol. 19, no. 4 (1999), pp. 531–543.

2. *Picturegoer* published a regular column on ballroom dancing, and in February 1930 ran a feature on dance in films. Fred Astaire gave advice to dancers over three issues in 1936: 'Advice to dancers', *Picturegoer*, 21 March 1936; 'Learn to dance by doing it', *Picturegoer*, 28 March 1936; 'Choose an individual style', *Picturegoer*, 4 April 1936. In the mid-1930s, the monthly *Film Fashionland* ran a regular column of dancing tips by George Raft. In 1935, *Film Weekly* published an interview with Buddy Bradley, 'the coloured genius with rhythmic legs', who was dance director on a number of British musicals: *Film Weekly*, 4 April 1935.

3. John Mueller, 'Fred Astaire and the integrated musical', *Cinema Journal*, vol. 24, no. 1 (1984), pp. 28–40; the quotation is from p. 30.

4. *Picturegoer*, 8 February 1936; *Film Pictorial*, 8 February 1936.

5. This and the foregoing quotations are from T95-111, Eileen Scott, Suffolk, 16 October 1995.

6. T95-112, Eileen Scott, Suffolk, 16 October 1995.

7. T95-132, Eileen Scott, Suffolk, 9 November 1995.

8. For this analysis, transcripts from 21 interview sets were looked at, these accounting for upwards of 30 informants. Taken together, they represent an even spread of responses across the four interview fieldwork locales: Glasgow (five transcripts), Harrow (five transcripts), Manchester (five transcripts) and East Anglia (six transcripts). Ten of the transcripts are of interviews with women, either alone or in pairs or groups; six are with men (all interviewed individually); and five are with married couples or mixed pairs or groups.

9. T95-149, Irene and Bernard Letchet, Harrow, 23 November 1995.

10. T95-32, Annie Wright, Manchester, 26 May 1995.

11. T95-97, Irene and Bernard Letchet, Harrow, 25 July 1995.

12. T95-4, Patrick McCambridge, Tommy Dunn, Tommy Adams, Sarah Louise Gale and Nancy Keyte, Glasgow, 24 January 1995.

13. T95-81, Olga Scowen, Harrow, 6 July 1995.

14. T95-123, Ethel Cullum, Norfolk, 25 November 1995; T95-146, Cliff Richard Temple, Norfolk, 20 November 1995; T95-117.

15. These include T95-48, Douglas Rendell, Manchester, 8 June 1995; T95-19, A.D. Houlston, Manchester, 26 April 1995; T95-27, Dorris Braithwaite, Vee Entwistle and Kath Browne, Bolton, 11 May 1995.

16. William and Hazel Pickess, Suffolk, 20 October 1995.

17. T95-37, Ellen Casey, Manchester, 31 May 1995.

18. T95-81, Olga Scowen, Harrow, 6 July 1995.

19. T95-133, George Turner, Suffolk, 10 November 1995.

20. Michel de Certeau, *The Practice of Everyday Life*, trans. Steven Rendall (Berkeley: University of California Press, 1984), Chapters 2 and 3.

21. T95-101, Nancy Carrington, Nancy Prudhoe and Elsie Horne, Harrow, 25 July 1995.

22. De Certeau, *The Practice of Everyday Life*, p. 40.

23. T94-8, Tom Walsh, Glasgow, 25 November 1994.

24. T95-2, Helen Smeaton, Glasgow, 23 January 1995.

25. T94-1, Norman MacDonald, Glasgow, 17 November 1994.

26. T95-141, Gloria Gooch, Norfolk, 16 November 1995.

27. T95-145, Hilda Bennett, Norfolk, 21 November 1995.

28. T95-37, Ellen Casey, Manchester, 31 May 1995.

29. J.P. Telotte, 'Dancing the depression: narrative strategy in the Astaire-Rogers films', *Journal of Popular Film and Television*, vol. 8, no. 3 (1980), pp. 15–24; the quotation is from p. 16.

30. De Certeau, *The Practice of Everyday Life*, p. 25.

31. Rick Altman, *The American Film Musical* (Bloomington, IN: Indiana University Press, 1984), p. 140.

32. Ibid., p. 159.

33. Jerome Delamater, *Dance in the Hollywood Musical* (Ann Arbor, MI: UMI Research Press, 1978), p. 53.

34. Telotte, 'Dancing the depression', p. 18.

35. T95-111, Eileen Scott, Suffolk, 16 October 1995; T95-132, Eileen Scott, Suffolk, 9 November 1995.

36. T95-133, George Turner, Suffolk, 10 November 1995.

37. T95-97, Irene and Bernard Letchet, Harrow, 21 July 1995.

38. The quotations which follow are from interviews with Mr Murray conducted on 9 May 1995 (T95-62) and 15 June 1995 (T95-56). Sadly, Mr Murray died in December 1995.

39. Giuliana Bruno, *Streetwalking on a Ruined Map: Cultural Theory and the City Films of Elvira Notari* (Princeton, NJ: Princeton University Press, 1993), p. 57; Michel Foucault, 'Other spaces: the principles of heterotopia', *Lotus*, vol. 48–49 (1986), pp. 9–17. On the motif of expansion in the musical, see Richard Dyer, 'The space of happiness in the musical', *Aura*, vol. 4, no. 1 (1998), pp. 31–45.

40. The reference here is to the belief structure characteristic of fetishism, discussed in Chapter 6.

41. Rene Cutforth, *Later Than We Thought: A Portrait of the Thirties* (Newton Abbot: David and Charles, 1976), p. 81.

42. For an analysis of the film's plot, see Edward Gallafent, *Astaire and Rogers* (Dumfriesshire: Cameron and Hollis, 2000), pp. 33–43.

43. Altman, *The American Film Musical*, p. 171.

44. Ibid., p. 173; see pp. 173–5 for a musical analysis of this number. See also Jim Collins, 'Toward defining a matrix of the musical comedy: the place of the spectator within the textual mechanisms', in *Genre; the Musical*, (ed.) Rick Altman (London: Routledge and Kegan Paul, 1981), pp. 134–146.

45. John Mueller, 'The filmed dances of Fred Astaire', *Quarterly Review of Film Studies*, vol. 6, no. 2 (1981), pp. 135–154; also see Mueller, 'Fred Astaire and the integrated musical'.

8

All My Life, and Beyond...

FANDOM, says John Fiske

> selects from the repertoire of mass-produced and mass-distributed
> entertainment certain performers, narratives or genres and takes
> them into the culture of a self-selected fraction of the people. They
> are then reworked into an intensely pleasurable, intensely
> signifying popular culture that is both similar to, yet significantly
> different from, the culture of more 'normal' popular audiences.[1]

Although the 1930s generation were keen cinemagoers and most had
their favourites among the film stars of the day, only a small minority
devoted themselves exclusively to one star, or joined a fan club or took
part in any of the other activities associated with fandom. While some
cinemagoers recall having been active followers of 'the pictures' in a
general way – reading film magazines, keeping scrapbooks, making lists
of films seen and so on – most now look on activities of this kind as
very much a thing of the distant past, with allusions to them in the present
being in the service of current relationships and activities. As, for
example, in the case of the sisters Margaret Young and Molly Stevenson,
whose memories of their youthful picturegoing, diary keeping and
magazine reading are, as noted in Chapter 3, largely directed at sustaining
their ongoing relationship in the present.

Among those who took part in the present inquiry, only one
interviewee and four of those who completed questionnaires say they

have ever been members of star fan clubs: the stars concerned are Deanna Durbin, Nelson Eddy, Jeanette MacDonald and Patricia Roc (a British star of the 1940s).[2] Fan clubs for Durbin, Eddy and MacDonald still remain active, and some of these informants are still involved in fan activities. But although such enduring fans of film stars of the 1930s form but a tiny fraction of their generation, the very intensity of their engagements with their chosen stars and films means that their testimonies yield illuminating insights into the interrelations between cultural memory, cinema memory and films. Enduring fans' distinctive memory-talk enacts distinctive thematic concerns and discursive modes, and these indicate that for this type of 1930s cinemagoer the picturegoing past is no foreign country but is ongoingly produced as a vital part of daily life in the present. While all forms of fandom are, in Fiske's words, 'semiotically productive', enduring fandom embodies distinctive modes of remembering and adds something of its own to the repertoire of fan productivity.

Among the most devoted enduring fans of 1930s stars are those of the singing stars Jeanette MacDonald and Nelson Eddy. MacDonald, whose film career was well established by the early 1930s, made her name in the Lubitsch romantic comedies discussed by Denis Houlston in Chapter 6. Eddy entered films in the mid 1930s, and between 1935 and 1942 appeared in five pictures. In those seven years, the two performers also starred together in eight operetta-style films, including *Naughty Marietta* (1935), *Rose Marie* (1936) and *Maytime* (1937). During the 1930s, films featuring MacDonald and/or Eddy were major box-office attractions in Britain: one or both performers was ranked among the *Motion Picture Herald*'s top ten moneymakers on British screens in every year between 1937 and 1942, and the stars themselves attracted a considerable fan following.

Though hugely successful in their day, the films of Jeanette MacDonald and Nelson Eddy, unlike those of Astaire and Rogers, have largely been consigned to critical and historical oblivion. Edward Baron Turk offers several explanations for this, ranging from the social-historical to the psychoanalytic.[3] What is not explained, though, is the fact that despite this, and notwithstanding the fact that the stars stopped making films in the late 1940s and died in the 1960s, fan clubs for MacDonald and Eddy – such as the Mac-Eddy Friendship Club and the Nelson Eddy Appreciation Society – still remain active today.

Members of the Mac-Eddy club who took part in the questionnaire survey also wrote letters expressing admiration for their favourite stars.

Mrs E. Martin, for example, thinks 'Nelson Eddy had a wonderful voice and was so tall and handsome'. She did not join a fan club in the 1930s, 'because in my family it was considered "not nice"', but joined the Mac-Eddy club later in life. Mrs D.M. Cummings, who 'saw all of their films that came over here' and loved their 'beautiful voices and electrifying chemistry on screen', also joined the fan club after the 1930s: 'We receive beautiful magazines and hold a weekend at Blackpool every year'. Joan Bice was so 'enamoured' of the pair that she 'wrote them enthusiastic letters – always receiving replies – and sat watching their films twice over (each time)'. She joined the fan club in the 1930s and is still a member: 'It is wonderful to know that, even though so many years have elapsed since Jeanette and Nelson passed away, there are so many admirers who still remember them with love'.[4]

The only member of a fan club among the interviewees belongs to the Nelson Eddy Appreciation Society, and an examination of this informant's interviews in conjunction with an analysis of one of MacDonald and Eddy's biggest hits, *Maytime*, suggests some culturally significant interconnections between expressions of memory in the form and content of films on the one hand and in the distinctive productions of memory of enduring fans on the other.[5] Even on its first release in 1937, *Maytime*, an MGM musical based upon an operetta first staged in 1917, was already a palimpsest of memory.[6] The film's narrative present harks back to the early years of the twentieth century; and the story is structured around the reminiscences of the central female character, and these in turn memorialise events some fifty years before that.

The plot of *Maytime* is wistfully romantic, with a hint of the 'too late' trope which characterises the melodramatic. The film opens in a small New England town at the turn of the twentieth century. A Spring festival is under way, and two elderly women are overheard in conversation: 'I was Queen of the May once', recalls one. Witnessing a tiff between young lovers, the other woman is moved to look back to her own youth and to the night of her glittering debut as a singer 'many, many years ago' in Paris, at the court of Louis Napoleon. When, dizzy with success and too restless to sleep, the young Marcia Mornay (MacDonald) ventures out into the night for a drive, she meets fellow American Paul Allison (Eddy), a talented but unambitious baritone. They strike up a brief acquaintance, which culminates in a perfect, and perfectly innocent, day at a May fair. In a duet ('Will You Remember?'), they declare their mutual love, but are immediately separated for seven

JEANETTE NELSON

MacDonald Eddy

in

MAYTIME

with JOHN BARRYMORE

Springtime—Lovetime—Maytime—and the most thrilling singing sweethearts the screen has ever known to bring you carefree rapture and romantic ecstasy...The tender romance of two souls that become one as their voices blend in love-swept song—golden melodies from the gifted pen of Sigmund Romberg...Following in the triumphant path of "Naughty Marietta" and "Rose Marie", Metro-Goldwyn-Mayer brings you another unforgettable picture with the same great stars, Jeanette MacDonald and Nelson Eddy, plus a brilliant cast including John Barrymore and Herman Bing. Directed and produced by the entertainment masters who thrilled you with "The Great Ziegfeld."

A METRO-GOLDWYN-MAYER PICTURE ★ *Produced by* HUNT STROMBERG ★ *Directed by* ROBERT Z. LEONARD

Maytime publicity

years, during which time Marcia enters a loveless marriage with her impresario, Nikolai, and scales the heights of operatic fame. Marcia and Paul meet again when cast in the leading roles in an opera in New York. Marcia at last resolves to elope with Paul, but it is too late: the jealous

Nikolai shoots Paul. Dying, he tells Marcia that their day together in Paris '*did* last me all my life'. As the aged Marcia concludes her story ('I found Paul too late'), the spectral figure of Paul appears before her, and Marcia's young self steps out of her dying body. United in death, the couple walk arm-in-arm into the distance, flanked by cherry trees in bloom.

Dorris Braithwaite is an avid enduring fan of Nelson Eddy:

> I am 73 yrs of age and have been a film fan all my life until the last ten years or so. The Cinema in my young days was a source of joy. We lost ourselves in the thrilling stories we watched on the screen. I loved the musicals and remember so well seeing "Naughty Marietta", a new kind of musical and introducing Nelson Eddy who became the well-loved singer and super star of that era. He and Jeanette MacDonald created a magic never before seen or since. They became known as "The Singing Sweethearts" and a fan club for each of them still flourishes today. I know because I belong to the Nelson Eddy Appreciation Society. I fell in love with him at the age of thirteen when I saw him in his first starring role. I wrote to him and have many letters and Xmas [sic] cards from him, plus autographed photos and five albums. I bought every record he made and now through writing to friends in America have a number of his radio shows on cassette.[7]

In her letter, Mrs Braithwaite offers an account not only of her youthful enjoyment of the pictures in general (phrases like 'we lost ourselves' are frequently used by informants) but also more unusually – and certainly more significantly for the informant herself – of her lasting devotion to one film star in particular. She records a lifetime's devotion to the baritone Nelson Eddy, from the day she first 'fell in love with him' to her current involvement with a fan club and her contacts with fellow fans overseas.

It appears to be characteristic of written memory accounts by enduring fans not only that the defining moment of 'falling in love' with the star is vividly recalled, but also that this moment is accorded motivating status in a narrative of lifelong devotion. Informants in Jackie Stacey's study of female filmgoers of the 1950s include a number of enduring fans of the juvenile singing star Deanna Durbin. Writing of the occasion when she first saw Durbin on the screen, one fan recalls:

In 1940 at the age of twelve, I was evacuated from my home in South London to Looe in Cornwall, and it was there that I was taken to the pictures for a special treat. There at last I saw her. The film, a sequel to her first, was *Three Smart Girls Grow Up*. The affect [*sic*] she had upon me can only be described as electrifying. I had never felt such a surge of admiration and adoration before. [...] My feeling for her was no passing fancy. The love was to last a lifetime.[8]

Another key feature of this form of fandom is that devotion to its object is sustained through relationships in the present. So, for example, Mrs Braithwaite establishes her credentials as a potential informant by mentioning her membership of a still-flourishing fan club, an organisation which provides plentiful opportunities for networking both at home and abroad. Closer to home, she is part of a creative writing group in Bolton, Lancashire, and it was through this connection that she became involved in the cinema culture project together with her friends and fellow writing group members Vee Entwistle and Kath Browne. All three women have lived most or all of their lives in Bolton.[9]

A native of Bolton, Kath Browne was born in 1921, the daughter of a regular soldier and one of two children. She left school at 16 and went to work in an office. Vee Entwistle was born in Bolton in 1926. The daughter of a miner and one of five children, she left school at 14 and worked in a variety of jobs, including weaving and chocolate manufacture. Mrs Entwistle names MacDonald and Eddy among her favourite stars, because of 'their superb singing voices'.[10] Dorris Braithwaite was born in Stockport in 1922; her father was an engineer and she is one of two children. The family moved to Bolton when Dorris was ten, and she left school at 14 and took jobs in a photographer's shop, as a machinist and as a typist. During the 1930s she collected autographs and photographs of her favourite stars, and later joined the Nelson Eddy Appreciation Society. The three women were interviewed together, and this was followed a few weeks later by a second interview, in which only Mrs Braithwaite and Vee Entwistle took part and in the course of which the informants and the interviewer watched *Maytime*.[11]

The first interview opens with informants' accounts of their early filmgoing, then moves quickly into recollections focused more specifically on Nelson Eddy and his films. In the latter, the informants shuttle freely between past and present, reliving their feelings as young women ('They were romantic'; 'Oh, I'm gone!'; 'It was sheer beauty') as they talk about the occasions in the present when they deliberately stage a re-entry into the past by viewing Eddy's films on videotape. A detailed résumé of the plot of *Maytime* gives way to more general fan talk about Nelson Eddy, and a disagreement between Dorris Braithwaite and Kath Browne about Eddy's acting skills:

Int   I've never seen *Maytime*, actually.

DB   Oh you must come!

VE   You'll have to come.

DB   Next time you come I'll put it on for you. You must! I've got every film.

Int   What's the storyline? Don't spoil the ending for me then. What happens in these films?

DB   Well, she's an opera singer. And this chap, who's John Barrymore, is her teacher.

VE   Teacher.

DB   And he's given all his pupils up just to, you know, see that she can get to the top. And she eventually gets to sing with the, what would you call him, Louis of eh? No, Napoleon, wasn't it? Of, not Napoleon. The song. Napoleon Joseph or something like that. What was his name? It wasn't Napoleon and Josephine. It was the other one. Louis Napoleon.

KB   Yes.

DB   Louis Napoleon. And she gets to sing with him and that's the highlight, you know. And he asks her to marry him. And she's so excited. She accepts. She doesn't love him and he knows that. But she's so grateful that he's got her to where she wanted. And she's so excited, she can't sleep. So she decides she'll get a carriage to take her just riding round the park.

And the horse breaks loose. And she's left while the feller goes running after the horse. And from a little cafe you can hear this voice singing. There was like a party going on. Of course it's him, you see, singing. And he sings *The Fat Prima Donna*, doesn't he? [*Laughs*] And of course, she's the Prima Donna, you see. So she goes in, listening. And, he gets carried to where she's sat. Starts a conversation. And, then there's a raid by the police. And he runs.

He makes her promise that, she'll have lunch with him the following day. And he shows her where he lives. And said, you must come.

So, she turns up. And then, he goes to see her in the opera. Of course, he's fallen in love with her by this time. And then he asks her to go to this May Day fair. And that was, it was a lovely scene, that.

VE Beautiful.

DB You know, it's all the typical old-fashioned May Day fair. And, of course, they finish up by singing *Will You Remember*. And, then he finds out that she's going to marry the other feller. So I won't tell you any... [*laughs*]

[*General laughter*]

Int Oh, I'll have to see it now.

VE Oh, you'll have to see that. It really is a nice film.

DB Well, it's all the blossom.

VE Yeah. The May blossom.

DB You know, the blossom.

VE It's beautiful.

[...]

Int You were saying that you preferred *Naughty Marietta*.

KB Yes, I think I did.

Int Yeah.

KB But that was the first one I saw. Well, I mean, I know it's heresy to, eh, but I have expressed that before. I thought Nelson Eddy was a bit of a wooden actor.

DB You're a...

Int [*Laughs*]

DB You can't say that because he wasn't wooden at all! [*Laughs*] He wasn't wooden at all. [*Voice rises*] You want to see him, his whole body's going when he's singing! His whole body is going!

KB Is it?

DB Yeah.

KB Right.

There is constant movement here between past and present as memories of past activities and feelings are brought back into the present in a manner which appears to mimic the informants' behaviour outside the interview situation: films viewed again and again, oft-repeated exchanges of talk about the star's life and personality, and so on. In the first interview, too, the informants recollect enjoying photographs of Eddy in magazines like *Film Weekly*. But then a viewing of one of Mrs Braithwaite's albums of photos of the star prompts Vee Entwistle to remind her that when Nelson got married Dorris had cut his wife out of the wedding photo which appeared in one of the magazines:

> *Int* His wife's not unlike Jeanette MacDonald, is she? In some ways. She's not as attractive as Jeanette MacDonald but…
>
> *VE* No, not really, no.
>
> *DB* She was nice.
>
> *Int* Yeah.
>
> *DB* She was a nice person.
>
> *VE* She was so nice that a friend of mine cut her off the picture.
>
> *DB* I were jealous! When he got married, I couldn't! That was in the *Picturegoer*. [*Laughs*]

They laugh off their youthful folly ('We all thought we were in with a chance, you see'[12]) and start to look back again at Nelson's entire career. This variant of the past/present trope, the use of memory to bridge past and present from the standpoint of the present, 'places time in the text' exactly in the manner of what Alessandro Portelli calls 'shuttlework'.[13]

The second interview, embarked on in earnest after the interviewer had been shown some of Mrs Braithwaite's substantial collection of Eddy memorabilia, focuses almost exclusively on Nelson Eddy and his co-star Jeanette MacDonald, and is very much about enduring fandom and its continuing meanings throughout the lives of the fans themselves. The interview includes a number of passages of 'insider' gossip about Eddy – anecdotes the informants must have shared with each other on numerous prior occasions and yet whose retelling now appears to be only partly for the interviewer's benefit. They talk about collecting Eddy memorabilia, about Mrs Braithwaite's writings on Eddy in fanzines and nostalgia magazines and about networking with fellow fans.

The interview then moves towards more profound issues, as the informants struggle to put into words their feelings about Nelson Eddy's special qualities and their feelings about the star:

DB It comes over. And I mean, to have come over on the screen, it must've been, you know, you're not seeing them personally. So to see that or feel that on screen, there's something there.

VE Oh yes.

DB And it's not just odd ones. Everyone, especially Nelson Eddy. Everyone that likes him have all experienced the same feeling. That there was something there behind his handsome looks and his good voice. That there was a, em, well a spiritual...

VE Yeah.

DB Kind of a spirituality. A good feeling.

VE I was telling Val coming up on the bus, our Hilda used to sit there absolutely gone and think he was just singing to her!

DB Well you did!

VE And you know, she was.

DB Yeah, yeah.

VE I used to keep watching her, you know. And when he was smiling she was, as though he was...

DB [*Laughs*]

VE Actually smiling at her. Any minute he would come off the screen and she would...

Dorris Braithwaite's talk here expresses a reliving of the feelings evoked, while her friend, who talks in the past tense about a third party's (our Hilda's) fantasy that Eddy was actually smiling at her, assumes a more detached stance. Talk of emotions and fantasies leads into accounts by both informants of dreams they have had about Nelson Eddy, the telling of which suggests these too have been recounted many times before. The interviewer then attempts to segue into a discussion about the informants' feelings and fantasies whilst watching the films:

Int Did you used to dream about him when you were seeing the pictures as well?

DB Eh [*pause: 2 seconds*]. I can't really remember that far back.

VE   No I don't think we actually *dreamt* it so much as, sort of imagined, you know. You could actually see the whole thing. And you would probably be saying the female's part, you know, to him, sort of thing. Just imagining that you was the female in the film.

Int   Yeah.

VE   Well I did. I don't know about you.

DB   Oh yes! Well my friend and I used to act them out. We used to act the films out. Because she liked Cesar Romero. Have you seen Cesar Romero? 'Tache and very dark. Well she was blonde. So if she went for the dark, I went for the fair, you see. And we used to act them in her cellar. We used to act the film. And she was Nelson Eddy because she was blonde and she had a deep wave. And she used to deepen it and draw her hair back. I wish I could find that photo. I took a photo of her once. And she's doing, like that [*demonstrates friend deepening wave*]. She's looking like him on it. Drew her hair back. And she was Nelson Eddy, see. And I acted Cesar Romero. [*Hilarious laughter*]

Mrs Braithwaite's reluctance to return to the past (she hesitates and claims that she cannot remember) supports the view that the foregoing dream narrations had been non-regressive, and thus that the informants' talk is very much in, and indeed for, the present moment of narration.[14] The informants themselves draw a distinction between dreams (which for them are still alive in the present) and the fantasy when watching the films as young women that they were 'the female in the film'. Their acting out of this fantasy in real life is laughingly dismissed as a piece of girlish nonsense, something that belongs firmly in the past. These observations are telling not only because they shed light on the workings of cinema memory but also because they flesh out discussions in previous chapters concerning the embodied quality of spectatorial engagements with cinema.

The interview soon moves off this tricky ground, returning to 'safe' insider fan gossip, some of which repeats material in the first interview. Mrs Braithwaite then shows the interviewer some newsletters of the Nelson Eddy Appreciation Society and letters received from the star between 1937, when she first wrote to him, and 1961. Informants and interviewer then view *Maytime* on videotape. Mrs Braithwaite, who does this quite often, makes a special occasion of the screening by closing the curtains and offering servings of tea and cake throughout the proceedings. The interviewer noted that

> everyone was enthralled although there were certain bits where it was thought all right to interject a... humorous comment. Especially at the expense of John Barrymore, who's... Nelson Eddy's love rival in the picture... So certainly they didn't feel they had to be totally uncritical of the film...[15]

After the viewing, interviewer and informants exchange some appreciative comments about the film, which in turn lead to the recounting of some further behind-the-scenes stories about its stars.

These observations are of interest in light of Henry Jenkins's definition of fandom, which 'recognises that part of what distinguishes fans as a particular class of textual consumers is the *social* nature of their interpretive and cultural activity'.[16] Jenkins contends that fans adopt a *distinctive mode of reception*, involving conscious selection and repeated consumption of material and translation of the material and its reception into a social activity (for example, through talk with other fans, membership of fan clubs, attendance at conventions, exchanges of letters and so forth). Also, says Jenkins, fandom *constitutes a particular interpretive community* – fan club meetings, newsletters and fanzines all offer a forum for collective negotiation of the meanings of texts – as well as an *alternative social community* ('the fans' appropriation of media texts provides a ready body of common references that facilitates communication with others scattered across a broad geographic area').[17] Jenkins also suggests that fandom *constitutes a particular 'Art World'*, wherein fans use their selected texts as bases for new cultural creation.

Each of these aspects of fandom is of relevance to an understanding of Dorris Braithwaite's enduring devotion to Nelson Eddy. She often listens to Eddy's songs and repeatedly watches the films, both alone and in the company of others (indeed the interview provided further occasion not only for this activity but also for the enjoyment of a wealth of fan talk). This is clearly, in Jenkins's terms, a distinctive mode of reception. Mrs Braithwaite's devotion to Nelson Eddy, having brought her into contact with people from various parts of the UK and around the world, also secures her membership of an alternative social community. However, to the extent that debates between his fans centre on Eddy's star persona and personal qualities rather than on interpretations of 'Eddy texts', Eddy fans perhaps constitute a social more than an interpretive community. Mention is made in one of the interviews of a sculpture of Nelson Eddy crafted by an American fan, and Mrs Braithwaite herself has produced an essay on MacDonald and Eddy and a book about Eddy.[18] Nelson Eddy fandom does then embody some aspects of what Jenkins terms an 'Art World'. That it emphasises social rather than interpretive activities may be a matter of gender and generation. Jenkins's definition arises from his study of devotees of *Star Trek*, a group of people that is relatively young and male-dominated. The evidence suggests, nevertheless, that a common set of structures underlies instances of fan behaviour and objects of fandom.

Jenkins's remarks refer to contemporary media fandom, however, whereas in the present instance we have to bear in mind the historical dimension of 'fannish' reception and use of media texts as well as the role of memory in enduring fandom. What, if any, specific productions of memory are at stake in enduring fandom, especially where, as in the present case, it involves near lifelong devotion to a star who is no longer alive? And in what ways do these productions connect with Fiske's and Jenkins's definitions? To what extent are the enduring fan's orchestrations of past and present peculiar to this mode of reception? What specific continuities and discontinuities between past and present are proposed in the memories of enduring fans? And how do the present-day imaginings of such fans continue to engage cultural products first consumed many years ago, texts indeed which outlive the object of the enduring fan's devotion?

Although Nelson Eddy died in 1967, he remains very much alive for Dorris Braithwaite, and undoubtedly for his other enduring fans as well. This must be, in part at least, because the element of fantasy in star worship does not necessarily require the sustenance of a living person's presence. The films, the photographs, the recordings remain as memorials, just as during the star's lifetime they were substitutes, standing in for something deeply desired and in the end unattainable. As Mrs Braithwaite says of Eddy's voice: 'It just did something. It still does to this day'. This 'something', deeply felt and impossible to put into words, transcends the passage of time. In a discourse which speaks very much in and from the present, Mrs Braithwaite's statement – like the dying word of the Eddy character in *Maytime* ('That day *did* last me all my life') connects past and present, weaving a thread of continuity between them.

But if this mode of memory production is characteristic of enduring fandom, it is not the only one. Loss is always already present in the enduring fan's investments: her investments not only in the star's persona but also in the tangible objects, the memorabilia, which stand in for the star. Loss is ever present, too, in *Maytime*: loss anticipated and loss relived pervade the story and its telling. From the standpoint of old age Marcia Mornay, the Jeanette MacDonald character, mourns a lost opportunity, a lost love, and the lost Maytime of her youth. She remembers the love of her life as something that never quite was, something which could only be lived in the anticipation of remembrance ('Will You Remember?'): love as loss, love as memory. Likewise, from the vantage of her own advancing years, the enduring fan may adopt a similar narrative standpoint as she looks back upon, and weaves into her own life story, a lifetime's devotion to 'her' star.

Writing of her admiration for her favourite star, the Deanna Durbin fan quoted above recalls the 'electrifying' moment when, decades earlier, she first saw the singer on screen. With the insistence that 'the love was to last a lifetime', however, she makes a smart shift into the present, suggesting that her devotion has been carried on unbroken through all the intervening years. In an exemplary statement, whose complex subjectivity and temporality exactly replicate those of *Maytime*'s 'Will You Remember?' duet, the future anterior ('was to') at once looks forward to looking back and locates the anticipated recollection in a past time. There is the future, then, and there is the past that will be remembered in the future: in this discourse, the present is always elsewhere.

If death is a central theme of *Maytime* (both of the central characters die in the story), in this instance death proposes possibility rather than closure, hope rather than defeat. In the film's plot the two deaths, though many years apart in the world of the story, are contiguous: the scene in which Paul, the Eddy character, dies marks the conclusion of Marcia's flashback and thus the point at which the film's enunciation returns to the narrative present as, with a reprise of 'Will You Remember?', Paul's ghost appears before a Marcia exhausted to the point of death by her reminiscences. Out of the old woman's dying body then steps the young Marcia; and the couple, reunited and restored in death to the springtime of their youth, finally grasp the love which had eluded them in life.

This literal putting into the image of what has already been proposed through the film's narrative discourse – that Marcia's aged appearance is no more than a cloak for the young woman she remembers herself to have been – echoes a point made by a number of informants: that, outward appearances notwithstanding, 'inside' they are still the young people they once were. For the enduring fan, though, this has a particular inflection: just as one's youthful self does not die as one ages, so the enduring fan's devotion survives the death of its object. In an essay written for the newsletter of the Nelson Eddy Appreciation Society, Mrs Braithwaite conveys something of this transcendence:

> Now Nelson is gone and so is my husband. But I play records and videos and they are both with me again and I feel just as young and in love as I was all those years ago.[19]

Youth lives on in old age, then, and love conquers death. The enduring fan's devotion, too, embodies something of this transcendent quality: Dorris Braithwaite speaks, for example, of a kind of spiritual quality lying behind Nelson Eddy's handsome looks and good voice. The tributes in a fanzine which appeared soon after Nelson Eddy's death eloquently convey this sense of the transpersonal, of 'higher things', and their feeling tone uncannily echoes that of the transcendent closing moments of *Maytime*:

> In the last, lingering note of the voice all of us knew and loved so well, there is an undying chord, a sound almost too exquisite to be borne, which will go on sounding through all the years so long as we who hear remember and cherish it.[20]

Through repeated re-viewings, *Maytime* – already in itself multilayered in its production of memory – accrues yet further layers of memory-meaning. Enduring fans of the film and its stars will perhaps recollect first seeing *Maytime* in the 1930s, and many years later might have memories of that first viewing to recall. But, true to the distinctive modes of reception associated with fandom, these fans will have viewed the film many times over since that first occasion. Memories of subsequent viewings will overlay and occlude each other and become informed by events and changes in the fans' own lives: Mrs Braithwaite, for instance, hints in the passage quoted above at a renewed mode of reception, new readings of Eddy texts, which became available to her after her husband's death.

In both content and narrative discourse, *Maytime* is already saturated in memory, 'like lavender in a long unopened drawer.'[21] As the text is appropriated and used by enduring fans, further layers of intertextual and extratextual memory-meaning continuously accrue. On all levels, *Maytime* speaks a very specific type of memory: nostalgia, a bittersweet longing for a lost or otherwise unattainable object. In the film, the scene of memory constantly retreats into an ever more distant past, a past from whose vantage point the future itself is anticipated with nostalgia.

The same is true, perhaps, of the enduring fan's use of media texts, especially if the performer who is the object of devotion is no longer living. The case of *Maytime* suggests that in this mode of reception the death of the star may be mapped onto the deaths of the film's central characters, and love produced as triumphing over death. Thus, like Paul and Marcia, the enduring fan remains forever young in an eternal Maytime, bearing witness to a devotion that lasts not merely 'all my life', but beyond life.

Notes

1. John Fiske, 'The cultural economy of fandom', in Lisa A. Lewis (ed.), *The Adoring Audience: Fan Culture and Popular Media* (London: Routledge, 1992), p. 30.

2. Annette Kuhn, 'Cinemagoing in Britain in the 1930s: report of a questionnaire survey', *Historical Journal of Film, Radio and Television*, vol. 19, no. 4 (1999), pp. 531–543; see p. 539.

3. Edward Baron Turk, 'Deriding the voice of Jeanette MacDonald: notes on psychoanalysis and the American film musical', *Camera Obscura*, nos 25–26 (1990), pp. 225–249.

4. 95-62-1, Mrs E. Martin, Cleveland, n.d. [1995]; 95-227-1, Mrs D.M. Cummings, West Midlands, 16 June 1995; 95-228-1, Joan Bice, Devon, 15 June 1995. There are several internet sites devoted to MacDonald and Eddy, including *Jeanette MacDonald Home Page*, http://members.aol.com/jmacfan (26 May 2001); *Jeanette MacDonald and Nelson Eddy Home Page*, http://www.maceddy.com (26 May 2001).

5. On *Maytime*'s British release during Coronation week in May 1937, exhibitors were preparing themselves for a big hit: *Kinematograph Weekly*, 13 May 1937, front cover and p. 25; *Today's Cinema*, 7 May 1937. Mark Glancy notes that *Maytime* was MGM's most expensive and successful film yet: Glancy, 'MGM film grosses: 1924–1949: the Eddie Mannix ledger', *Historical Journal of Radio, Film and Television*, vol. 12, no. 2 (1992), pp. 127–44. In the Mass-Observation (M-O) Archive, a number of filmgoers' letters in praise of MacDonald and Eddy are preserved: M-O Archive: TC Films, Boxes 5 and 6.

6. 'A nostalgic thing set to music', according to the *Photoplay* reviewer: *Photoplay*, May 1937, p. 53.

7. 95-38-1, Dorris Braithwaite, Bolton, to Annette Kuhn, 17 February 1995.

8. Jackie Stacey, *Star Gazing: Hollywood Cinema and Female Spectatorship* (London: Routledge, 1994), pp. 139–42.

9. In the late 1930s Bolton, as 'Worktown', was the subject of a number of Mass-Observation investigations of cinemagoing: see M-O Archive: Worktown, Boxes 35 and 36; 'Cinema-going in Worktown', in Jeffrey Richards and Dorothy Sheridan (eds), *Mass-Observation at the Movies* (London: Routledge and Kegan Paul, 1987); Jeffrey Richards, 'Cinemagoing in Worktown: regional film audiences in 1930s Britain', *Historical Journal of Film, Radio and Television*, vol. 14, no. 2 (1994), pp. 147–66. Filmgoing in Bolton is also discussed in Leslie Halliwell's autobiography, *Seats in All Parts: A Lifetime at the Movies* (London: Grafton Books, 1986); and by John Sedgwick, 'Film "hits" and "misses" in mid-1930s Britain', *Historical Journal of Radio, Film and Television*, vol. 18, no. 3 (1998), pp. 333–47. A Bolton cinema manager, interviewed in late 1938, mentions that *Maytime* had by then achieved eight runs in the town: see *Mass-Observation at the Movies*, p. 29.

10. 95-51-1a, Questionnaire, Vee Entwistle, Bolton, n.d. [1995].

11. The first interview took place on 11 May 1995 (T95-27, T95-71), the second on 5 June 1995 (T95-42, T95-43).

12. A photograph of Mrs Braithwaite's late husband suggested to the interviewer that he bore a marked resemblance to Nelson Eddy: T95-71, Interviewer's fieldnotes, 11 May 1995.

13. Alessandro Portelli, *The Death of Luigi Trastulli and Other Stories: Form and Meaning in Oral History* (Albany, NY: State University of New York Press, 1991), p. 64.

14. For a discussion of the functions of time in oral history, see ibid., pp. 59–76.

15. T95-43, Interviewer's fieldnotes, Dorris Braithwaite and Vee Entwistle, Bolton, 5 June 1995.

16. Henry Jenkins, '"Strangers no more, we sing": filking and the social construction of the science fiction fan community', in Lisa A. Lewis (ed.), *The Adoring Audience: Fan Culture and Popular Media* (London: Routledge, 1992), p. 209 (emphasis added).

17.　Ibid., p. 213.

18.　95-38-19, 'Evergreen melodies: the singing sweethearts', *Evergreen*, Summer 1991, pp. 18–28; 95-38-29, *The Golden Voice of Nelson Eddy* (1997).

19.　95-38-21, Spring Supplement to 'The Golden Star', 1977, p. 8.

20.　95-38-22, Marguerite Malatesta in *The Shooting Star*, memorial edition 1967 (published by the Nelson Eddy Music Club), p. 10.

21.　Nelson Eddy obituary, *Evening Standard* (London), 7 March 1967.

9

Oh! Dreamland!

WHAT was the attraction of the pictures for the 'movie-made' generation of the 1930s? Why did they go to the cinema, and what did they get out of it? In today's conventional wisdom, the answer to these questions can be summed up in a single word: escape. There is undoubtedly some truth in the view that cinema provided a distraction from the dreary conditions in which many British people lived in the 1930s. But a closer looks reveals that things are not quite so simple. And considered in all its shade and nuance the story is, in sometimes surprising ways, highly revealing about cinema culture as it was lived by the 1930s generation and about how their memories have been shaped by it.

During the 1930s there was considerable public debate about cinema and its place in society, and much of this was of an anxious nature. Contemporary investigations of the cinema audience such as the inquiries into children's cinemagoing looked at in Chapter 4 were invariably conducted by pressure groups and other policy-oriented bodies. While the voices of the cinemagoers themselves are not entirely absent from these inquiries, they are inevitably mediated and modulated by the institutional discourses around public morality and child welfare which inspired them. Academic or independent scholarly research directed at accessing the cinemagoer's point of view was largely unheard-of in Britain before the 1940s.

However, an interview-based study of unemployed men conducted in London in the early 1930s by the American sociologist E. Wight Bakke did give serious attention to cinema as it was experienced by the jobless. Bakke found that 'The unemployed, and especially the skilled, were unwilling to forgo the cinema unless they were forced to do so': these men would happily curtail expenditure on other amusements rather than stop going to the pictures.[1] Asked 'What attracts you to the cinema?', interviewees replied: 'The pictures help you live in another world for a little while. I almost feel I'm in the picture'; and '[Pictures] make you think for a little while that life is all right'.[2] These responses are interesting in a number of respects. Firstly, they are surprisingly frank, and bear no trace of deference or formulaic politeness: perhaps the researcher's rapport with his working-class informants was helped by his being American. Secondly, there is a strong sense of immediacy about these responses: by definition, they are uncoloured by hindsight or popular memory as replies to questions about cinemagoing in the 1930s might be today.

Four key, and related, points about cinema's attraction are encapsulated in the experiences of Bakke's informants: a sense of entering or living in another world; a sense of oneself being 'inside' the picture; a feeling that life seems 'better' while one is at the pictures; and an acknowledgement of the temporariness of this immersion ('for a little while'). Only at most one of these points ('life is all right') may be readily linked to the speaker's joblessness, and even this idea is readable as expressing an 'all-rightness' that embraces more than just one's employment situation. The idea of 'escape' is present, too; but already 'escape' seems to embody a range of potential meanings and depths of investment on the cinemagoer's part.

Britain's first in-depth academic researches on the cinema audience were conducted in the 1940s by the German *émigré* sociologist, J.P. Mayer. For his ethnographic studies of British cinemagoers, Mayer drew on letters and essays produced by readers of the popular film magazine, *Picturegoer*. For his book *Sociology of Film*, he appealed to *Picturegoer* readers to write about the influence they felt the pictures had exerted on their daily lives and on their nighttime dreams. One man wrote:

> When I am watching [films featuring the tropical isles], I seem to forget the present world, in which I am living, lost in a kind of spell that is enchanted by the impression of my being actually there.[3]

In the mid-1940s, unemployment was virtually non-existent, and Mayer notes that this respondent was employed in a manual job. And yet the notions of being in another world ('I seem to forget the present world') and of being inside the film ('actually there') are present in this man's account, just as they were in the responses of Bakke's unemployed men a decade and a half earlier. The words 'lost' and 'spell' are significant, implying as they do magic and – in the old sense of the word – ecstasy, or an out-of-body state. Significantly, perhaps, this state also characterises certain forms of religious experience.

The letters Mayer received in response to his *Picturegoer* appeal are published verbatim and uncorrected, and so may be taken as raw, un-mediated, data. For his other major study, *British Cinemas and their Audiences*, Mayer adopted a method devised in the 1930s for the US Payne Fund Studies of young cinemagoers: the 'motion picture auto-biography'. Again, readers of *Picturegoer* were approached, this time to write about the history of their interest in films,[4] and again the responses were published in unedited form. Some of the essays are clearly by people unused to expressing themselves in writing, and are arguably the more valuable as evidence for that. A 20-year-old factory hand writes:

> I were going to the Cinemas with an elderly girl friend when I were around 7yrs. old, seeing Nelson Eddy and Jeanette McDonald films, but weren't so keen then, so when I found myself a boy pal, we used to go to the pictures twice per week. Was then I became very interested in films. My favourite pictures used to be 'Westerns' and those weeping films of Shirley Temple's during the 1930's... [sic][5]

To return to the 1930s, and to move to the other end of the social spectrum, an essay about the attraction of the pictures by a noted writer betrays a very similar set of investments. In 1937, Elizabeth Bowen published her account of 'Why I go to the cinema' in which, speaking as 'a fan, not a critic', she explains why she enjoys the pictures. She writes of eagerly looking forward to an occasion which she knows will be special, outside the humdrum: 'I am giving myself a treat – or being given a treat'; 'I go empty but hopeful... The approach tunes me up for pleasure... [L]ike a chocolate-box lid, the entrance is... voluptuously promising: sensation of some sort seems to be guaran-teed.'[6]

She also puts into words the lived experience of what cinema alone, as against any other type of entertainment, can offer: 'being subject to glamour', she writes, 'I experience a sort of elevation'; and '[stars] live for my eye. Yes, and I not only perceive them but *am* them'.[7] The key features of Bowen's attraction to the pictures, then, are anticipation, sensation and elevation: not so very different in fact from the investments of Bakke's unemployed men and Mayer's film lovers.

This sought-after sensation of immersing yourself in a different and better world, or of being a better person, may stay with you after you leave the cinema, feeling uplifted. The desire to be occasionally taken out of oneself, even if only 'for a little while', is a widespread if not a universal one, and it has been met in a variety ways in different times and places. But if the wish itself transcends time and place, the material on which it draws, and indeed the content of the wish, are always culturally and historically situated. As Sally Alexander notes: 'fantasy draws on the immediate and historical for aspects of its content, form, and context, and the conditions of these are always changing'.[8] For the 1930s generation, the 'content, form, and context' of the wish was provided by cinema.

Contemporary accounts, written or spoken 'on the pulse', of 1930s and 1940s cinemagoers' investments in the pictures may well reference an element of fantasy in the sense of an unconscious wish scenario. But they are perhaps better understood as investments which in their content, expression and intensity range between ordinary consciousness through reverie to ecstasy. The recurrence of certain themes and turns of phrase in these contemporary accounts suggests, too, that a collective imagination is at work in them. To this extent, they may be interpreted as expressions of cultural as much as of individual engagements. In like manner, 1930s cinemagoers' recollections of their youthful investments in cinema also bear the hallmarks of collective, cultural memory.

Everyone who gave interviews for this study was asked some version of the question: 'What did going to the pictures feel like for you in the 1930s?' While this deliberately open question was interpreted in a range of different ways, it was always taken as an invitation to look back on life and assess the role played in it by cinema. The appropriate moment for putting this question normally presented itself towards the end of the final interview, for at this point interviewees seemed automatically to settle themselves into a 'looking back on life' mode. In this context, a request to think about and recollect past feelings seems natural; and although for some interviewees – those perhaps who had never before attempted to put these things into words – answers did not come readily, everyone did their best to give the question due consideration and to offer an answer of some sort, albeit sometimes with further encourage-ment from the interviewer, and albeit sometimes in conventional turns of phrase. Without benefit of prompting, a number of letter-writers also took the opportunity to reflect on what a trip to the cinema had meant to them so long ago.

All informants give more eloquent expression to these feeling-memories than they themselves might imagine: even being at a loss for words can speak volumes. Again, the power and the value of these memories as evidence lies less in what they reveal about the individuals articulating them – it is neither helpful nor proper in an inquiry of this kind to attempt to psychoanalyse informants – than in the insights they yield about the collective imagination of a generation. For, taken as a whole, informants' accounts of their investments in cinema yield a surprisingly consistent pattern of response.

In these testimonies, inevitably, the conventional wisdom of hindsight does surface: there is a certain amount of talk about escapism and hard times, for example. Such talk, delivered as it characteristically is in a detached or impersonal discursive mode, is in marked contrast to the tone which pervades informants' attempts to put their own feelings and engagements into words. Here, there is a sense that the speaker is getting inside the feeling-memory, perhaps even re-experiencing the feeling in the telling. Sometimes, too, detached and engaged modes of response sit side-by-side in a single testimony. Bernard Goodsall, for example, begins his lengthy letter by observing that

> The cinema offered us a temporary haven of comfort. They were our 'Dream Palaces', a make believe world, a glittering [kaleido-scope] of movement, magic and madness. For a couple of pence we could exchange our drab surroundings of an unheated home for the luxury of the super cinema and fulfil our wildest dreams.

The collective enunciation notwithstanding ('we could exchange our drab surroundings'), this is a detached observation about a historical moment rather than a direct expression or reliving of the writer's feelings. Some of the expressions used, too ('Dream Palaces' versus 'drab sur-roundings', for example) are formulaic turns of phrase which betray the intervention of hindsight and the operation of popular memory. Having set the historical scene, though, Mr Goodsall lets slip something of his own remembered feelings of excitement at the prospect of a visit to the pictures:

> The anticipation of the feast to come started as you approached the cinema, the lights, the uniformed commissionaire and it didn't matter what was on the screen.

The letter ends by returning to a detached observation of a different sort, from the standpoint of a reassessment of the writer's life story: 'for me going to the pictures in the 1930s will remain with me as a most exciting memory'.[9] Beneath these discursive shifts, however, a consistent investment in cinema is apparent in expressions such as 'kaleidoscopic movement', 'magic and madness', 'wildest dreams', 'exciting'. For this informant, it seems, the feeling-memory is coloured by a sense of fast, intoxicating movement – by kinesis, in other words. This relation to cinema may or indeed may not contain elements of the conventional 'escape'; but expressed from the inside, from the standpoint of the writer's own experience, it offers a fresh slant on the nature of the investment involved. The freshness is perhaps a matter of nuance, of depth and feeling tone more than of content or substance.

In this context, a range of types and degrees of engagement are apparent in 1930s cinemagoers' memory-talk. At one extreme, some accounts deal with matters which may seem relatively superficial and which informants rarely seem to have difficulty putting into words. At the other extreme, some testimonies betray an intensity of engagement which touches on the transcendent; and where words fail here, the feeling may find expression in circumlocutions as well as in hesitations, silences and other nonverbal modes of expression. The majority of remembered attachments appear to lie between these two poles, and along the continuum between them are observable broadly three types of feeling-memory. Firstly, memory-talk which suggests a down-to-earth, 'of the moment', sense of cinema's place in the daily routines and amusements of the 1930s; secondly, talk which evokes the lived experience of being in the cinema theatre; and thirdly, accounts which touch on the wider and deeper meanings of cinema throughout the informant's life.

On cinema's place in daily life, many informants note that in the 1930s cinema was, in the words of one interviewee, 'the main attraction'. Cinema was important and meaningful in people's lives because nothing else then available offered quite so desirable a way of spending one's spare time. As Olga Scowen notes:

> But, em, no, it was, the cinema was really the centre of our lives in those days. Certainly, during the thirties. When I was, what was I? Twelve, when I went to the county school. And my friends and I were all interested in films. Nothing else to do.[10]

A number of informants with working-class backgrounds add that, while entertainments such as the theatre felt socially 'off-limits', the pictures seemed accessible to them. They remember a sense of entitlement attaching to the pictures, a feeling that the cinema somehow belonged to them, was *their* 'main attraction'. As Thomas McGoran remembers:

> There was no other means of entertainment for, for the uneducated masses! No, there was theatres in the city and there was dance halls. Dance halls for the teenagers. Once you grew up a bit, you went to the dance. The theatres, probably, for people that has money. But the cinemas was for the poor people.[11]

The idea of cinema's being the 'main attraction' shades into a sense of its being at the very cutting edge, the up-to-the-minute place to be. This conceit embraces two separate but related themes: the modernity of the attraction itself, and the irresistibly magnetic force it seemed to exert. On the latter point, numerous informants mention that in the 1930s the cinemas were nearly always full and that it was invariably necessary to queue to get in. This conveys a feeling of busy-ness, activity and energy about these places. Cinemas, in this account, were 'attractions' in the sense that people were irresistibly drawn to them.

The sense of novelty and energy associates in turn to feelings of excitement. Bernard Goodsall, quoted earlier, is far from alone in talking about going to the pictures as a 'most exciting memory'. Ashley Bird also recalls this feeling: 'Em, you know, we were so excited as kids, it was so new'.[12] Letter-writer Sheila Black explains what it was that made cinema so exciting for her, offering a telling comparison with present-day attractions:

> We went because it was such a magical invention packing our lives with glamour and action, with history, reality and non-reality. It was all new and wonderful, just as internet and computing are today.[13]

The feeling of newness, wonder, and barely-containable excitement pervading these memories clearly has something to do with what was on the cinema screen. But it seems to be attached much more strongly to the experience of cinemagoing in its entirety, including – indeed especially – the prospect of going to the pictures and the journey to the cinema. These, to paraphrase Elizabeth Bowen, tuned one up for pleasure. Interviewee Mickie Rivers remembers the regular outings to the cinema she and her husband made early in their married life as 'something to look forward to all the week'.[14] For Bernard Goodsall, it did not even matter what was on the screen: the 'anticipation of the feast to come as you approached the cinema' was evidently, again in Elizabeth Bowen's words, 'voluptuously promising' enough. Cinema was the main attraction, then, because it was exciting, and it was exciting because it was new and modern, because it was the fashionable place to go, and because going there was always anticipated with relish.

Memories about the experience of being inside the cinema vary in tone according to the nature and intensity of the experience recollected. At the more down-to-earth end of the spectrum, many informants simply recall how warm and comforting it felt to be inside the cinema, how it induced sensations of bodily ease. John Cooper remembers well the sense of relief after enduring a long wait outside in the cold:

> But when we did get in, it was always nice and comfortable in most of them. And I think that the warmth and the, eh [*pause: 1 second*], kind of comfort. And the plush seats. The darkness and everything. Had a strong, an appeal to us. As the actual films themselves. It was an oasis of comfort and warmth in most of them.[15]

Bernard and Irene Letchet are among many informants who draw comparisons between the comforts of the cinema and the austerity of home:

BL   Well that was another thing of course, the cinema was...

IL   Lovely and warm!

BL   Very comfortable.

IL   Warmer than at home probably.[16]

Letter-writer Bob Surtees eloquently recalls the experience of bodily ease that went with being in the cinema, associating this with pleasurable memories of loving closeness with his girlfriend: 'an evening at the cinema with your girlfriend. The comfort! warmth! the nearness and love'.[17] In informants' memory-talk, this kind of feeling-memory of comfort and ease is always set against its opposite: the physical discomforts of the world outside the cinema walls – the chilly, wet street where you stood waiting in the queue, a sparsely-furnished, unheated home. Mr Surtees's comparison is between the comforting and comfortable memory of closeness in the pre-war cinema and the loneliness, separation and stresses of wartime: 'Until '39!'.

Many informants offer vivid accounts of the feelings of awe inspired by the decor and furnishings of the luxurious new cinemas that were built in the 1930s. Most striking of all, in terms of the frequency with which it is mentioned and the kind of language used, are memories of the delight and wonder inspired by the cinema organ. Writing about cinemagoing in his memoir of the 1930s, the cultural commentator Rene Cutforth recalls 'the "Mighty Wurlitzer" – which from time to time rose from the depths like a submarine and filled you right up to the top with… "In a Monastery Garden" or some similar fantasy of blessing and stability before submerging once more into the basement'.[18] A surprisingly large number of informants offer their own memories of cinema organs, and in terms remarkably similar to Cutforth's:

MR Because, at the Regent, they'd got a wonderful organ as well. And the organ used to provide a break in the film you see. Between the two films. Used to come out of the ground. And all the *lights*. And all the *colours*. [*Transported voice*][19]

VE That's from the Odeon that. A programme…
NW Yeah.
VE From our Odeon.
NW Used to have an organ.
VE Yeah. I told you about it, didn't I? Used to come up.
NW Half time, at the interval, used to come up, didn't it?
VE Yeah. Oh it was beautiful. It was all white.[20]

J. Charles Hall remembers 'the magic of the organist arising from the depths', while Olive Johnson recalls how 'the multi-coloured organ would rise from the floor to great applause from the audience'. Myra Schneidermann writes: 'The "grand" cinemas had an organist who used to appear magically from some subterranean "kingdom" smiling and waving'. Joan Donaghue remembers that 'A Compton Wonder Organ would arise from the floor with its lights changing colours while the organist played'. And Valerie Shute recollects 'The great Wurlitzer [that] came up from somewhere down below and played popular tunes'.[21]

The intensity and emotional tone of memories of the cinema organ attach themselves with particular insistence to the magical appearance of the instrument in all its splendour from apparently nowhere, and to its ascending movement. The organ came out of the ground, arose from the depths, appeared from some subterranean kingdom, came up from somewhere down below. The sense of wonder attaching to these memories is apparent, too, in references to the beautiful flashing lights and the changing colours that accompanied the organ's appearance. Informants offer no precise memories of the music the organist would be playing, or of whether the organ music afforded the kind of beneficence Cutforth refers to, but a sense of 'blessing and stability' would certainly be of a piece with the feelings of comfort and ease remembered as induced by being in the cinema.

In the magical ambience of the cinema auditorium, time as well as space take on new dimensions, and time spent in the pictures is remembered as qualitatively different from ordinary time. It is more elastic, more flexible, more giving. While time-memories are rarely explicitly articulated in these terms, repeated allusions in informants' accounts to a particular way of organising cinema time are revealing in this respect. Nearly everyone mentions the 1930s policy of 'continuous programming' in cinemas. Patrons could enter the cinema at any time, even in the middle of the main feature film, and were technically free to remain in their seats throughout the rest of the day's screenings of the programme. Interviewees from Bolton and Harrow explain:

Mr A And then I don't know what year it would be, we got continuous showing.

Ms X Yeh.

Mr A So you could go in early and stay till, whenever you want.

Ms X What you had to do, you had to sit through till...

Mr A Yes.

Ms X If you went in half way through you sat in till you got to the bit where you came in.

AB And then you...

Ms X   Went out! [*laughs excitedly*]

[*All laugh*]

LB   If you weren't thrown out!

Mr A   [You used to get some people?] who went in early and stopped till closing time.[22]

EB   When you in em, you didn't wait particularly for the programme to begin. You just went in anytime. It could've been halfway through or whatever. An then you sort of sat through the programme and then waited to see the bit that you'd missed. [*Sound of scaffolding in background*] [*Beginning inaudible*] it went up when you came in.

Int   Mmm.

EB   That was quite usual. And on the other hand some people stayed and watched the programme through twice if they felt like it. You didn't have to leave. Once the thing was going, you know, you could just stay.[23]

Phyllis Bennett remembers the pleasure of feeling free to sit through several screenings of a particularly enjoyable film:

PB   Cause that used to be continuous in them days.

Int   A-ah.

PB   You see. But now they're performances. You have to come out, don't you?

Int   Yeah.

PB   But then, I mean, you could sit in and see it three times round if you wanted.

Int   And was that still something that you...

PB   [*Laughs*]

Int   That you did. [*Laughs*]

PB   If that was a picture I liked, you know.

Int   Yeah.

PB   I'd say, oh, I'll see some more of that.[24]

A sense of generosity attaches to memories of the continuous programme: some informants remember their feelings of incredulity on first learning that it was quite permissible to stay in the cinema through more than one screening of a film. Two further aspects of the continuous programme are of salience to an understanding of how cinema time was experienced by 1930s cinemagoers. Firstly, the fact that it was quite usual to begin watching a feature film part way through the story meant that it was a common part of the cinemagoing experience to see the end of a film before the beginning. This mode of spectatorship has fascinating implications as regards narration and narrativity in film, and certainly challenges the concept of the self-contained and linear narrative. With continuous programming, narrative time, narrative trajectory and narrative closure are modified; and narrative time and viewing time are potentially thrown out of alignment. This, in combination with the opportunity afforded by continuous programming of remaining inside the cinema for hours on end, seeing the same programme several times over, lends remembered cinema time a quality of expansiveness and circularity. One letter writer says of her favourite films that she 'never wanted them to finish'.[25] The continuous programme went a long way towards making such a wish come true.

The expansive, non-everyday quality of time in the cinema is perhaps allied with the experience recollected by many informants of being 'carried away' whilst watching films:

Int   I mean one thing that I did want to ask was, it sounded obviously as if you had a lot of pleasure out of going to the pictures. Em, how did it actually feel when you were there?

HP   Really great. [*Enthusiastic voice*] You got carried away.[26]

This experience is expressed at several levels, from memories that reference an abstract sensation of being transported (the pictures, says Mickie Rivers, 'transported you to another world', it gave you 'a break from life. It transported you away from the dull things'[27]), through memories expressing a sense of passing through the veil of the cinema screen and stepping into the world of the film, to a remembered sensation of being singled out and addressed individually by characters on the screen.

The words 'carried away' and 'transported', which arise repeatedly in memories of the experience of watching films, imply both movement or travel and passivity: the film takes you on a journey, and you just let it happen. The journey, in another recurrent turn of phrase, is to 'another world', a world utterly different from the 'dull things' of everyday life:

So the cinema just was your only real [*pause: 2 seconds*]. To take you away from life as it was. As your life was. You went in there and then you were into another world, looking at people clothed and dressed.[28]

I was [in] a family of ten, youngest but 2, as you can imagine not very well off. At the cinema I lived in a fantasy world for [a] few hours. It was great.[29]

For some, this pleasurable sense of being transported has to do with the cinemagoing experience in its own right, without reference to the 'real world'. Tessa Amelan, for example, speaks of being carried away whilst watching a film, and of the feeling remaining with her for some while afterwards:

Int   What was it about going to the pictures that you liked so much?

TA   Well, I tell you what it was. It's like being in another world. Which it is. And I enjoyed it. And then when I come out, I'm a bit, you know, kind of ooh! [*Laughs*] A bit, eh, carried away. [*Laughs*] And eh, then I come down to earth eventually. That's why I like the pictures. Take you out of this world.[30]

Bill Pickess describes the sensation of being carried away as one of being 'glued on the screen':

Int   Ah. I mean one thing that I did want to ask was, it sounded obviously as if you had a lot of pleasure out of going to the pictures. Em, how did it actually feel when you were there?

HP   Really great. [*Enthusiastic voice*] You got carried away.

WP   Well, yes. That's what I going say. Eh, you're glued on the screen and eh...

HP   Yeah.

WP   That was it. I mean if you were together you didn't have no interest in each other. You were [*laughs*] glued on the screen.

HP   You were absorbed in it.

WP   Yeah.[31]

The feeling tone of this remembered experience is of willingly allowing oneself to be swept up and pulled into the world portrayed on the screen, and of becoming completely caught up in it, ensnared to the exclusion of all else. Being 'absorbed' in the world on the screen, one seems to become part of that world and of the characters inhabiting it. One makes the transition, as Elizabeth Bowen puts it, from perceiving them to *being* them. Jim Godbold does not find it easy to put this experience into words, but nonetheless comes up with a telling phrase:

> *Int* I mean, how did you feel when you were at the pictures? How did, how did going to a picture make you feel? Em, how did you feel when you were actually watching it?
>
> *EG* Oh, you sort of live the part, don't you? I mean eh, the gangsters and that. I can't explain it really.[32]

There is a point at which the experience of passively letting oneself be transported shifts into a sensation of passing through the veil of the cinema screen and actually entering into the picture. For Irene and Bernard Letchet, the intensity of this experience is in direct proportion to the magnitude of the cinema screen and the larger-than-life scale of the world portrayed on it:

> *IL* You know. But, em, if you were really enjoying it you did, you did, em, yes.
>
> *BL* Ooh yes. Got right into it.
>
> *IL* Mm.
>
> *BL* Which is a thing you cannot do with television. Part of it is the physical size of it.

Prompted by the interviewer, the Letchets agree enthusiastically that what the large screen allows one to do is to enter imaginatively into the world of the film:

> *Int* So did you actually...
>
> *BL* You have a screen about that size [*laughs*].
>
> *Int* Did you ever actually imagine yourself *in* the films?
>
> *BL* *Oh yes!*
>
> *IL* *Oh yes!*
>
> [*Both respond extremely positively and enthusiastically at the same time.*][33]

Annie Wright makes an implicit association between being in love and imagining oneself 'living the part' as a protagonist in the romantic action on the cinema screen:

And of course, you was in love and of course, that enhanced the feeling. All these films were sort of made for you. You know you could see yourself in. Well I did anyway.[34]

The idea of films being 'made for you' adds a further dimension to the feeling-memory of being carried away. It is as if the film singles the viewer out from the rest of the audience and, speaking to her alone, beckons her into its world. This type of involvement is often associated with fan worship or cinephilia. Former cinema usherette Isobel Bullock is one of several informants whose testimony suggests that this experience was particularly intense when one's favourite star was, it seemed, singing to one, or inviting one to dance:

> as I was standing at the back while Nelson Eddy was singing his love song *to me* the ice cream used to melt. I danced with Fred Astaire while Ginger Rogers watched.[35]

Finally, some investments have to do with the deeper meanings of cinema in the context of informants' whole lives – as opposed, that is, to its significance at a particular life stage such as childhood or adolescence. Although this is an aspect of engagement with cinema which many find particularly difficult to put into words, in context it is susceptible to observation. For some 1930s cinemagoers, such attachments are clearly very important.

The tonic effect of an evening at the pictures is fairly often mentioned. Gloria Gooch offers the briskly detached observation that 'it was a morale booster really... to see the more cheerful things'. Ethel Cullum reaches for the core of the cinema's attraction for her with a telling comparison: 'Oh yeah, that's as good as a dose of medicine going to the pictures. I mean, there wasn't much else for us to do was there then'.[36] Jim Godbold describes the 'little lift' he felt as a kind of injection of psychological energy that, far from being an escape, helped him and others like him to cope with the rigours and demands of their daily lives:

> *Int* I mean, how did you feel when you came out the cinema? Em, you're saying...
>
> *EG* Oh, you feel refreshed and eh. Like eh, you know, you've had an experience and you, you know, you went home and you thought, well, I've had a nice night. Enjoyed the cinema and that.

And you was ready for work the next day.

[...]

EG Specially when you think you lived in a small market town and nothing ever happened. And people just went to work and girls went into service. And got half a crown a week. Just one half day off and that. You've gotta think in them terms, you see. And you would be impressed by eh, going to cinema and seeing how gangsters went about. And Fred Astaire and Ginger Rogers and all that. Very impressive and that. It put sorta new heart into you really, you know.[37]

Others use more abstract language in articulating the sense of freedom and elation a visit to the pictures could bring about. For Irene Letchet, 'It was a form of release really'; while Doreen Lyell explains how this feeling remained with you after leaving the cinema, and how you could sometimes hang onto it until the next time you went to the pictures:

Int I mean, when you say it was, eh, a sort of release from your everyday life, how did you actually feel when you came out the cinema?

DL Well we felt elated you know. And that sort of stayed with us till the next time we went to the cinema [*laughs*]. I don't think it made us feather-headed you know.[38]

Mrs Lyell is adamant that while the elation afforded by cinema was highly pleasurable, film lovers like herself never lost touch with reality ('I don't think it made us feather-headed'), and even derived some useful lessons for life from the pictures:

Int How did you feel when you were at the pictures?

DL Oh lovely. You know. It was really uplifting. Really. It was really uplifting. And then again it was, it was, em, there was always a moral message. I mean the good people didn't have much but in the end they were happy and contented. And the bad people seemed to get away with something for a time but in the end, the morals were always there.[39]

In *British Cinemas and their Audiences*, J.P. Mayer concludes from his informants' motion picture autobiographies that 'films appear as a dominating "educational" influence on a [sic] human life'; and indeed, like some of Mayer's informants, Doreen Lyell claims to have learned moral lessons from films, with their valuation of the virtues of being a 'good egg'. Mayer accurately, if cynically, describes this as 'the value patterns of the Hays Code-*pur sang*';[40] but it is apparent that Mrs Lyell at least has something bigger in mind than a simple lesson in doing the right thing. This 'something' is the possibility films seemed to proffer that anyone, no matter how poor, could 'make themselves better than they are... it gave you hope'.[41]

As Mrs Lyell expresses it, it seems that the hope was coloured to some extent by Hollywood's version of the American Dream. However, other informants' talk about this feeling of hope suggests that something more profound is at issue: that there is an armature of desire, or wanting, onto which cinema hangs itself, so that the armature is clad with cinematic content, in the manner described by Sally Alexander. A half-expressed sense of a wish for something 'better' emerges in a number of informants' accounts of their investments in cinema. And when these accounts are taken together, the outward clothing of the desire begins to look somewhat contingent.

Peggy Kent and her friends, for example, talk together around the idea of something better, approaching it from several directions:

BH Well up to a point because we, what you saw, that, all that lovely way of living, especially all that lovely old song and dance.

PK Yeh.

GK Oh, I love those song and dance films.

BH They seemed to have such a easy life, don't they, you know?

GK Well we did, we...

[*Unintelligible: overtalking*]

BH Perhaps one day life will be like that.[42]

The abstract notion of better things, or a better life, is given content in the shape of the 'way of living', the 'lovely' singing and dancing, and the 'easy life' enjoyed by people in films. At last, though, the underlying wish – both more and less than a desire for lovely things and an easy life – is baldly stated: 'perhaps one day life will be like that'.

While Mrs Kent and her co-interviewees approach their recollections of wanting something 'better' in a lighthearted spirit, there is a potentially serious sentiment underlying this sense of yearning. For it combines the memory of youthful hopes that life will one day be wonderful with a remembered feeling, or a certainty in retrospect, that one is or was unentitled to better things, that such a lovely life is unachievable for people like oneself:

DL Well I really was immersed in the cinema. My day.

Int Yeah.

DL Because, eh, that was part of your dreams, you know.

Int Mm.

DL You didn't expect them to come true.[43]

This perhaps encapsulates a class-based and peculiarly British experience of the dream of a better life. The words 'lovely' and 'beautiful' are often used, particularly by women, in recollections of feelings experienced when watching films. Read in context, such words articulate exactly the mix of desire and acceptance of its impossibility that is embodied in the type of wishing or wanting encapsulated in the idea of yearning. The dreams and the hopes might have been strong, but if you did not understand it then, you certainly do now, that opportunities for fulfilling them were limited.

Words often seem inadequate, too, when those 1930s cinemagoers for whom cinema was the locus of general dreams and aspirations offer their reflections and retrospections on the meaning of cinema in their lives. For Doreen Lyell, for instance, cinema was certainly the site of her dreams: she was, she says, 'immersed' in it. When she says that 'the cinema was everything to us really. It was to me',[44] she appears to be offering a profound statement about the place of cinema in her inner life. The idea of films being 'everything' surfaces in other informants' accounts, and these too may be read in context as referencing some deep and abiding aspect of one's inner life.

Asked whether she looked forward to going to the pictures, Phyllis Bennett replies emphatically: 'Yeah, oh, yeah. Yeah. Yeah, my films were everything to me. Yeah.' And the intensity of Thomas McGoran's investment in cinema is as apparent in the way he talks as in the actual words he uses:

Oh it was *great*! Cause the life, the cinema life then it was *everything*! [*with great emphasis and emotion*][45]

For Doreen Lyell, Phyllis Bennett and Thomas McGoran, 'everything' seems to connote an inexpressible and all-encompassing investment in cinema.

Sometimes, the commonly expressed idea of being 'taken out of oneself' appears to gesture towards a more profound experience, as Phyllis Bennett's words suggest:

Int   I mean how did you actually feel when you were at the pictures?

PB   I, I, I used to lose myself in the pictures.[46]

In the context of her testimony as a whole, Mrs Bennett's highly self-implicated statement, along with her hesitation as she searches for the right expression, speak of a loss of self, a transcendence of ego, a standing outside oneself: precisely a state of ecstasy.

It is only for a small minority, however, that cinema is so intensely and profoundly meaningful, so central in giving significance to their lives. For these people, expressions of longing for beauty in life, for an indefinable something better, assume the quality of a secular quest for transcendence, and this in turn finds promise of fulfilment in cinema.

Most commonly in 1930s cinemagoers' accounts of their investments in cinema, a narrative of a sort emerges: one of anticipation, transportation and elevation:

I can still remember the excitement of eventually going through the door after waiting in the rain or snow for an hour… For 3 hours the outside world was forgotten, worries… disappeared as we lived through the screen.

Standing in the street queuing in pleasant anticipation of what the next couple of hours had to offer, as the lights dimmed and the screen lit up away we went transported into a world of fantasy.[47]

This is a story of a journey from 'real life' to the pictures and back again, from outside the cinema to inside and then back to an outside world which, for a while at least, will be imbued with the magic encountered and left behind in the cinema: an outside which then becomes the starting place for another journey, another cycle of return and (temporary) uplift and transformation.

Over a valedictory cup of tea at the end of her final interview, Beatrice Cooper tells as full, rounded and eloquent a version of the story as Elizabeth Bowen had done 60 years earlier, complete with vivid detail, incident, and relived feelings; but now overlaid with the *pentimento* of memory:

Int   [*Laughs*] I mean, how did you actually feel when you were watching the films in the thirties?

BC   Oh, well. It was a whole wonderful world. I mean there was no TV an, em, what was there? You know, I didn't go that much to the theatre either at that age. I mean if I went to the theatre it was an event. And if I went once a year it was, you know. Em, so film was a marvellous escape world. Em, I think in the previous one you [*inaudible*]. I told you my mother used to go in for sixpence. And she's have two films. An A film and a B film and tea. And the organ would [*laughs*] come up.

Int   Ah.

BC   And all that. Yeah, it was a, a fantastic way of spending either a whole afternoon or an evening. [*Coughs*] And eh, how did I feel? Oh, excited. Terribly excited. You'd go into this dark, dark place. And the films then of course were continuous. You know, they wasn't, they weren't [*pause: 1 second*] set to programmes. [*Coughs*] Sorry. [*Pause: 2 seconds*] And eh, so, it didn't matter when you went in. [*Puts cup on saucer*] You didn't mind coming in halfway through. And then you could sit it round again, for as often as you'd want to. Nobody pushed you out. [*Laughs*]

Int   [*Laughs*]

BC   And em, oh yes! Oh, wonderful atmosphere. But very smoky. Full of smoke. And em, always packed! Always packed. And usually queues. Mm. Specially if it was, you know, a good film. And most of them were. You know. Fairly popular. Em, it was just exciting. Terribly exciting [*laughs*] you know. Specially if it was, you know, somebody you really wanted to see, like Garbo or, or eh, you know, Grace Moore. One of those good stars. Eh, yes. It was a thrill.

Int   Mm.

BC   Cinema was a real thrill in those days. Mm. Yeah. Talking about it I can almost feel how I felt. Yeah. Yeah. [*Laughs*] Mm. It was wonderful.[48]

Notes

1. E. Wight Bakke, *The Unemployed Man: A Social Study* (London: Nisbet and Co. Ltd, 1933), p. 263.
2. Ibid., p. 182.
3. J.P. Mayer, *Sociology of Film: Studies and Documents* (London: Faber and Faber, 1946), p. 181; p. 185.
4. J.P. Mayer, *British Cinemas and their Audiences: Sociological Studies* (London: Dennis Dobson Ltd, 1948), p. 14.
5. Ibid., p. 75.
6. Bowen, 'Why I go to the cinema', in Charles Davy (ed.), *Footnotes to the Film* (London: Lovat Dickson Ltd., 1937), p. 210; p. 212.
7. Ibid., p. 213; p. 214 (emphasis in original).
8. Sally Alexander, 'Becoming a woman in London in the 1920s and 1930s', in Gareth Stedman Jones and David Feldman (eds), *Metropolis-London: Histories and Representations* (London: Routledge, 1989), pp. 245–71 (quotation is on pp. 248–9).
9. 95-81-1, Bernard Goodsall, Avon, to Annette Kuhn and Valentina Bold, n.d. 1995.
10. T95-80, Olga Scowen, Harrow, 6 July 1995.
11. T94-12, Thomas McGoran, Glasgow, 30 November 1994.
12. T95-104, Ashley Bird, Harrow, 26 July 1995.
13. 95-267, Questionnaire, Sheila Black, London, December 1995.
14. T95-109, Leonard and Mickie Rivers, Suffolk, 11 October 1995.
15. T95-58, John and Marion Cooper, Bolton, 8 May 1995.
16. T95-150, Irene and Bernard Letchet, Harrow, 23 November 1995.
17. 95-96-1, Bob Surtees, Gwent, to Annette Kuhn and Valentina Bold, 6 February 1995.
18. Rene Cutforth, *Later Than We Thought: A Portrait of the Thirties* (Newton Abbot: David and Charles, 1976), p. 82.
19. T95-109, Leonard and Mickie Rivers, Suffolk, 11 October 1995.
20. T95-70, Norman Wild (Vee Entwistle interpreting), Bolton, 16 May 1995.
21. 95-55, Questionnaire, J. Charles Hall, Dyfed, February 1995; 95-60-1, Olive Johnson, West Midlands, to Annette Kuhn and Valentina Bold, 14 February 1995; 95-77-1, Myra Schneidermann, Cardiff, to Annette Kuhn and Valentina Bold, 10 February 1995; 95-87-1, Joan Donaghue, Cardiff, to Annette Kuhn and Valentina Bold, 11 February 1995; 95-113-1, Valerie Shute, Hampshire, to Annette Kuhn and Valentina Bold, 17 February 1995.
22. T95-61, Westhoughton History Society, Bolton, 9 May 1995 (AB: Ada Bellis; LB: Lois Basnett; Mr A: Mr Ackers; Ms X: unnamed female interviewee).
23. T95-91, Eileen and Joe Barnett, Harrow, 18 July 1995.
24. T95-144, Phyllis Bennett, Norfolk, 17 November 1995.
25. 95-299, Questionnaire, Ivy Royal, Norfolk, December 1995.
26. T95-138, Hazel and William Pickess, Suffolk, 14 November 1995.
27. T95-109, Leonard and Mickie Rivers, Suffolk, 11 October 1995; T95-130, Leonard and Mickie Rivers, Suffolk, 8 November 1995.
28. T95-72, Helen Smeaton, Glasgow, 26 June 1995.
29. 95-319, Questionnaire, Doris English, Cambridgeshire, December 1995.
30. T95-158, Tessa Amelan, Manchester, 28 May 1995.
31. T95-138, Hazel and William Pickess, Suffolk, 14 November 1995.
32. T95-113, E.J. Godbold, Suffolk, 17 October 1995.
33. T95-149, Irene and Bernard Letchet, Harrow, 23 November 1995.

34. T95-33, Annie Wright, Manchester, 26 May 1995.

35. 95-236-1, Isobel Bullock, Nottinghamshire, to Cinema Culture in 1930s Britain, n.d. 1995.

36. T95-142, Gloria Gooch, Norfolk, 16 November 1995; T95-139, Ethel and George Cullum, Norfolk, 14 November 1995.

37. T95-113, E.J. Godbold, Suffolk, 17 October 1995; T95-129, E.J. Godbold, Suffolk, 27 November 1995.

38. T95-149, Irene and Bernard Letchet, Harrow, 23 November 1995; T95-135, Doreen Lyell, Suffolk, 13 November 1995.

39. T95-116, Doreen Lyell, Suffolk, 19 October 1995.

40. Mayer, *British Cinemas and their Audiences*, p. 151.

41. T95-135, Doreen Lyell, Suffolk, 13 November 1995.

42. T95-115, Peggy Kent, Hilda Green, Hilda Catchpol, Barbara Harvey and Gladys Kent, Suffolk, 18 October 1995.

43. T95-116, Doreen Lyell, Suffolk, 19 October 1995.

44. T95-135, Doreen Lyell, Suffolk, 13 November 1995.

45. T95-144, Phyllis Bennett, Norfolk, 17 November 1995; T94-12, Thomas McGoran, Glasgow, 30 November 1994.

46. T95-144, Phyllis Bennett, Norfolk, 17 November 1995.

47. 95-111-1, Margaret Houlgate, Hampshire, to Annette Kuhn and Valentina Bold, 20 February 1995; 95-232-1, Raymond Aspden, Lancashire, to Valentina Bold, n.d. 1995.

48. T95-153, Beatrice Cooper, Harrow, 27 November 1995.

Epilogue

THIS book has covered a great deal of ground on its journey around and through cinema and cultural memory, and in the course of the journey some new directions have been explored and some lessons about the conduct of inquiries into popular culture learned.

Film studies

This inquiry has aimed to consider in tandem films, their spectators and audiences, the times and places in which films have been consumed and the place of cinema in the lives of those who consumed them. With such a wide-ranging remit, it has been forced to scrutinise and reformulate the methods and objects of film studies, and indeed those of other disciplines devoted to the study of culture.

Spectatorship in cinema

For example, looking at the consumption and reception of cinema and films from the standpoint of the experience of the cinemagoer entails a rethinking of theories and models of the relationship between film texts and spectators. This has involved relativising theories which privilege the role of vision and looking in this cinema-spectator relationship, and admitting a broader range of embodied engagements into that relationship.

The cinema audience

This in turn permits a deeper understanding of the point at which modes of spectatorship intersect with the feelings and behaviours of social audiences; of how, for instance, the feelings and imaginings on which cinema draws may inform people's daily activities and interactions with family members and peers.

Canonicity

When cinemagoers are given central stage as producers of cultural meanings, preconceived notions about popular cinema and films immediately shift: in this instance we can see beyond the 1930s films and stars celebrated today to a rather different canon arising from a highly distinctive cinema culture.

Cultural memory

Examining the detail and the discursive registers of memory stories of 1930s cinemagoers throws into relief the distinctive qualities of cinema memory. Also, and more generally, it enhances, deepens and modifies understandings of the nature and operations of cultural memory.

Memory work

Exploring ways of working with memory and analysing memory-stories highlights the value of memory work in itself, for the people who are remembering as well as for those wishing to understand how acts of memory organise personal and collective imaginations.

Childhood

Looking at childhood memories of cinemagoing from the standpoint of the adult offers a productive way into understanding how children and young people, past and present, engage with popular culture and media as part of the process of growing up.

Ageing

The content and the discursive registers of the cinema memory-stories of the 1930s generation throw light on the cultural as well as the psychical processes involved in ageing.

Elders' stories

The memory-stories told in this book are in many different ways interesting, informative, revealing, instructive, entertaining, surprising, and thought-provoking. They are a reminder, much-needed in an ageist society, of the cultural treasure that lies in our elders' memories.

APPENDIX

Cinema Culture in 1930s Britain: Ethnohistory of a Popular Cultural Practice

Research Design, Methods and Sources

1. The ethnographic inquiry

This part of the project, guided by the methodological protocols of interpretive sociology, ethnography and oral history, was devoted to gathering data from surviving cinemagoers of the 1930s. This began at the start of the project in 1991, and still continues. However, the main period of data gathering was between 1994 and 1996, when the project was funded by a grant from the Economic and Social Research Council and staffed by a Research Fellow and a secretary.

Three types of data or materials have been gathered in the course of the ethnographic inquiry: interviews, questionnaires, and other materials generated by 1930s cinemagoers.

1.1 Interviews

Cinemagoers of the 1930s were interviewed in four UK locations: Glasgow, Greater Manchester, East Anglia and the London suburb of Harrow. These were carefully chosen to give a spread of settlement patterns and class and regional cultures. Interviews were piloted in the city of Glasgow in the southwest of Scotland, where the project was at that time based. In the 1930s a centre of shipbuilding and other heavy industry, this self-styled 'movie-mad' city was reputed to have Europe's highest number of cinema seats per head of population. The nineteenth-century city of Manchester, in the northwest of England, was still a centre of the cotton industry in the 1930s and boasted many cinemas, old and new: in 1933, for instance, there were 109 cinemas for a population of 770,000. The Greater Manchester fieldwork area incorporated Bolton, a small industrial town about six miles north of Manchester city centre and the site of Mass-Observation's famous 'Worktown' studies of the 1930s. Situated to the north-west of London, Harrow underwent considerable growth during the 1930s, becoming transformed from a semi-rural area to a prosperous metropolitan suburb boasting several new supercinemas. In the 1930s as today, the predominantly rural counties of Suffolk and Norfolk in East Anglia featured a variety of settlement patterns, including small towns and seaside resorts, as well as villages of various sizes; and farming was the area's main industry.

Interviewees were sought in several ways. The majority of the Glasgow interviewees were selected from people who had been in contact with the project from its beginning and from contacts of the Research Fellow's in educational groups, day centres and homes for the elderly. Interviewees in the other three areas were sought through media appeals in which people who went to the cinema in the 1930s were asked to get in touch with the project. A total of 37 local radio broadcasts and announcements in local newspapers and publications for the elderly were made. Approaches were also made to institutions and organisations of various kinds (local history societies, friendship groups, housebound library users' services, residential homes for the elderly, and so on).

Interviewees were chosen from amongst these 'first contacts' with a view to balancing several demographic factors: location – the aim was to interview more-or-less equal numbers of people in each of the four fieldwork locales; type of contact – a mix of self-selected volunteers and others was aimed at; and also gender, social class in the 1930s (judged on the basis of terminal education age, first occupation and parents' occupations) and ethnicity. A quota in terms of class and gender was estimated, on the basis of contemporary data on the composition of the cinema audience, at two-thirds women and two-thirds working class. The ethnicity quota was less straightforward, because no data are available on the ethnic composition of the 1930s cinema audience in Britain. Although approaches to multicultural community organisations and similar groups in Glasgow, Manchester and London generated few contacts, a number of Jewish people were interviewed.

A total of 78 core informants were selected for interview, the largest single group of whom had responded to media appeals (Table 1). The 78 are fairly evenly spread across the four fieldwork locations (Table 2). The rough social class and gender quotas aimed at were satisfactorily achieved (Tables 3 and 4).

Table 1: Mode of contact

Personal Contact (Glasgow)	10
Responded To Media Appeal	33
Volunteer From Local Organisation	13
Volunteer From Day Centre	12
Volunteer From Residential Home	10
TOTAL	78

Table 2: Location

Glasgow	17
Greater Manchester	22
East Anglia	21
Harrow	18

Table 3: Gender

Male	28
Female	50

Table 4: Social class during 1930s

Working	42
Working/Middle	6
Middle	29
Upper Middle	1

Interviewees' dates of birth range between 1897 and 1928, with the majority clustered between 1917 and 1923. The median year of birth is 1919. A cut-off year of 1925 was aimed for on the grounds that those born after that date would remember little of the 1930s. In the event, several people born in the later 1920s were interviewed (Table 5).

All but three of the 78 core informants were interviewed more than once, with the majority being interviewed on two occasions. Forty-five people were interviewed on their own, and the rest were interviewed in couples or groups: these involved siblings, married couples, friends, and members of clubs, associations, residential homes, and so on.

Table 5: Year of birth

1897	1
1902 to 1910	12
1911 to 1915	11
1916 to 1920	27
1921 to 1925	20
1926 to 1928	7

Interviews were conducted by the project's Research Fellow, Valentina Bold, an experienced oral history researcher. Most of the meetings took place in interviewees' homes, and a few in day centres, residential homes, or group meeting places. While the interviews covered preset topics (Table 6), the interviewer never visibly consulted the checklist, questions were open and non-directive and informants were not dissuaded from straying into other areas. The pattern of questioning was to move from the specific to the abstract: for example from discussions of local cinemas to discussions of feelings about the cinema. For the first interviews, the interviewer prepared a selection of memory stimulants, including photographs of local cinemas and 1930s film stars. These were used discreetly, and only where the interviewer was sure they would not be 'leading' or intrusive. In first interviews, informants were keen to be recorded and to offer facts 'for posterity', listing cinema names and locations, for instance. Some informants had done preparatory research of their own. First interviews lasted between one and three hours.

Second and subsequent meetings, with rapport established, were freer and, rather than information flowing in one direction, were closer to exchanges between interviewer and interviewee. On this occasion the interviewer would follow up issues arising in the informant's first interview, and take along contemporary film annuals and popular reference books as memory stimulants. Most informants responded with enthusiasm when handling this material from the 1930s. More peripheral and contextual detail emerged during second interviews, often giving deeper insight into the informant's attitudes and outlook. Second interviews lasted about two hours.

A total of 186 hours of tape-recorded interview material was gathered. In all but a few cases (where sound was of very poor quality, for example), interviews with the core informants have been transcribed, together with the interviewer's fieldnotes.

To analyse the interview transcripts, the qualitative data analysis software QSR NUD*IST (Non-numerical Unstructured Data Indexing Searching and Theorizing) was used. This software supports storing, managing, indexing, searching, and theorising with, qualitative data. A coding frame was derived initially from transcripts of pilot interviews, and indexing and analysis of the interviews began during the project's funded period.

Table 6: Checklist of questions for first interviews

Cinemas attended: when, where, how often (describe; a cafe)?
How often did the programmes change?
When did you go (day/time of day)?
Time of year (summer/winter differences)?
Cost/payment in kind?
Differences in local cinemas: 'posh'? types of films?
Go into town for the pictures?
Staff: commissionaires; usherettes; managers; organist
Live acts? (singing to 'the dot')

Who did you go with (friends/dates)?
What did you wear (makeup? hairstyle? 'dress up'?)
Did you eat and/or drink during the films?
How did you/other people behave? (if enjoying/not enjoying the picture)
How did you feel? (before/during/after)

Favourite films: likes and dislikes; what makes a 'good' film or a 'bad' film
Favourite stars
Differences/changes in taste (Children/Men/Women)
First experience of sound/colour pictures
Shorts; news
European films

How did you choose films?
In a fan club? collect photos? read magazines? film society?
In a cinema club? (children?)
Did you sing songs from the films? Buy sheet music?

Other forms of entertainment you enjoyed in the 1930s?
Did you go to the cinema on holiday?

What did going to the cinema mean to you (how did you feel?)

1.2 Questionnaire

In the course of the search for interviewees, hundreds of letters, enquiries and offers of information were received from all over Britain, and it became apparent that the project had generated much more interest than could be accommodated through interviews alone. Though not originally planned, it was decided to ask those correspondents who were not interviewed to take part in a postal questionnaire survey.

The questionnaire was kept short and simple, and designed – through the choice, framing and ordering of questions – to stimulate recall of events and experiences of more than 60 years before. Questionnaires were sent out in two batches: 129 in May 1995 and 97 in December 1995. Of these 226 questionnaires, a total of 186 were returned, representing a response rate of over 82 per cent. Questionnaires were processed using SPSS, a software package widely used for quantitative data in the social sciences.

Three-quarters of the questionnaire respondents found out about the project through announcements in a local newspaper or a specialist publication for the elderly (Table 7). Although no gender balance was planned or intended, respondents divided themselves more or less equally as to gender: of the 186, 91 (49 per cent) were male and 95 (51 per cent) female. Some six in ten were born between 1915 and 1924, the median year of birth being 1922 (Table 8). Nearly one-third of all respondents lived in the southeast of England during the 1930s (Table 9), and the majority lived in larger towns and cities as opposed to small towns and rural areas.

Table 7: Mode of contact

	No.	%
Personal contact	13	(7.1)
Local radio	4	(2.2)
Newspaper (eg *Manchester Evening News*)	75	(41.2)
Specialist press (eg *Mature Tymes*)	62	(34.1)
Local history/film society	4	(2.2)
Unknown	24	(13.2)

Table 8: Year of birth

	Male		Female		All	
	No.	%	No.	%	No.	%
1903–1914	6	(7.0)	10	(10.5)	16	(8.6)
1915–1924	51	(56.0)	59	(62.1)	110	(59.1)
1925–1934	34	(37.0)	26	(27.4)	60	(32.3)
Median y.o.b.	1923		1922		1922	
Range	1906–32		1903–34		1903–34	

Table 9: Region of domicile in the 1930s

	No.	%
Southwest England	14	(17.5)
Southeast England	61	(32.8)
East Anglia	34	(18.3)
Midlands	12	(6.5)
Yorkshire/Humberside	9	(4.8)
Northwest England	22	(11.8)
North England	5	(2.7)
Scotland	11	(5.9)
Northern Ireland	1	(0.5)
Wales	15	(8.1)
Unknown	2	(1.1)

Just over half of the respondents finished their full-time education at the age of 14 or below; that is, at the minimum school-leaving age for this generation, for whom education beyond elementary school was a minority experience. The women, however, were rather more likely than the men to have received a secondary education. At the end of their full-time education, the largest single group of men and women entered jobs classified as skilled: these include secretarial and clerical occupations (which account for more than 27 per cent of all respondents) as well as certain types of administrative and craft jobs. A substantial additional group found work in sales occupations, and another group in agriculture and other primary occupations. In general, as might be expected of a self-selected sample, the people taking part in this survey appear to have had slightly more formal education, and to have worked in jobs requiring greater skill and/or more training, than would be expected in their age group as a whole.

For a copy of the questionnaire and a report on the findings of the survey, see Annette Kuhn, 'Cinemagoing in Britain in the 1930s: report of a questionnaire survey', *Historical Journal of Film, Radio and Television*, vol. 19, no. 4 (1999), pp. 531–543.

1.3 Other informant-generated material

Nearly all the 1930s cinemagoers who responded to appeals to take part in the project, both at the beginning and during the main period of data gathering, made initial contact in writing. Many of these people sent long letters with descriptions of favourite cinemas, lists of films and stars and memories of their cinemagoing days. Others enclosed essays, poems and other writings about 'the pictures' in the 1930s, press clippings, drawings and photographs. Some of those who took part in the questionnaire survey also enclosed material of this kind with their completed questionnaires. In all, there are upwards of 300 of these as yet uncounted items. All this material has been archived, but not yet catalogued, transcribed or added to the NUD*IST database.

A number of interviewees also donated their collections of cinema memorabilia (scrapbooks, copies of 1930s film weeklies and film annuals, fanzines and so on) to the project.

Where this informant-generated material is drawn on for the ethnographic inquiry, selection and analysis have been conducted manually.

1.4 Citation conventions for ethnographic materials

Every interviewee, questionnaire respondent and correspondent has been assigned a unique reference number under which all materials from or relating to that individual are archived.

Citations of memorabilia, correspondence and similar materials include the informant's reference number and the accession number of the item concerned. For example, in a letter cited as

> 95-100-1, Lewis Howells, Gwent, to Annette Kuhn and Valentina Bold, 9 February 1995

the informant's reference number is 95-100 and the 1 refers to the letter. A reference to an item of memorabilia such as

95-38-21, Spring Supplement to 'The Golden Star', 1977

incorporates the reference number of the informant who donated it (95-38) and the number of the item as listed within that person's file (21).

References to individual questionnaires use the same convention, for example:

95-324, Questionnaire, Mrs A. Close, Lincolnshire, December 1995.

Extracts from interviews are referred to by archive transcript number, with name(s) of interviewee(s), location and date of interview; for example:

T94-17, Margaret Young and Molly Stevenson, Glasgow, 5 December 1994.

2. The Historical Inquiry

Source materials for the historical inquiry include primary published and unpublished documents, with an emphasis on material by, for or about cinemagoers of the 1930s. They include: the popular film press and other mass-circulation periodicals of the period, including women's magazines; film industry sources such as trade journals, directories and almanacs; contemporary official and semi-official inquiries and reports on cinemagoing; and box-office figures, popularity polls and audience surveys, both published and unpublished. Historical source materials also include information on local cinemas in the areas where interview fieldwork was conducted, letters and diaries written by filmgoers in the 1930s, and 1930s cinema memorabilia. Notes on much of this material have been added to the NUD*IST database (see 1.3 above).

2.1 The Popular Press

An exhaustive review of the popular film press of the 1930s was undertaken (Table 10), and this yielded information about the films and stars that were popular at the time, as well as affording a general impression of the 'structure of feeling' of 1930s cinema culture.

The most important British popular film magazines of the 1930s were *Film Pictorial, Picturegoer, Film Weekly* and *Picture Show*. All but *Film Pictorial* (which was started in 1932) were published throughout the decade and until the outbreak of the Second World War, when *Film Weekly* was absorbed by *Picturegoer*, and *Film Pictorial* by *Picture Show*. All of them were weeklies, with the exception of *Picturegoer*, which was monthly until May 1931, when it too went weekly. In the mid-1930s, these four journals enjoyed a combined weekly circulation of more than 300,000 copies, indicating a readership in excess of one million. In addition to the big four, a large number of more ephemeral fan periodicals appeared at various times during the decade, perhaps the most important of these being a weekly called *Girls' Cinema*, which after a change of title (to *Film Star Weekly* eventually merged in the mid 1930s with *Picture Show*.

These journals offer a useful source of information on the popularity, with critics and to a certain extent with cinemagoers, of different films and stars. *Film Pictorial*, *Film Weekly* and *Picturegoer* all, at various points during the 1930s, had scales for rating the films they reviewed. *Film Weekly* ran an annual readers' poll for Best British Films and performances; and from 1932 *Picturegoer* awarded its Gold Medal annually for the best film performances by male and female performers.

Women's magazines, especially towards the end of the 1930s when the new weekly *Woman* was launched, also published occasional or regular features on cinema and film reviews. Two film monthlies, *Film Fashionland* and *Woman's Filmfair*, are in fact hybrids of the woman's magazine and the film magazine.

Table 10: Popular film periodicals consulted

British Film-Studio Mirror	1931–32	Monthly
Cinema Express	1932–33	Weekly
Cinegram	1937–39	Fortnightly
Cinegram Preview	1939–40	Fortnightly
Fan Fare	1935	Monthly (1 Issue)
Film Fashionland	1934–35	Monthly
Film Favourites	1932	Monthly (2 Issues)
Film Pictorial	1932–39	Weekly
Film Souvenir	1935	Monthly (2 Issues)
Film Star Weekly	1932–34	Weekly
Film Weekly	1930–39	Weekly
Girls' Cinema	1930–32	Weekly
Movie Fan	1931	Monthly (8 Issues)
Picture Show	1930–37	Weekly
Picturegoer	1930	Monthly
Picturegoer	1931–39	Weekly
Screen Pictorial	1937–39	Monthly
Woman's Filmfair	1934–35	Monthly

Table 11: Women's magazines consulted

Woman	1937–39	Weekly
Woman's Journal	1936	Monthly
Woman's Weekly	1930, 1934	Weekly

2.2 Film Trade Publications

The film trade press is a useful source of material on the popularity of films and stars from the distributor's, and more especially from the exhibitor's, point of view. From 1936, the American trade weekly *Motion Picture Herald* and its companion publication, the annual *Motion Picture Almanac*, ran listings of money-making stars (but not pictures) in Britain, in two categories: all star (British and Hollywood stars); and stars in British-made pictures only. However, the British trade press lagged somewhat behind the American in collecting and publishing information on audiences' choices at the box office, and it was not until 1937 that the British trade paper *Kinematograph Weekly* began publishing its annual survey of the biggest box-office attractions of the previous year. From around 1936, therefore, it is possible to obtain a reasonably clear picture from published British and American trade sources of the popularity of particular stars and films in Britain, as measured by box office receipts.

Table 12: Film trade publications consulted

Kinematograph Weekly	1937–40	Weekly
Kinematograph Year Book	1930–10	Annual
Motion Picture Almanac	1933–40	Annual

2.3 Other Contemporary Material

Other historical source materials include contemporary published and unpublished materials of various kinds. These include official records on regulations governing children's admission to cinemas and on the censorship of 'horrific' films; inquiries into children's cinemagoing conducted by local authorities, pressure groups and others; popularity polls such as the questionnaire surveys organised by the cinema impresario Sidney Bernstein in 1931, 1934 and 1937; surveys and observations of film audiences conducted under the aegis of Mass-Observation from 1937; letters, essays, diaries and other material produced in the 1930s by cinemagoers; and photographs and film 'documents' such as photographs of cinemas and newsreel footage of cinema openings.

Also included under this heading are books and essays published during the 1930s on the state of Britain in general and on cinema in particular. These contemporary published source materials are listed in the Bibliography under a separate heading.

2.4 Libraries and archives

Popular press, film trade press and other contemporary source materials were consulted in various general and specialist libraries, local, regional and national specialist archives, local record offices and local history collections (Table 13), as well as in the project's own memorabilia collection.

Table 13: Libraries and archives visited

Bolton Local History Library
British Film Institute, Library
British Film Institute, Special Collections
British Library, London
British Library, Newspaper Division, Colindale
Cinema Museum, Ronald Grant Archive, London
East Anglian Film Archive, University of East Anglia
Harrow Civic Centre Library, Local History Collection
Manchester Central Library, Arts Library
Manchester Central Library, Local Studies Unit
Mass-Observation Archive, University of Sussex
Mitchell Library, Glasgow
North-West Film Archive, Manchester
Public Record Office, Kew
Scottish Film Archive, Glasgow
Suffolk Record Office, Ipswich

3. Films

Feature films were selected for inclusion in the inquiry using two methods: firstly, from an analysis of historical source materials; and secondly, on the basis of testimonies of 1930s cinemagoers gathered for the ethnographic inquiry. Nearly all the films were viewed, and detailed notes taken. Film analysis began with narrative breakdowns and proceeded to examination of cinematic elements (mise en scene, lighting, editing and so on) and in selected instances detailed shot breakdowns were carried out. Films not viewed are denoted with an asterisk (*).

3.1 Films from 1930s sources

A list of 20 films which were popular in Britain in the 1930s (ten British, ten Hollywood) was compiled early in the project with a view to ascertaining the tastes of British audiences and reviewers at the time, and to assess changes of taste over the period. The list was produced by triangulating data from several contemporary sources: reviews in and awards given by the popular film press, newspapers and other mass-circulation publications; film and star popularity polls conducted among filmgoers; and data on box-office attractions gathered by the film industry. The popularity of individual stars with reviewers and filmgoers and at the box office was also taken into account in compiling the list in Table 14.

Because there is a paucity of data for the earlier years of the decade, titles given for the years up to 1935 are less likely to be reliable than the later ones. The list is not intended to suggest that these were the most popular films in Britain during the 1930s, but rather to serve as a broad indicator of contemporary tastes.

Table 14: Films Popular in Britain, 1930–39
(dates are for British general release)

Year	British	Hollywood
1930	Rookery Nook	The Love Parade*
1931	Sally in Our Alley	A Free Soul
1932	Sunshine Susie	Arrowsmith
1933	I Was a Spy	Cavalcade
1934	Private Life of Henry VIII	Queen Christina
1935	Escape Me Never	Lives of a Bengal Lancer
1936	The Ghost Goes West	Mr Deeds Goes to Town
1937	Victoria the Great	Stowaway
1938	It's in the Air	Snow White and the Seven Dwarfs
1939	The Citadel	Three Smart Girls Grow Up

For further details and additional findings, see Annette Kuhn, 'Researching popular film fan culture in 1930s Britain', in Jostein Gripsrud and Kathrin Skretting (eds), *History of Moving Images: Reports from a Norwegian Project* (Oslo: Research Council of Norway, 1994).

3.2 Informants' films

Included in the list of informant-generated film titles are pictures which interviewees have memories of seeing (a passing reference to a film did not qualify it for inclusion); titles listed by significant numbers of questionnaire respondents in answer to the question 'Do you recall any films that made a particularly strong impression on you?'; and films to which detailed reference is made in correspondence.

This is not a straightforward exercise, however, because informants rarely offer detailed memories of particular films, and where they do they do not always remember the film's title correctly, or indeed at all. This is especially apparent with the earliest memories of films, which are often simply of isolated images or scenes. Where informants refer to serials or series films without mentioning specific titles (for example, the Fu Manchu films), indicative titles have been added to the list only where the films are discussed at length by informants and/or are frequently mentioned (Table 15). It is perhaps worth noting that with the exception of *The Thirty-nine Steps*, no British film is mentioned by name by any of the informants.

Table 15: Films named by informants

Title	(Director, Country, Year)
All Quiet on the Western Front	(Lewis Milestone, US, 1930)
Blue Angel/Der blaue Engel	(Josef von Sternberg, Germany, 1930)
Dr Jekyll and Mr Hyde	(Rouben Mamoulian, US, 1932)
42nd Street	(Lloyd Bacon, US, 1933)
Four Sons	(John Ford, US, 1928)
Frankenstein	(James Whale, US, 1931)
It Happened One Night	(Frank Capra, US, 1934)
The Kid	(Charles Chaplin, US, 1921)
King Kong	(Cooper/Schoedsack, US, 1933)
The Mask of Fu Manchu	(Charles J. Brabin, Jr, US, 1932)
Maytime	(Robert Z. Leonard, US, 1937)
The Mummy	(Karl Freund, US, 1933)
The Mystery of Dr Fu Manchu – serial	(A.E. Colby, GB, 1923)
The Mystery of the Wax Museum	(Michael Curtiz, US, 1933)
Night Must Fall*	(Richard Thorpe, US, 1937)
Ramona*	(Edwin Carewe, US, 1928)
Seven Keys to Baldpate	(William Hamilton, US, 1935)
Seventh Heaven	(Frank Borzage, US, 1927)
Snow White and the Seven Dwarfs	(Walt Disney, US, 1937)
The Thirty-nine Steps	(Alfred Hitchcock, GB, 1935)
Three Smart Girls	(Henry Koster, US, 1936)
Top Hat	(Mark Sandrich, US, 1935)

There are several possible explanations for the divergences between this list and the one derived from contemporary source materials. Firstly, for informants born before about 1923, the earliest and most memorable cinemagoing experiences usually involved silent films: in consequence, the informants' list contains a number of pre-1930s films. Secondly, the 1930s preferences would have included those of older age groups, and are biased towards critics', as opposed to cinemagoers' choices. Thirdly, the informants' list is based on memory, which is inevitably selective, and hindsight and popular memory might have had some impact on the contents of the list.

Links for further information about Cinema Culture in 1930s Britain

ESRC Data Archival Resource Centre (Qualidata):
http://www.essex.ac.uk/qualidata/ (21 June 2001)

Institute for Cultural Research:
http://www.lancs.ac.uk/users/cultres/research/htm (21 June 2001)

Regard:
http://www.regard.ac.uk/regard/home/index (21 June 2001)

Bibliography

Contemporary documents: theses, reports, articles, books

Bakke, E. Wight, *The Unemployed Man: A Social Study* (London: Nisbet & Co. Ltd, 1933)

Bath Children's Cinema Council, *Report on a Questionnaire Drawn Up by the British Film Institute as Applied to Seven Bath Schools* (Bath: Bath Children's Cinema Council, 1936)

Birkenhead Vigilance Committee, *A Report of Investigations, June–October 1931* (Birkenhead: Birkenhead Vigilance Committee, 1931)

Birmingham Cinema Inquiry Committee, *Notes of Meeting Held on November 7 1930* (Birmingham: Birmingham Cinema Inquiry Committee, 1930)

Birmingham Cinema Inquiry Committee, *Report of Investigations, April 1930–May 1931* (Birmingham: Cinema Inquiry Committee, 1931)

Blumer, Herbert, *Movies and Conduct* (New York: MacMillan, 1933)

British Film Institute, *Films for Children: a First List of Films Recommended for Special Performances for Children in Cinema* (London: British Film Institute, 1937)

British Film Institute, 'Report of the conference on films for children, November 20th and 21st, 1936', in *Films for Children* (London: British Film Institute, 1936)

Browning, H.E. and A.A. Sorrell, 'Cinemas and cinema-going in Great Britain', *Journal of the Royal Statistical Society,* vol. 117, no. 2 (1954), pp. 133–168

Calder-Marshall, Arthur, 'The Film Industry', in *The Mind in Chains: Socialism and the Cultural Revolution*, (ed.) C. Day-Lewis (London: Frederick Muller, 1937), pp. 57–79

Cameron, C. et al, *Disinherited Youth: a Survey, 1936–1939* (Fife: Carnegie United Kingdom Trust, 1943)

Coglan, W.N., *The Readership of Newspapers and Periodicals in Great Britain*, (London: Incorporated Society of British Advertisers, 1936)

Commission on Educational and Cultural Films, *The Film in National Life* (London: George Allen & Unwin, 1932)

Dale, Edgar, *The Context of Motion Pictures* (New York: MacMillan, 1935)

Davy, Charles, (ed.) *Footnotes to the Film* (London: Lovat Dickson Ltd., 1937)

Durant, Henry, *The Problem of Leisure* (London: George Routledge & Sons Ltd, 1938)

Farr, William, 'Films for children—plea for co-operation', *Cinematograph Times*, no. 12 (1936)

Farr, William, 'Analysis of questionnaire to adolescents 14–18 years', (London: British Film Institute, [1939])

Ford, Richard, *Children in the Cinema* (London: Allen & Unwin, 1939)

Forman, Henry James, *Our Movie-Made Children* (New York: MacMillan, 1933)

Griffith, Hubert, 'Films and the British public', *The Nineteenth Century*, vol. 212, no. 66 (1932), pp. 190–200

Handel, Leo A., *Hollywood Looks at its Audience* (Urbana, IL: University of Illinois Press, 1950)

Herring, Robert et al, *Cinema Survey* (London: Blue Moon Press, 1937)

Jennings, Hilda and Winifred Gill, *Broadcasting in Everyday Life: a Survey of the Social Effects of the Coming of Broadcasting* (London: BBC, 1939)

Jennings, Humphrey and Charles Madge, *Mass-Observation Day-Survey: May 12th 1937* (London: Faber and Faber, 1987)

Jephcott, A.P., *Girls Growing Up* (London: Faber and Faber, 1942)

Knowles, Dorothy, *The Censor, the Drama and the Film, 1900–1934* (London: Allen & Unwin, 1934)

League of Nations: International Educational Cinematograph Institute, *The Social Aspects of the Cinema*, (Rome: International Educational Cinematograph Institute, [1934])

Lewis, A. Maxwell, 'The Theory and Practice of Film Observation: an Experimental Investigation into the Child's Attitude to Educational and Entertainment Films' (MA, University of London, 1938)

London County Council: Education Committee, *School Children and the Cinema*, (London: London County Council, 1932)

London School of Economics and Political Science, *The New Survey of London Life and Labour, Vol. ix: Life and Leisure* (London: P.S. King and Son Ltd., 1935)

MacKie, John, *The Edinburgh Cinema Enquiry: Being an Investigation Conducted into the Influence of the Film on Schoolchildren and Adolescents in the City* (Edinburgh: Edinburgh Cinema Enquiry Committee, 1933)

Madge, Charles and Tom Harrisson (eds), *First Year's Work, 1937–38, by Mass-Observation* (London: Lindsay Drummond, 1938)

Madge, Charles and Tom Harrisson, *Britain by Mass-Observation* (Harmondsworth: Penguin, 1939)

Madge, Charles and Tom Harrisson, *Mass-Observation Series, no 1* (London: Frederick Muller Ltd, 1937)

Mass-Observation, *The Pub and the People: a Worktown Study* (London: Gollancz, 1943)

Mayer, J.P., *British Cinemas and their Audiences: Sociological Studies* (London: Dennis Dobson Ltd, 1948)

Mayer, J.P., *Sociology of Film: Studies and Documents* (London: Faber and Faber, 1946)

Middleton, T.M., 'An Enquiry into the Use of Leisure amongst the Working Classes of Liverpool' (MA, University of Liverpool, 1931)

Moss, Louis and Kathleen Box, *The Cinema Audience: an Inquiry made by the Wartime Social Survey for the Ministry of Infomation* (London: Ministry of Information Wartime Social Survey, 1943)

Mowat, C.L., *Britain Between the Wars, 1918–1940* (London: Methuen, 1955)

Orwell, George, *The Road to Wigan Pier* (London: Victor Gollancz, 1937)

Priestley, J.B., *English Journey* (London: William Heinemann Ltd, 1934)

Reynolds, Frank, *Off To The Pictures* (London: Collins, 1937)

Rowson, Simon, *The Social and Political Influence of Films* (London: British Kinematograph Society, 1939)

Rowson, Simon, 'A statistical survey of the cinema industry in Great Britain in 1934', *Journal of the Royal Statistical Society,* vol. 99, no. 1 (1936), pp. 67–129

Seldes, Gilbert, *Movies for the Millions* (London: B.T. Batsford Ltd, 1937)

Shand, P. Morton, *The Architecture of Pleasure 1: Modern Theatres and Cinemas* (London: B.T. Batsford, 1930)

Sheffield Social Survey Committee, *A Survey of Juvenile Employment and Welfare in Sheffield* (Sheffield: Social Survey Committee, 1933)

Stone, Richard and D.A. Rowe, *The Measurement of Consumers' Expenditure and Behaviour in the United Kingdom, 1920–1938,* vol. 2 (Cambridge: Cambridge University Press, 1966)

Struthers, J., 'Leisure Activities of Schoolchildren in a Middlesex Secondary (Mixed) School' (MA, University of London, 1939)

Thorp, Margaret Farrand, *America at the Movies* (New Haven, CT: Yale University Press, 1939)

United Kingdom: Home Office, *Children and 'A' Films* (London: HMSO, 1933)

Winchester, Clarence, (ed.) *The World Film Encyclopedia: a Universal Screen Guide* (London: Amalgamated Press, 1933)

Other documents: a selection

Agar, Michael, 'Stories, background knowledge and themes: problems in the analysis of life history narrative', *American Ethnologist,* vol. 7, no. 2 (1980), pp. 223–239

Aldgate, Tony, 'Comedy, class and containment: the British domestic cinema of the 1930s', in *British Cinema History,* (ed.) James Curran and Vincent Porter (London: Weidenfeld & Nicolson, 1983), pp. 257–271

Aldred, N.L., 'Working Class Women's Leisure Activities in Bolton in the Interwar Era: Focussing on the Pub and the Cinema' (BA Dissertation, Oxford Polytechnic, 1989)

Alexander, Sally, 'Becoming a woman in London in the 1920s and 1930s', in *Metropolis — London: Histories and Representations,* (ed.) Gareth Stedman Jones David Feldman (London: Routledge, 1989), pp. 245–271

Allen, Robert C., 'From exhibition to reception: reflections on the audience in film history', in *Screen Histories: a Screen Reader,* (ed.) Annette Kuhn and Jackie Stacey (Oxford: Oxford University Press, 1998), pp. 13–21

Allen, Robert C. and Douglas Gomery, *Film History: Theory and Practice* (New York: Alfred A. Knopf, 1985)

Altman, Rick, *The American Film Musical* (Bloomington, IN: Indiana University Press, 1984)

Altman, Rick, (ed.) *Genre; the Musical* (London: Routledge & Kegan Paul, 1981)

Atwell, David, *Cathedrals of the Movies: a History of British Cinemas and their Audiences* (London: Architectural Press, 1980)

Austin, Bruce A., *The Film Audience: An International Bibliography of Research* (Metuchen, NJ: Scarecrow Press, 1983)

Baxter, Peter, 'On the naked thighs of Miss Dietrich', *Wide Angle,* vol. 2, no. 2 (1978), pp. 19–25

Beddoe, Deirdre, *Back to Home and Duty: Women between the Wars, 1918 – 1939* (London: Pandora, 1989)

Berenstein, Rhona J., *Attack of the Leading Ladies: Gender, Sexuality and Spectatorship in Classic Horror Cinema* (New York: Columbia University Press, 1996)

Bergfelder, Tim, 'Negotiating exoticism: Hollywood, film Europe and the cultural reception of Anna May Wong', in *'Film Europe' and 'Film America': Cinema, Commerce and Cultural Exchange, 1920–1939*, (ed.) Andrew Higson and Richard Maltby (Exeter: University of Exeter Press, 1999), pp. 302–324

Bertaux, Daniel, *Biography and Society: the Life History Approach in the Social Sciences* (Beverley Hills, CA: Sage, 1981)

Biesty, Patrick, 'The myth of the playful dancer', *Studies in Popular Culture*, vol. 13, no. 1 (1990), pp. 73–88

Bloome, David et al, *Reading Mass-Observation Writing: Theoretical and Methodological Issues in Researching the Mass-Observation Archive*, (Brighton: University of Sussex Library, 1993)

Bourget, Jean-Loup, *'Seventh Heaven'*, *Monogram*, vol. no 4 (1972), pp. 24–25

Bowers, Ronald, 'Shirley Temple', *Films in Review*, vol. 27, no. 10. (1976), pp. 577–594

Branson, Noreen and Margot Heinemann, *Britain in the 1930s* (London: Weidenfeld & Nicolson, 1971)

Bruno, Giuliana, 'Site-seeing: architecture and the moving image', *Wide Angle*, vol. 19, no. 4 (1997), pp. 8–24

Bruno, Giuliana, *Streetwalking on a Ruined Map: Cultural Theory and the City Films of Elvira Notari* (Princeton, NJ: Princeton University Press, 1993)

Buckingham, David, *Moving Images: Understanding Children's Emotional Responses to Television* (Manchester: Manchester University Press, 1996)

Calder, Angus and Dorothy Sheridan, (eds.) *Speak For Yourself: a Mass-Observation Anthology* (London: Jonathan Cape, 1984)

Casey, Edward S., *Remembering: a Phenomenological Study* (Bloomington, IN: Indiana University, 1987)

Castanza, Philip, *The Films of Jeanette MacDonald and Nelson Eddy* (New Jersey: Citadel Press, 1978)

Certeau, Michel de, *The Practice of Everyday Life*, trans. Steven Rendall (Berkeley: University of California Press, 1984)

Clifford, James and George E. Marcus, eds. *Writing Culture: the Poetics and Politics of Ethnography* (Berkeley: University of California Press, 1986)

Cohan, Steven, '"Feminizing" the song-and-dance man: Fred Astaire and the spectacle of masculinity in the Hollywood musical', in *Screening the Male: Exploring Masculinities in Hollywood Cinema*, (ed.) Steven Cohan and Ina Rae Hark (London: Routledge, 1993), pp. 46–69

Cordova, Richard de, 'Ethnography and exhibition: the child audience, the Hays Office and Saturday matinees', *Camera Obscura*, no. 23 (1990), pp. 91–106

Corrigan, Philip, 'Film entertainment as ideology and pleasure: towards a history of audiences', in *British Cinema History*, (ed.) James Curran and Vincent Porter (London: Weidenfeld & Nicolson, 1983), pp.24–35

Cross, Gary, *Worktowners at Blackpool: Mass-Observation and Popular Leisure in the 1930s* (London: Routledge, 1990)

Cutforth, Rene, *Later Than We Thought: A Portrait of the Thirties* (Newton Abbot: David & Charles, 1976)

Davies, Andrew, 'Cinema and broadcasting', in *Twentieth-century Britain: Economic, Social and Cultural Change*, (ed.) Paul Johnson (London: Longman, 1994), pp. 263–280

Davies, Andrew, *Leisure Gender and Poverty: Working-class Culture in Salford and Manchester, 1900–1939.* (Milton Keynes: Open University Press, 1992)

Delamater, Jerome, *Dance in the Hollywood Musical* (Ann Arbor, MI: UMI Research Press, 1978)

Dentith, Simon, 'Contemporary working-class autobiography: politics of form, politics of content', in *Modern Selves: Essays on Modern British and American Autobiography*, (ed.) Philip Dodd (London: Frank Cass, 1986), pp. 60–80

Dickinson, Margaret and Sarah Street, *Cinema and State: The Film Industry and Government, 1927–34* (London: British Film Institute, 1985)

Dumont, Herve, 'Jacob's ladder, or love and adversity', *Griffithiana*, no. 46 (1998), pp. 88–101

Dunne, Michael, 'Fred Astaire as cultural allusion', *Studies in Popular Culture*, vol. 16, no. 2 (1994), pp. 9–19

Dyer, Richard, 'The space of happiness in the musical', *Aura*, vol. 4, no. 1 (1998), pp. 31–45

Eckert, Charles, 'Shirley Temple and the house of Rockefeller', *Jump Cut*, vol. no. 2, no. 1 (1974), pp. 17–20

Eco, Umberto, *The Role of the Reader: Explorations in the Semiotics of Texts* (London: Hutchinson, 1981)

Everson, William K., 'The career of Deanna Durbin', *Films in Review*, vol. 27, no. 9 (1976), pp. 513–529

Everson, William K., 'Serials with sound have steadily declined in quality and quantity', *Films in Review*, vol. 4, no. 4 (1953), pp. 269–276

Ferguson, M., *Women's Magazines and the Cult of Femininity.* (London: Heinemann, 1983)

Field, Audrey, *Picture Palace: a Social History of the Cinema* (London: Century Books, 1974)

Figlio, Karl, 'Oral history and the Unconscious', *History Workshop*, no. 26 (1988), pp. 120–132

Fischer, Michael M.J., 'Ethnicity and the post-modern arts of memory', in *Writing Culture: the Poetics and Politics of Ethnography*, (ed.) James Clifford and George E. Marcus (Berkeley, CA: University of California Press, 1986), pp. 194–233

Foucault, Michel, 'Other spaces: the principles of heterotopia', *Lotus*, vol. 48–49 (1986), pp. 9–17

Fox, Julian, 'Colman (part 1)', *Films and Filming*, vol. 18, no. 6 (1972), pp. 26–32

Fox, Julian, 'Colman (part 2)', *Films and Filming*, vol. 18, no. 7 (1972), pp. 34–39

Freeman, Mark, *Rewriting the Self: History, Memory, Narrative* (London: Routledge, 1993)

Gagnier, Regenia, *Subjectivities: A History of Self-Representation in Britain* (New York: Oxford University Press, 1991)

Gallafent, Edward, *Astaire and Rogers* (Dumfriesshire: Cameron & Hollis, 2000)

Gansberg, Alan L., *Little Caesar: A Biography of Edward G. Robinson* (Sevenoaks: New English Library, 1983)

Geraghty, Christine, 'Cinema as a social space: understanding cinemagoing in Britain, 1947–63', *Framework*, vol. no.42 (2000). http://www.frameworkonline.com/index2.htm [17 August 2001]

Ginzburg, Carlo, 'Microhistory: two or three things I know about it', *Critical Inquiry*, vol. 20, no. 4 (1993), pp. 10–35

Glancy, Mark, 'MGM film grosses: 1924–1949: the Eddie Mannix ledger', *Historical Journal of Radio, Film and Television*, vol. 12, no. 2 (1992), pp. 127–144

Gloversmith, Frank, *Class, Culture and Social Change: a New View of the 1930s* (Sussex: Harvester Press, 1980)

Gomes, Maryann, *The Picture House: a Photographic Album of Film and Cinema in Greater Manchester, Lancashire, Cheshire and Merseyside* (Manchester: North West Film Archive, 1988)

Graves, Robert and Alan Hodge, *The Long Weekend* (Harmondsworth: Penguin, 1971)

Greene, Graham, *The Pleasure Dome: Collected Film Criticism 1935–40* (London: Secker & Warburg, 1972)

Gripsrud, Jostein, 'Film audiences', in *The Oxford Guide to Film Studies*, (ed.) John Hill and Pamela Church Gibson (Oxford: Oxford University Press, 1998), pp.202–211

Gripsrud, Jostein, 'Moving images, moving identities: texts and contexts in the reception history of film and television' (Los Angeles: Society for Cinema Studies, Annual Conference, May 1991)

Gurney, Peter, (ed.) *Bolton Working Class Life in the 1930s* (Brighton: University of Sussex Library, 1988)

Hagedorn, Roger, 'The serial as a form of narrative presentation', *Wide Angle*, vol. 10, no. 4 (1998), pp. 4–12

Halliwell, Leslie, *Seats in all Parts: a Lifetime at the Movies* (London: Grafton Books, 1986)

Hansen, Miriam Bratu, 'The mass production of the senses: classical cinema as vernacular modernism', *Modernism/Modernity*, vol. 6, no. 2 (1999), pp. 59–77

Hartley, John, '"Text" and "audience": one and the same? methodological tensions in media research', *Textual Practice*, vol. 13, no. 3 (1999), pp. 487–508

Hendrick, Harry, *Children, Childhood and English Society, 1880–1990* (Cambridge: Cambridge University Press, 1997)

Hendrick, Harry, 'Constructions and reconstructions of British childhood: an interpretative survey, 1800 to the present', in *Constructing and Reconstructing Childhood: Contemporary Issues in the Sociological Study of Childhood*, (ed.) Allison James and Alan Prout (Brighton: Falmer Press, 1990), pp. 35–59

Hiley, Nick, 'British Cinema Fan Magazines in 1936' (Unpublished paper, 1991)

Hiley, Nicholas, '"Let's go to the pictures": the British cinema audience in the 1920s and 1930s', *Journal of Popular British Cinema*, vol. 2 (1999), pp. 39–53

Hirsch, Foster, *Edward G. Robinson* (New York: Pyramid, 1975)

Jackson, Alan A., *Semi-detached London: Suburban Development, Life and Transport, 1900–39* (London: George Allen & Unwin, 1973)

Jeffrey, Jaclyn and Glenace Edwall, (eds.) *Memory and History: Essays on Recalling and Interpreting Experience* (Lanham, MD: University Press of America, 1994)

Johnson, Tom, *Censored Screams: the British Ban on Hollywood Horror in the 1930s* (Jefferson, NC: McFarland, 1997)

Jones, Stephen G., *Workers at Play: a Social and Economic History of Leisure, 1918–1939* (London: Routledge & Kegan Paul, 1986)

Kenyon, Norman, *Bolton Memories* (Manchester: Neil Richardson, 1993)

Klenotic, Jeffrey F., 'Class markers in the mass movie audience: a case sudy on the cultural geography of moviegoing, 1926–1932', *Communication Review*, vol. 2, no. 4 (1998), pp. 461–495

Knowles, Eleanor, *The Films of Jeanette MacDonald and Nelson Eddy.* (London: Tantivy Press, 1975)

Kuhn, Annette, 'Cinema culture and femininity in the 1930s', in *Nationalising Femininity*, (ed.) Christine Gledhill and Gillian Swanson (Manchester: Manchester University Press, 1996), pp. 177–192

Kuhn, Annette, *Cinema, Censorship and Sexuality, 1909–1925* (London: Routledge, 1988)

Kuhn, Annette, 'Cinemagoing in Britain in the 1930s: report of a questionnaire survey', *Historical Journal of Film, Radio and Television*, vol. 19, no. 4 (1999), pp. 531–543

Kuhn, Annette, 'A journey through memory', in *Memory and Methodology*, (ed.) Susannah Radstone (Oxford: Berg, 2000), pp.179–196

Kuhn, Annette, 'Memories of cinema-going in the 1930s', *Journal of Popular British Cinema*, vol. no 2 (1999), pp. 100–120

Kuhn, Annette, 'Researching popular film fan culture in 1930s Britain', in *History of Moving Images: Reports from a Norwegian Project*, (ed.) Jostein Gripsrud and Kathrin Skretting (Oslo: Research Council of Norway, 1994), pp. 85–95

Kuhn, Annette, 'Smart girls: growing up with cinema in the 1930s', in *Moving Images, Culture and the Mind*, (ed.) Ib Bondebjerg (Luton: University of Luton Press, 2000), pp.31–42

Kuhn, Annette, "That day *did* last me all my life': cinema memory and enduring fandom', in *Identifying Hollywood's Audiences: Cultural Identity and the Movies*, (ed.) Richard Maltby and Melvyn Stokes (London: British Film Institute, 1999), pp.135–146

Kuhn, Annette, 'Women's genres', *Screen*, vol. 25, no. 1 (1984), pp. 18–28

Lant, Antonia, 'The curse of the pharaoh, or how cinema contracted Egyptomania', in *Visions of the East: Orientalism in Film*, (ed.) Matthew Bernstein and Gaylyn Studlar (New Brunswick, NJ: Rutgers University press, 1997), pp. 69–98

Leader, Raymond, 'From Pearl White to Superman: forty years of movie serials', *ABC Film Review*, vol. 3, no. 5 (1953), pp. 10–11

Lefebvre, Henri, *The Production of Space*, trans. Donald Nicholson-Smith (Oxford: Blackwell, 1991)

Lefebvre, Henri, *Writings on Cities*, selected, translated and introduced by Eleonore Kofman and Elizabeth Lebas (Oxford: Blackwell, 1996)

LeMahieu, D.L., *A Culture for Democracy: Mass Communication and the Cultivated Mind in Britain Between the Wars* (Oxford: Clarendon Press, 1988)

Light, Alison, *Forever England: Femininity, Literature and Conservatism between the Wars* (London: Routledge, 1991)

McBain, Janet, *Pictures Past: Scottish Cinemas Remembered* (Edinburgh: Moorfoot Publishing, 1985)

Marcus, Laura, 'Psychoanalysis, history and autobiographies', *History Workshop*, no. 21 (1986), pp. 203–204

Massey, Anne, (ed.) *Romancing Hollywood* (Southampton: Southampton Institute, 1997)

Mercer, Neil, 'Mass-Observation 1937–40: the Range of Research Methods', *Working Papers in Applied Social Research*, University of Manchester, no. 16 (1989)

Miles, Peter and Malcolm Smith, *Cinema, Literature and Society: Elite and Mass Culture in Interwar Britain* (London: Croom Helm, 1987)

Mueller, John, 'The filmed dances of Fred Astaire', *Quarterly Review of Film Studies*, vol. 6, no. 2 (1981), pp. 135–154

Mueller, John, 'Fred Astaire and the integrated musical', *Cinema Journal*, vol. 24, no. 1 (1984), pp. 28–40

Muggeridge, Malcolm, *The Thirties* (London: Fontana, 1971)

Murphy, Robert, 'Coming of sound to the cinema in Britain', *Historical Journal of Film, Radio and Television*, vol. 4, no. 2 (1984), pp. 143–160

O'Brien, Margaret and Allen Eyles, (eds.) *Enter the Dream House: Memories of Cinemas in South London from the Twenties to the Sixties* (London: British Film Institute, 1993)

Ohmer, Susan, 'Female spectatorship and women's magazines: Hollywood, *Good Housekeeping*, and World War Two', *The Velvet Light Trap*, vol. 25 (1990), pp. 53–68

Olden, Norman, *Sixty-three Years a Movie Fan* (Sussex: The Book Guild, 1991)

Oltean, Tudor, 'Series and seriality in media culture', *European Journal of Communication*, vol. 8, no. 8 (1993), pp. 5–31

Parish, James Robert, *The Jeanette MacDonald Story* (New York: Mason/Chanter, 1976)

Parish, James Robert and Alvin H. Marril, *The Cinema of Edward G. Robinson* (New York: A.S. Barnes, 1972)

Passerini, Luisa, 'Memory', *History Workshop*, no. 15 (1983), pp. 195–196

Peart, Stephen, *The Picture House in East Anglia* (Lavenham, Suffolk: Terence Dalton Ltd, 1980)

Perks, Robert, *Oral History: Talking about the Past* (London: Oral History Society, 1992)

Peter, Bruce, *100 Years of Glasgow's Amazing Cinemas* (Edinburgh: Polygon, 1996)

Plummer, Ken, *Documents of Life: an Introduction to the Problems and Literature of a Humanistic Method* (London: George Allen and Unwin, 1983)

Polanyi, Livia, 'Literary complexity in everyday storytelling', in *Exploring Orality and Literacy*, (ed.) Deborah Tannen (Norwood, NJ: Ablex Publishing Corp., 1982), pp. 155–170

Poole, Julian, 'British cinema attendance in wartime: audience preference at the Majestic, Macclesfield, 1939–1946', *Historical Journal of Film, Radio and Television*, vol. 7, no. 1 (1987), pp. 15–34

Portelli, Alessandro, *The Death of Luigi Trastulli and Other Stories: Form and Meaning in Oral History* (Albany, NY: State University of New York Press, 1991)

Portelli, Alessandro, 'The peculiarites of oral history', *History Workshop*, no. 12 (1981), pp. 96–107

Portelli, Alessandro, 'The time of my life: functions of time in oral history', *International Journal of Oral History*, vol. 2, no. 3 (1981), pp. 162–180

Porter, Vincent and Sue Harper, 'Throbbing hearts and smart repartee: the reception of American films in 1950s Britain', *Media History*, vol. 4, no. 2 (1998), pp. 175–193

Power, James, 'Aspects of Working-Class Leisure During the Depression Years: Bolton in the 1930s' (MA Thesis, University of Warwick, 1980)

Richards, Jeffrey, *The Age of the Dream Palace: Cinema and Society in Britain 1930–39* (London: Routledge & Kegan Paul, 1984)

Richards, Jeffrey, 'Boy's own Empire: feature films and imperialism in the 1930s', in *Imperialism and Popular Culture*, (ed.) John M. MacKenzie (Manchester: Manchester University Press, 1986), pp. 140–164

Richards, Jeffrey, 'The British Board of Film Censors and content control in the 1930s', *Historical Journal of Film, Radio and Television*, vol. 1, no. 2 (1981), pp. 95–116; vol. 2, no. 1 (1982), pp. 38–48

Richards, Jeffrey, 'The cinema and cinemagoing in Birmingham in the 1930s', in *Leisure in Britain 1780–1939*, (ed.) John K. Walton and James Walvin (Manchester: Manchester University Press, 1983), pp. 31–52

Richards, Jeffrey, 'Cinemagoing in Worktown: regional film audiences in 1930s Britain', *Historical Journal of Film, Radio and Television*, vol. 14, no. 2 (1994), pp. 147–166

Richards, Jeffrey, 'Controlling the screen: British cinema in the 1930s', *History Today*, March 1983, pp. 11–17

Richards, Jeffrey, 'Ronald Colman and the cinema of Empire', *Focus on Film*, no. 4 (1970), pp. 42–55

Richards, Jeffrey, (ed.) *The Unknown 1930s: an Alternative History of the British Cinema, 1929–39* (London: I.B. Tauris, 1998)

Richards, Jeffrey, *Visions of Yesterday* (London: Routledge & Kegan Paul, 1973)

Richards, Jeffrey and Dorothy Sheridan, (eds.) *Mass-Observation at the Movies* (London: Routledge & Kegan Paul, 1987)

Rigby, Brian, 'Bolton and the cinema: from Mass-Observation to the diaries of a nobody', *Manchester Region History Review*, vol. 5, no. 2 (1991–2), pp. 3–12

Robinson, Edward G., *All My Yesterdays: An Autobiography* (New York: Hawthorn Books, 1973)

Rosen, Philip, 'Difference and displacement in *Seventh Heaven*', *Screen*, vol. 18, no. 2 (1977), pp. 89–104

Ross, Bruce M., *Remembering the Personal Past: Descriptions of Autobiographical Memory* (New York: Oxford University Press, 1991)

Samuel, Raphael and Paul Thompson, *The Myths We Live By* (London: Routledge, 1990)

Scheiner, Georganne, *Signifying Female Adolescence: Film Representations and Fans, 1920–1950* (Westport, CT: Praeger, 2000)

Seaman, L.C.B., *Life In Britain Between the Wars* (London: Batsford, 1970)

Sedgwick, John, 'Film 'hits' and 'misses' in mid-1930s Britain', *Historical Journal of Radio, Film and Television*, vol. 18, no. 3 (1998), pp. 333–347

Sedgwick, John, 'The market for feature films in Britain, 1934: a viable national cinema', *Historical Journal of Film, Radio and Television*, vol. 14, no. 1 (1994), pp. 15–36

Sedgwick, John, *Popular Filmgoing in 1930s Britain* (Exeter: University of Exeter Press, 2000)

Sedgwick, John, 'Regional distinctions in the consumption of films and stars in 1930s Britain', *Electronic Seminars in History*, http://ihrinfo.ac.uk/ihr/esh/star.html (7 April 2001)

Shafer, Stephen Craig, 'Enter the Dream House: The British Film Industry and the Working Classes in Depression England, 1929–1939' (PhD, University of Illinois, 1982)

Sharp, Dennis, *The Picture Palace and Other Buildings for the Movies* (London: Hugh Evelyn, 1969)

Siikala, Anna-Leena, *Interpreting Oral Narrative* (Helsinki: Academia Scientiarium Fennica, 1990)

Skal, David, *The Monster Show: a Cultural History of Horror* (London: Plexus, 1993)

Smith, Richard Candida, 'Popular memory and oral narratives: Luisa Passerini's reading of oral history interviews', *Oral History Review*, vol. 16, no. 2 (1988), pp. 95–107

Spender, Humphrey, *Britain in the 30's [sic]: Photographs by Humphrey Spender with an Introduction and Commentary by Tom Harrisson* (London: Royal College of Art, 1975)

Spender, Humphrey, *Worktown People: Photographs from Northern England, 1937–38* (Bristol: Falling Wall Press, 1982)

Stacey, Jackie, *Star Gazing: Hollywood Cinema and Female Spectatorship* (London: Routledge, 1994)

Stacey, Jackie, 'Textual obsessions: method, memory and researching female spectatorship', *Screen*, vol. 34, no. 3 (1993), pp. 260–274

Staiger, Janet, 'The handmaiden of villainy: methods and problems in studying the historical reception of film', *Wide Angle*, vol. 8, no. 1 (1986), pp. 19–28

Staiger, Janet, *Interpreting Films: Studies in the Historical Reception of American Cinema* (Princeton, NJ: Princeton University Press, 1992)

Staiger, Janet, 'The perversity of spectators: expanding the history of classical Hollywood cinema', in *Moving Images, Culture and the Mind*, (ed.) Ib Bondebjerg (Luton: University of Luton Press, 2000), pp. 19–30

Staiger, Janet, 'Writing the history of American film reception', in *Hollywood Spectatorship: Changing Perceptions of Cinema Audiences*, (ed.) Melvyn Stokes and Richard Maltby (London: British Film Institute, 2001), pp. 19–32

Staiger, Janet and Martin Barker, 'Traces of interpretations: Janet Staiger and Martin Barker in conversation', *Framework, no.42 (2000)*, http://www.frameworkonline.com/42jsmb.htm (17 August 2001)

Stead, Peter, *Film and the Working Class: the Feature Film in British and American Society* (London: Routledge, 1989)

Stead, Peter, 'Hollywood's message for the world: the British response in the 1930s', *Historical Journal of Film, Radio and Television*, vol. 1, no. 1 (1981), pp. 19–32

Stead, Peter, 'The people and the pictures', in *Propaganda, Politics and Film, 1918–45*, (ed.) N. Pronay and D.W. Spring (London: MacMillan, 1982), pp. 77–97

Stearns, Marshall and Jean Stearns, *Jazz Dance: the Story of American Vernacular Dance* (New York: MacMillan, 1968)

Street, Sarah, 'The Hays Office and the defence of the British market in the 1930s', *Historical Journal of Film, Radio and Television*, vol. 5, no. 1 (1985), pp. 37–55

Studlar, Gaylyn, 'The perils of pleasure? fan magazine discourse as women's commodified culture in the 1920s', *Wide Angle*, vol. 13, no. 1 (1991), pp. 6–33

Tagg, Stephen K., 'Life story interviews and their interpretation', in *The Research Interview: Uses and Approaches*, (ed.) Michael Brenner, Jennifer Brown and David Cantor (London: Academic Press, 1985), pp. 163–199

Taylor, Helen, *Scarlett's Women: Gone With The Wind and its Female Fans* (London: Virago Press, 1989)

Telotte, J.P., 'Dancing the depression: narrative strategy in the Astaire-Rogers films', *Journal of Popular Film and Television*, vol. 8, no. 3 (1980), pp. 15–24

Thompson, Kristin, *Exporting Entertainment: America in the World Film Market, 1907–34* (London: BFI Publishing, 1985)

Thompson, Paul, *The Voice of the Past: Oral History*, second edition (Oxford: Oxford University Press, 1988)

Thomson, Alistair et al, 'The memory and history debates: some international pespectives', *Oral History*, vol. 22, no. 2 (1994), pp. 33–43

Tonkin, Elizabeth, *Narrating Our Pasts: the Social Construction of Oral History* (Cambridge: Cambridge University Press, 1992)

Turk, Edward Baron, 'Deriding the voice of Jeanette MacDonald: notes on psychoanalysis and the American film musical', *Camera Obscura*, nos 25–26 (1990), pp. 225–249

Tydeman, William E., 'Tom Mix: king of the Hollywood cowboys', in *Back in the Saddle: Essays on Western Film and Television Actors*, (ed.) Gary A. Yoggy (Jefferson, NC: McFarland & Co, 1998), pp. 25–42

Urry, John, *Consuming Places*, International Library of Sociology (London: Routledge, 1995)

Walvin, James, *Leisure and Society, 1830–1950* (London: Longmans, 1978)

Wexman, Virginia Wright, *Creating the Couple: Love, Marriage and Hollywood Performance* (Princeton, NJ: Princeton University Press, 1993)

White, Cynthia L., *Womens Magazines, 1693–1968* (London: Michael Joseph, 1970)

Zinman, David, *Saturday Afternoon at the Bijou* (New Rochelle, NY: Arlington House, 1973)

Index of Informants

General Index

Mask of Fu Manchu, The (1932), 85–87, 91, 253
Mass-Observation, 241, 250
matinees, 38, 40, 46–47, 50–51, 51–52, 55–60, 82
Mayer, J. P., 216–217, 218, 230–231
Maytime (1937), 197, 198–200, 201, 202–203, 206, 209–211, 212, 253; 'Will You Remember?', 198, 209
memory discourse, 9–11, 12, 40–41, 60–62, 238; and class, 10–11, 22–23, 46, 232; and gender, 10–11, 100–101, 110, 138; regional differences, 10–11; *see also* anecdotal memory discourse; impersonal memory discourse; past/present memory discourse; repetitive memory discourse
memory, *see* cinema memory; collective memory; memory discourse; men's memories; nostalgia; women's memories
men's memories, 101–110; and class, 108–109; clothes, 106–107, 108–109; cowboys and indians, 102–103; dancing, 103–104; impersonations, 103–107; 'making do', 101–102
methods, *see* research methods
Mix, Tom, 101, 108
money, 47, 48–54
Motion Picture Almanac, 250
Motion Picture Herald, 197, 250
Mr Deeds Goes to Town (1936), 252
Mueller, John, 169, 192
Mummy, The (1933), 66, 71, 76, 84, 87–91, 95, 253
musicals, 154, 155–157, 168–169, 198; backstage, 169, 181, 182; fairy tale, 181, 186; integrated, 168–169, 181–182
Mutiny on the Bounty (1935), 101
Mystery of the Wax Museum, The (1933), 73–75, 92–96, 253

Naughty Marietta (1935), 197, 203
Neagle, Anna, 158

Nelson Eddy Appreciation Society, 197–198, 200, 201, 206, 211
New York Times, 162
Night Must Fall (1937), 69, 71, 76, 253
North West Passage (1940), 72
nostalgia, 212

Old Dark House, The (1932), 69, 71
One Hour With You (1933), 167n45
organ, see cinema organ
Orientals in film, 85–94, 96

parental veto, 47, 48, 75
past/present memory discourse, 10, 20, 30–31, 34–35, 55, 67, 134, 139, 149–150, 164–165, 178, 204
Payne Fund Studies, 84, 217
Picture Show, 248, 249
picture palaces, *see* supercinemas
Picturegoer, 117, 120, 124, 127, 153, 156, 158, 169, 204, 216, 217, 248, 249
place-memory, 16–36, 41–43, 61, 110, 139, 141, 185; memory discourse, 17–28; regional variations, 28; walking, 33–36
Portelli, Alessandro, 11, 60, 204
Powell, Dick, 155
Priestley, J. B., 2
Private Life of Henry VIII, The (1933), 252
Production Code, 154, 158, 168, 181, 186

Queen Christina (1933), 252

Raft, George, 105
Ramona (1928), 149, 253
repetitive memory discourse, 10, 40–41, 46–47, 52, 62, 78–79, 139, 178–179, 181, 182–185
research methods, 3–9, 12, 237, 240–254; interviews, 8, 240–244; questionnaire, 245–247; triangulation, 7, 12, 252; *see also* ethnography; ethnohistory
Richards, Jeffrey, 2
Roc, Patricia, 197

Rogers, Ginger, 111, 113, 118, 120, 132,
    170, 175–176, 229, 230; *see also*
    Astaire/Rogers
romance, *see* courtship; romantic films
romantic comedy, 154, 155, 157, 197
romantic films, 144, 147–148, 174–175,
    228–229
Romero, Cesar, 206
Rookery Nook (1930), 252
Rose Marie (1936), 197

Sally In Our Alley (1931), 252
Saturday matinees, see matinees
serials, 56–58, 61–62, 87, 253; *Clutching
    Hand, The*, 84; *Elmo the Mighty*, 56;
    Flash Gordon, 56, 84; about Fu
    Manchu, 56; *Mystery of Dr Fu
    Manchu, The*, 87, 253; *see also*
    cliffhangers
Seven Keys to Baldpate (1935), 71, 253
Seventh Heaven (1927), 253
Seventh Heaven (1937), 149–50
sex, 144, 147, 149, 155, 181, 186, 192
Sheffield Social Survey, 82
silent films, 39, 45, 55
Simmel, Georg, 35
Singing Fool, The (1928), 144–145
singing, 170; during interview, 172
Snow White and the Seven Dwarfs
    (1937), 252, 253
social class, *see* class
spectator vs audience, 4, 238
Stacey, Jackie, 6, 200
Staiger, Janet, 5, 7
Steedman, Carolyn, 130–131
Stowaway (1936), 252
Sunshine Susie (1931), 252
supercinemas, 28, 55, 83, 141–142, 146,
    147, 153, 223

Taylor, Helen, 6
Telotte, J. P., 181, 182
Temple, Shirley, 169, 217
That Certain Age (1938), 119
Thirty-nine Steps, The (1935), 161–162, 253

Three Smart Girls (1936), 118, 119, 120,
    253
Three Smart Girls Grow Up (1939), 119,
    124, 201, 252
time-memory, 224–226
Todd, Thelma, 155, 158, 164
Top Hat (1935), 53, 120, 169, 172, 173,
    174, 176, 179–80, 182, 253 ,'Cheek to
    Cheek', 151, 180, 186–192; 'Isn't This
    a Lovely Day...', 170
topographical memory, *see* place-
    memory
Turk, Edward Baron, 197

uncanny, 96; Europe as, 95–96; Oriental
    as 85–94, 96

Victoria the Great (1937), 252
voyeurism, 157, 162, 163

walking, 33–36
Werewolf of London, The (1935), 70, 76
westerns, 55–56, 101, 108, 217; see also
    cowboys and indians
Wills, Nadine, 157
Woman, 123, 124, 126, 249, 250
Woman's Filmfair, 123, 249
Woman's Journal, 250
Woman's Weekly, 124, 250
women's magazines, 123–124; *see also
    Film Fashionland; Woman; Woman's
    Journal; Woman's Filmfair; Woman's
    Weekly*
women's memories, 110–133; and class,
    118, 130–132; clothes, 113–116,
    124–129, 130–132; and consumerism,
    120; copying stars, 110–111, 113;
    courtship, 148–149, 152–153;
    hairstyles, 111–113, 129. 170; makeup,
    111–112, 175–176; 'making do', 116,
    120; regional variations, 118
Wray, Fay, 77
Wyman, Jane, 124

yearning, 130–132, 231–232